RED DUST

Ma Jian is a writer, painter and photographer. He left China for Hong Kong soon after finishing his journey, but moved to Europe at the hand-over of Hong Kong in 1997. He now lives in London.

Ma Jian

RED DUST
A Path Through China

TRANSLATED FROM THE CHINESE BY
Flora Drew

VINTAGE

Published by Vintage 2002

10 9

Copyright © Ma Jian 2001
English translation © Flora Drew 2001

First published in Great Britain in 2001 by
Chatto & Windus

Vintage
Random House, 20 Vauxhall Bridge Road,
London SW1V 2SA

Random House Australia (Pty) Limited
20 Alfred Street, Milsons Point, Sydney
New South Wales 2061, Australia

Random House New Zealand Limited
18 Poland Road, Glenfield,
Auckland 10, New Zealand

Random House (Pty) Limited
Endulini, 5A Jubilee Road, Parktown 2193,
South Africa

The Random House Group Limited Reg. No. 954009
www.randomhouse.co.uk

A CIP catalogue record for this book
is available from the British Library

ISBN 0 09 928329 8

Printed and bound in Great Britain by
Bookmarque Ltd, Croydon, Surrey

Contents

1. RED WALLS   1

53 Nanxiao Lane
The Frozen Blue Sky
A Man of Thirty
Men in the Dark
Writing my Self-Criticism
Mixing Blood and Urine
Launch of the Campaign Against Spiritual Pollution
Back in the Public Security Bureau
Leaving Nanxiao Lane

2. DUST STORM   59

Emerging from the Gate of Hell
First Steps
Living in the Night
The Gold-Digger
Stuck in Suoyang
Resting in the Gale
The Living and the Dead
Lure of the Distance

3. DRIFTING THROUGH THE WEST   103

Hairdressing in Golmud
Fishing on Qinghai Lake
Racing down the Ravine
Meeting Ma Youshan
The Girl in the Red Blouse

4. A COUNTRY IN FERMENT   133

Back to the City
Night Sprinkler
River of Ghosts

5. THE WIND-BLOWN SOIL 167

City of Tombs
Lost in the Wastes
Flies in Scrambled Eggs

6. WANDERING DOWN THE COAST 203

House of Memories
Time is Money
Day and Night
Building a Park within a Park
The Opening Ceremony becomes the Closing Ceremony
Walking to the End of the World

7. THE ABANDONED VALLEYS 231

The Silent Beat of the Drum
Entering a Strange Circle
Abyss of Desire
Rain over the Leprosy Camp
Mountains behind Mountains

8. LIFE AT THE BORDER 261

Old Shabalu
Into the Jungle
From Traveller to Fugitive
Selling Chiffon Scarves in a Traffic Jam

9. A LAND WITH NO HOME 289

Buddha and the City
Same Path, Different Directions
The Woman and the Blue Sky
In the Sky, on the Road
Road and Direction

A Note on Names

In Chinese, surnames precede first names. Surnames have one syllable; first names have one or two. Each syllable is a transcription of a Chinese character and each character has a meaning and a sound. It is customary in English to write the two syllables of a first name as one word, for example, Guoping.

Transcriptions are pronounced as they read, with the following four exceptions: q is *ch*; x is *hs*; zh is *j*; c is *ts*.

The characters in this book are based on real people, but, except for Ma Jian's daughter, their names have been changed.

Friends and acquaintances featured most prominently:

MEN
Li Tao	Poet; bank clerk.
Hu Sha	Poet; activist; teacher of history at Beijing Steelworks University.
Fan Cheng	Short-story writer; tax officer.
Da Xian	Abstract painter; womaniser.

WOMEN
Guoping	Ma Jian's wife; dancer in Yanshan propaganda troupe.
Xi Ping	Accountant at All-China Federation of Trade Unions; film actress.
Lu Ping	Prima ballerina at Central Ballet Company.
Wang Ping	*Hangzhou Daily* reporter; short-story writer.
Chen Hong	Poet; doctor; Fan Cheng's girlfriend.
Lingling	Literary editor at Guangzhou Press publishing house.
Yang Ming	Editor of Chengdu's *Star* magazine; poet; Hu Sha's lover.

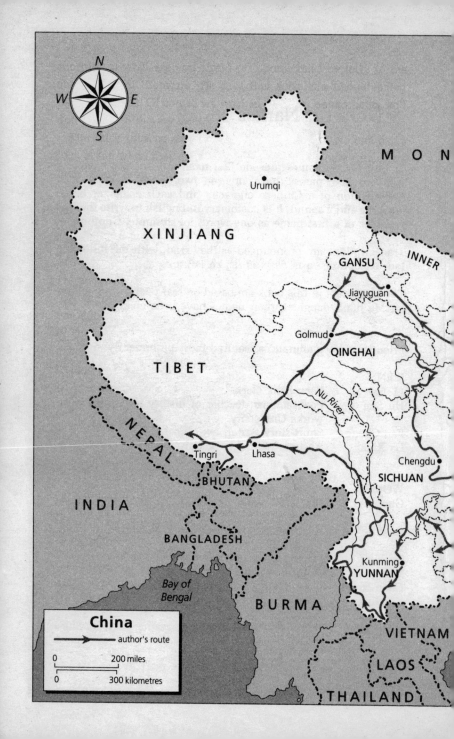

N
W · E
S

MON

Urumqi

XINJIANG

GANSU

INNER

Jiayuguan

Golmud

QINGHAI

TIBET

Nu River

NEPAL

Tingri   Lhasa

Chengdu

BHUTAN

SICHUAN

INDIA

BANGLADESH

Kunming
YUNNAN

Bay of
Bengal

BURMA

VIETNAM

China

→ author's route

0   200 miles

0   300 kilometres

LAOS

THAILAND

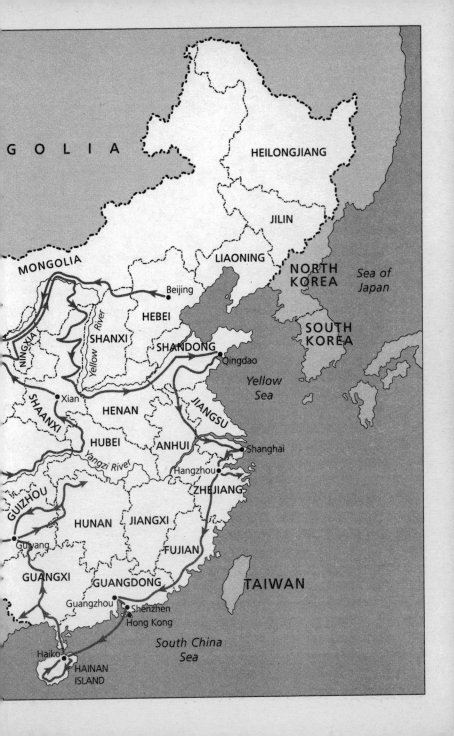

1.

Red Walls

53 Nanxiao Lane

Last year, in the spring of 1981, my work unit moved me from the staff dormitory block to a small house in Nanxiao Lane. Number 53. The house is squeezed between Dongsi Eleventh Street and Dongsi Twelfth Street in the Eastern District of Beijing – a hundred metres from the former residence of Liang Qichao, a member of the 1898 Reform Movement, whose calls for modernisation so enraged Empress Cixi that he fled the country and spent fourteen years in exile. The old locust tree outside his gate twists up a narrow gap between a wall and a telegraph pole. Nanxiao Lane lies twenty metres from my front door at the end of a narrow passage and is just wide enough for two buses to scrape past one another. At eight in the morning and four in the afternoon, the lane fills with people and bicycles, and everything comes to a halt.

From my sofa, I can hear buses stop and a conductress bang on a window and shout, 'Wait for the next one if you can't squeeze in. Hey! You with the gold wristwatch! Yes, you! Where's your ticket? All right, smug bastard. Take a cab if you're so high and mighty. Filthy rag . . .'

The house is surrounded on three sides by red-brick apartment blocks. When kitchen windows open, eggshells, cabbage leaves and plastic bags drop onto my roof and roll into the yard. On one occasion I received a plate of fried kidneys – someone up there must have smelt they had gone off and wanted me to deal with them. When I hang out my clothes to dry, pigeons nesting on the third floor splatter them with shit.

The yard is just two metres square. In autumn, the locust tree behind the back wall scatters it with twigs and branches. In the summer months, watermelon skins and empty ice-cream cartons fall from the flats and attract swarms of flies and mosquitoes, so I

3

tend to stay indoors. Winter is the best season as my neighbours seal their windows. And when the snow falls, my mean little house even recaptures some of the charm of old Beijing.

I use the house to paint, write and sleep. My wife and daughter still live in my old flat in the compound of Yanshan Petrochemical Plant, a two-hour bus drive away. For four years I was the plant's publicity photographer, while my wife danced in the propaganda troupe. Then three years ago, my photographs won a prize in a national competition and I was transferred to the capital to work for the foreign propaganda department of the All-China Federation of Trade Unions. The job keeps me so busy, I seldom get a chance to return to Yanshan.

The house may be a crumbling old shack, but the tap in the yard and the private gate give me an independence and freedom I never had in the dormitory block. A band of writers, painters, poets, dissidents and hangers-on use the house as a meeting point. We talk into the night about art and politics. We discuss the new 'Household Contract Responsibility System' and 'Socialism with Chinese Characteristics'. We play tapes of the Taiwanese singer Deng Lijun and distribute mimeographed copies of underground poetry. Sometimes we disguise a foreign journalist in balaclava and overalls, and sneak him into the house to show him our paintings and hear his stories. Many improbable plans have been debated between these four walls.

The room is filled with my paintings, I even use one as a rug. When I hold exhibitions here, many pictures go missing. But a man from the US Embassy actually bought one once. He paid me forty dollars.

My neighbours' prying eyes inevitably focus on my house. But the loud music and stream of visitors have also aroused the interest of the local police force. My friends all own keys to my front door. They try to arrive before dark so as not to attract attention. But when it is time to leave in the middle of the night no one's safety can be assured. So they either sleep over, or leave separately at five-minute intervals.

4

One night, I invited a colleague back to the house – a girl called Xi Ping who works in accounts. After supper, we talked for a while then I offered to walk her home. We had barely stepped two hundred metres from my gate when the police descended on us. Fortunately I had my identity card with me. I said I lived nearby, said we had been chatting and forgotten the time, said lots of polite things and at last they let me off. They let Xi Ping off too, but she had to walk back to the dormitory block through the long dark lanes all by herself.

Another night, my friends and I had been drinking too much and we collapsed in a heap in the yard. Five minutes later a police van screeched to a halt outside the gate, four officers herded us into the room and demanded to see our documents. Li Tao was behind the bed curtain by that time, having a cuddle with his wife Mimi. An officer raised the curtain, Li Tao pulled it down, then the officer raised it again. This continued for some time until Li Tao opened his eyes at last and saw the five gold stars on the policeman's hat. They were both interrogated of course. Neither of them could produce their marriage certificate, so they were taken away in the van.

Six years have passed since the death of Mao Zedong and the end of the Cultural Revolution. Deng Xiaoping is back in power, calling for 'Four Modernisations', private enterprise and foreign investment. He has liberated the economy, but continues to clamp down on all forms of dissent. When the activist Wei Jingsheng said the Four Modernisations were meaningless without the Fifth – democracy – he was arrested, put on trial and sentenced to fifteen years in jail.

The door has been opened to the outside world though, and people have started to think for themselves. In 1979, the No Name Group – communist China's first independent art association – held an inaugural exhibition in Beihai Park. The Star Group followed in its wake, and marched through the streets of Beijing demanding the right to hold private exhibitions. A team of Beijing photographers then set up the April Group with a revolutionary mission to photograph the country as it really is.

Everything is starting to change. China feels like an old tin of beans that having lain in the dark for forty years, is beginning to burst at the seams.

The Frozen Blue Sky

One winter afternoon of 1982, my daughter walks in from school. The strap of her bag is so long it almost reaches her knees.

Guoping and I have divorced, but she has agreed to let Nannan stay with me this term. She will come down from Yanshan on Saturday and take her back for the weekend, but today is only Tuesday. Nannan does not smile much any more. I am not happy either. My marriage is over, my girlfriend Xi Ping betrayed me twice this summer, and my work unit is threatening to rectify me again.

Nannan sidles up to me. 'Jianjian, Lili has a mountain spirit to help her with her homework. She's very pretty.'

'Where does she live?' I turn from the easel, my hands covered in paint.

'Inside Lili's pencil case. I saw her.' Her eyes look sore. 'Daddy – I mean, Jianjian – you've seen a spirit, haven't you?'

'Come here, Nannan. I will draw one for you.' I put down my brush, walk to the washbowl behind the door and clean my hands.

'You have a spirit, I know you have.' She leans over the desk and purses her lips.

I open the drawer, take out a stone I picked up on a beach, stroke Nannan's silky hair and switch on the lamp. 'Look, Nannan, this is where my spirit lives. This is her face, this is her red skirt, and this is her long black hair.'

She holds the translucent stone to the light and studies it in minute detail. At last she says she cannot see her, only heard her whisper something.

'The spirit is waiting for you to finish your homework.' I watch Nannan carefully lower the stone into her pencil box. 'When your homework is done, she will come out and take you flying around the room.'

The apartment blocks outside my window seem to merge into a single black wall. Lights shining from a few rooms glint like the eyes of a wolf. The government has unleashed a new campaign against 'Bourgeois Liberalisation' and my name has come up. My leaders at the foreign propaganda department have labelled me a 'questionable youth'.

I hear people pass through the wind outside. Men and women. The women's steps are lighter, but when the soles of their shoes crush against the sand, it sends needles through my skin.

On my way to fetch supper from the staff cafeteria this afternoon I bumped into Zhao Lan, a colleague who belongs to my art discussion group. She told me the security department called her in yesterday to ask why she visits my house and who she has seen there.

I retreated behind a heap of cabbages, and whispered, 'Don't mention the dance we went to, and whatever happens, don't tell them about the life drawings I did at Da Xian's house.' Last month, a group of friends clubbed together and hired a model for two yuan an hour. I left my easel at home and just took a sketchbook. The model had soft skin, large eyes, and thighs as smooth as glass. She sat in the middle of the room cracking sunflower seeds between her teeth, gazing at the men circled around her. Now and then, a husk fell from her mouth and landed on the black hair between her legs.

I heat up the meatballs I brought back from the cafeteria and serve them to Nannan. The room smells of pork and coriander. I glance at my unfinished painting: pale vertical branches cover half the canvas, a cloud moves through the black sky behind.

Nannan's picture hangs beside it. Last month, we walked down the lane to paint a tree bathed in sunlight. Nannan splashed green leaves onto her canvas and dotted them with specks of white light. The picture was small but much more alive than mine. She finished it in a matter of minutes, and when people stopped to take a look she said, 'Don't look at me, look at my father. He is the painter.' We worked until dark, then traipsed off to a dumpling restaurant and ordered two large bowls of egg soup.

When I return from the latrines, I hear Nannan whispering to the stone.

There are just a few coriander leaves left in her bowl. 'Where have the meatballs gone?' I ask her.

'I've eaten them,' she says, gazing at me with wide eyes.

There were two meatballs in her bowl before I left. The room still smells of pork. She must have hidden them somewhere. I sniff around and trace the smell to its source behind the bedside table. When I pull the table out, two squashed meatballs plop onto the cement floor. She opens her mouth and stares at mine in terror. I tell her to throw the meatballs in the bin, and she starts scuttling about the room like a frightened chicken.

Her body is so small and fragile, I feel helpless. I am sure her mother knows what to feed her.

'What does your mother give you to eat, Nannan?'

She looks up through her long tangled fringe. 'Fried bean sprouts and dofu.'

'You won't get fat on that. Come on, put your coat on and I'll take you out for some lamb hot-pot.' I check my pockets and stand up.

An hour or so later I turn off the main light and put my daughter to bed. The lamp on my desk shines on a heap of unfinished manuscripts, contact sheets and some stamps I am collecting for Wang Ping, a friend who writes for the *Hangzhou Daily*. The lampshade I made from cinema film smells of burnt glue. Below it lies the letter I have written to Guangxi Film Studio, and a Jushilin Temple textbook open at page ten: 'Sentient beings, lost in the red dust of the world, come to the Western Paradise of Amitabha, Buddha of Infinite Light . . .' I have attended weekly ceremonies at the temple for a while now. I spend hours memorising the sutras, but when the time comes to recite them I can never remember a word. Still, in the quiet of the temple I can forget myself. I watch the incense smoke drift to the sky and I follow it through the white clouds and see that above the clouds there is blue sky everywhere. I trail behind the disciples as they circle the shrine chanting sutras to the beat of a wooden fish drum. I fantasise about taking the Buddhist vows one day and roaming the country as a mendicant monk. When I leave the temple afterwards and see the crowds in the street outside, my stomach turns.

'Daddy, is Mummy coming this week?' Nannan's head peeps above the quilt.

'Call me Jianjian – Daddy sounds silly.'

'All my friends say Mummy and Daddy. Why can't I?'

'Because I'm not like a proper daddy. My life is a mess.'

'Daddy – I mean, Jianjian – when is Mummy coming to fetch me?'

'Saturday, as usual. You want your mummy, don't you? You don't want daddy any more.' I think of Guoping's face under her new perm. The tight curls make her chin look bigger. Sometimes she arrives on the back of her boyfriend's motorbike. The night before our divorce came through I went back to see her in Yanshan. I lay in bed beside her, breathing the warm scent of her hair. In the three years since I had moved to Beijing, we had slowly drifted apart. I knew she had a boyfriend called He Nong and she knew about my friendship with Xi Ping. The passion had gone, but when I thought that the next day this woman would no longer be my wife, I could not help feeling sad.

'I want you both. When is Xi Ping coming?'

'She won't be visiting any more.'

Xi Ping will never come here again. But she is still inside me, like a stuck fishbone rotting at the back of my throat. Why did it go wrong? Although I dared not believe in love after the failure of my marriage, she was the only woman I cared about. Her voice cut through the numbness in my heart. I loved her still features and quiet forehead.

I first noticed her last year in the cafeteria. She was standing in front of me in the queue for lunch. I asked her which department she worked in, and she said, 'Accounts. You should know. I've helped you twice with your expenses.' When we started going out together, I felt my life take a new turn. Sometimes I hated her, but the hate came from within me, it was a boil that grew from my despair. She understood me. When I told her I was considering giving up my job to go travelling around the country, she kissed my ear and whispered, 'Wherever you go, you can always come back to me. My body is your sunset.'

I can almost see her now, sitting on the orange sofa reading her book, then leaning over to pinch me with her damn little hands. I hated that. Women should be as gentle as water – warm water, of course. When we kissed, she waited until I was fully relaxed, then dug her teeth into my tongue like a mousetrap, biting harder and harder. She thought it was funny. When it was over she would giggle and kiss away my tears.

I put up with her bites and pinches. After all, what kind of girl can you hope to find in this mixed-up country? Clever girls are too busy opening restaurants and trying to make money. University graduates expect their men to be like the heroes in romantic novels who explore the wilds of Tibet. All the nice girls are in the countryside, but when they move to the cities they are too preoccupied with the cosmetics counters to have any time for you. Xi Ping was different though. She liked music and art, and her classical Chinese was better than mine. We both liked the colour brown and shared a recurring dream of being chased by a huge rock while our feet were glued to the ground. And neither of us liked to wash – we would only visit the public showers once a month.

I could take her anywhere and she would never complain. Once we were stuck on a hill after dark, so we just lay on the ground and waited for dawn to break. If she saw me lower my paintbrush and stare into space, she would write messages to me on her hand: 'I do exist you know', 'Hemingway topped himself in the end' or 'Where there's a will there's a way.' If that didn't work, she would pour a cup of tea over my canvas.

In July she was cast to play a nurse in a film about the Eighth Route Army that was to be shot in the hills of Guangxi. A week before she was due to leave, I discovered she had slept with Qiuzi and told her I never wanted to see her again. She was distraught, and I could not take the pain, so we made up in a flood of tears. I buried my anger in love. The night before she left Beijing, I pulled out a filing knife and told her to open her mouth.

'If you want to kill me, at least use something a little sharper.' When she looked into my eyes I could never tell what she was thinking.

'Come closer,' I said. She kneeled between my legs. I lifted the lampshade and let the light fall on her face. A cluster of freckles coloured her nose. I moved my hand into her mouth. Her breath felt warm and damp.

'I'll just straighten your front teeth.'

She sunk her teeth into my hand and looked up. The lower rims of her eyes were two streaks of red. 'Do you know how strong my teeth are?'

I pulled my hand free and shook the pain away. 'This front tooth is longer than the other, it will show when you smile on camera.'

'The nurse never smiles. It's a tragic role. She ends up being shot by a Japanese firing squad.'

11

'Then they will need to film your mouth when you scream in pain . . . Mm, your teeth are very strong.' I slowly scraped at the enamel, and this time she didn't flinch.

'What about Lu Ping? When is she coming?' Nannan is staring at the paper ceiling.

'Lu Ping won't be coming here for a while.'

Last week two officers visited Lu Ping at the Central Ballet Company and interrogated her late into the night. The next morning she came to my room and said, 'They asked about the photographs you took of me. They wanted to know if you kissed me. They told me never to model for you again.' She burst into tears. Her eyes were grey from lack of sleep.

Nannan has shut her eyes.

I remember accompanying Xi Ping to the train station the day she left for the shoot in Guangxi. We stood inside the crowded tram, our faces almost touching. She could sense I was still upset about the affair, so she said, 'Qiuzi wanted my address in Guangxi, but I refused to give it to him.'

'You mean you met him this week? You promised you would never see him again!' I looked at her face in disbelief.

'I've not left your sight for seven days – except the time I visited my aunt in Tongxian. I told you I was sorry. You said you'd forgiven me. But it seems you still don't trust me.' She stared out of the window and I looked at the slogan sprayed on the glass: 'Safe trip to work, happy ride home!'

'I will go to him when you've gone and find out the truth.' My eyes and throat felt as though they were clogged with cotton wool.

She glanced up at me. I looked into her eyes and saw the eyes that lay behind – mysterious globes that glowed one moment then were as dead as the dark waters of a well. It was still her face, but it no longer resembled her. The plucked eyebrows looked false. I had never studied her in such detail. Before, when her eyes met mine I saw blue skies, when the corner of her mouth twitched, I yearned to kiss it. But now the dream was broken. Her face was pale, the features seemed frozen. Her cheeks were dry and chapped.

Then I looked at her mouth and panicked, because I knew I had emptied all my love into it.

'My stomach aches.' She stepped off the tram. We clasped hands and pushed into the crowd.

'You can ask the conductor for a painkiller once you're on the train.' I took a deep gulp of air.

'Don't believe anything Qiuzi says. He's a hooligan, he will lie to you.' Her face looked ugly as it squeezed through the crowd. Our hands were still locked together.

'I just hope you're not lying to me again,' I said, pulling a suitcase that I longed to press down onto her head.

She never smiled after that, not even when I waved at her from the platform. As the train pulled away my heart clenched.

I went straight to Mimi's restaurant. I knew Qiuzi was a regular customer, I always saw his bike parked outside the door. When Xi Ping resigned from her job and started helping with the restaurant's accounts, Li Tao hinted that something was going on. But I ignored him – I was in love, and could not believe Xi Ping would go off with a man just because he had a motorbike. Besides, she was with me almost every day. When I discovered she had slept with him, I slapped her face and told her to leave. But that night, I saw her in Mimi's room. She was crying her eyes out, Tchaikovsky was booming from the radio, the room was dark, so we fell into each other's arms. The last thing I wanted to do now was to talk to Qiuzi.

At about five in the afternoon, he turned up. He was short, had a scar across his face and a leather jacket with shiny brass studs. He'd spent twelve years behind bars for hooliganism and sold petrol coupons on the black market. He'd bought Xi Ping black stockings, taken her on his bike to a friend's house and screwed her. When he went for a piss, his friend grabbed her. She screamed for help, but Qiuzi shouted, 'Do him a favour, will you, he's just out of prison.'

He walked towards me jangling a large ring of keys.

'Hey, Ma Jian! How's life treating you?'

The restaurant had four tables and a single bed at the back. There were no customers yet.

I lifted the door curtain and said, 'Come in, Qiuzi.'

He tucked his sunglasses into his pocket and made for the bed. A large motorbike was printed on the back of his leather jacket. The skin on his neck hung loose.

'If this blade doesn't kill you I'll turn myself in!' There was a knife in my hand and a spare one under the mattress. He struggled to his feet but I pressed him back down. 'Blink and I'll stab you!' My knife was pointing straight into his eye.

Mimi ran over from the counter. 'Ma Jian! Don't fight!'

'Stay away, Mimi!' I shouted, without turning round.

'There's no need for this. I'll tell you everything.' Qiuzi's face resembled the frozen chicken that was lying on the floor.

'I didn't do it much with Xi Ping. Once, at my friend's house. Three times in my room – my wife works during the day . . .'

'I know all that. Just tell me what happened this week.'

'She said she was going away. I took her to Beitaipingzhuang market, bought her two pairs of nylon tights. We went to the woods, she pulled down her trousers . . . Sunday I drove her to Tongxian to see her aunt, we did it twice. I dropped her at a station outside Beijing, she took the train for one stop, said you'd be waiting for her at the terminus . . . Yesterday, I gave her some travel money. We didn't go the whole way. She sucked me for a while but her teeth hurt, she said you'd cut them with a filing knife . . . Look, I'm sorry, I won't see her again. Don't be upset, women are all the same. I'll fix you up with someone else tonight, if you like . . .'

I left the restaurant and wandered through the streets for hours. I walked from Yuetan Road to Tiananmen Square, and from

Jianguomen Avenue to Ritan Park, then returned to the Square, and wandered past Mao's Mausoleum and the Museum of the Chinese Revolution. When I next looked up, I was at the turning into Nanxiao Lane. But I couldn't go home, because her slippers were on the floor, her black straw hat was on the wardrobe, and the windowsill was piled with her empty yoghurt bottles. She drank two or three bottles a day.

So I kept walking. The wall on my right followed me, then caught up and merged into the red walls of the Forbidden City. I was back at the Square again. I climbed up to the viewers' podium and lay on the cement floor below the portrait of Mao Zedong. Xi Ping's face was still shaking before my eyes. The day she went to her aunt I bought her some hawthorn jelly and loaded her cassette player with a recording of her favourite song, 'The Same Old Days'. That evening I waited on the station platform. She stepped off the Tongxian train and complained about the exhausting journey. When we got home, I took off her shoes, pressed my face onto her stomach, inhaled her musty smell, pushed her onto the bed . . .

'Get up, you wretched dog! What are you doing? Where are you from?' There were three policemen standing by my head.

'I missed the last train. My head hurts.' My voice disgusted me.

'Bullshit! Get out of here!' At least they didn't kick me.

My eyes swim across the room. Xi Ping's belongings are still stuffed in a plastic bag behind the door. As I stare at it, the bag appears to breathe.

'Go to sleep now, Nannan. You have to be up at seven tomorrow.'

'I am asleep.' Tufts of her black hair peep above the quilt.

'How can you talk if you're asleep?'

'I'm sleep-talking.' She curls up like a little rabbit.

I pull out my letter to the Guangxi Film Studio, and read it again. '. . . I am writing to you about my girlfriend, Xi Ping. I have recently discovered that she has been conducting an illicit relationship with a Beijing hooligan. She is cast to play the heroine of the film, a nurse devoted to the cause of the Party. I hope you will inform the director at once, and tell him that Xi Ping is entirely unsuitable for the part of . . .'

I take the letter to bed. Nannan crawls sleepily onto my chest. She needs her mother, not me. I have no breasts. I don't know how to cuddle her or brush her hair.

I turn off the light. The sky outside has cleared. Stars always shine brighter when a wind blows through the night. I will post the letter tomorrow. Never trust a woman again. If I listen to her excuses and take her back I will only have myself to blame. I told her I didn't believe in love, so why am I so upset? There is a gang of hooligans waiting for me at work. I will murder someone if they try to rectify me again. Fuck the Communist Party! Fuck its eighth bloody ancestor!

I shut my eyes and see myself lying on a cement floor. I have fallen to my death this time. My head is soaking in a pool of blood. Amitabha, Buddha of Infinite Light. Amitabha, Amitabha . . .

A Man of Thirty

Today is 18 August 1983. My thirtieth birthday. Before I am out of bed someone bangs on my gate. 'Ma Jian, hurry! Phone for you!' I grunt, slip into my flip-flops and stand up. The footsteps walk away. A radio booms down from the apartment block. At the gate I check my pockets, then go back to fetch my wallet, and grab my notebook too while I am about it.

A bus must have just passed, the dust feels hot underfoot. The left side of the lane is in dazzling sunlight, a few people stand in the shade on the right. The owner of the grave-clothes shop is sitting in his doorway. He holds the wooden doorframe with one hand and strokes his bare stomach with the other. 'Hey! Mr

Writer! You're up early today!' I grunt a reply and look away. I hate the sound of his voice. Ever since I quizzed him about grave-clothes and funerary objects he keeps asking me whether my book is finished yet. 'You've done well there,' he says, 'writing about the dead – they're much nicer than the living.' The public telephone rests on the windowsill of a small restaurant. A woman in a skirt is standing beside it, waiting to make a call.

Li Tao's voice rattles through the earpiece. 'It's your birthday today, I'll come round tonight.'

'Don't bother, I have nothing to celebrate.'

'Nonsense. You are having a party whether you like it or not. I'll bring the food, you get on the phone and ask some friends round. See you tonight.'

I glance at my wallet and notice the woman's calves shaking impatiently. Blue veins run down her feet and disappear under the black pigskin of her shoes.

'I'll pay for this one later, Aunty,' I say to the old woman seated by the telephone. 'I have a few more to make. I'll just let this lady make hers.'

The grocery store owner next door brings out a tray of sliced watermelon. A boy in a white vest snatches a slice then charges down a turning to the right.

'Fine. I'll send you the documents. End of the month. Of course they're imported, I have the receipts. Came back from Guangzhou last month. Great. Don't forget to bring the application forms . . .' The woman is still talking to the telephone.

Back in my room, I search for the sheepskin camera case I was awarded for a photograph exhibited at the Workers' Palace. It is too good to use, so I store it in a cardboard box under my bed. I open the zip and pull out a page of newspaper. It is dated 1 May 1982, the month before my divorce came through. I kept it because my prize-winning photograph, 'Sunset over Yanshan Petrochemical Plant', is printed on one side, and a review of Guoping's prize-winning Korean dance, 'Joy at the Great Harvests of the Agricultural Contract System', is printed on the other.

17

I saw her perform that dance in a propaganda show in the Temple of Heaven Park. After she came off stage I went to look for her in the changing pavilion. She was chatting with Hong Ye, laughing and swaying her hips. When she saw me, her face froze.

'I took ten pictures of you, they should turn out well,' I said.

'Hope they're better than the last ones.'

Hong Ye said, 'Stop bickering, you two. Come on, Ma Jian, take some photos of us while we still have our make-up on.' She is a few years younger than Guoping. Five girls rushed out onto the grass and practised their poses. Guoping raised her hands in the air and danced in a circle. In the sun her Korean skirt was as blue as the sky.

A large soprano stepped onto the stage and burst into song: 'Good manners and civilised behaviour are very important in life . . .' Her voice reverberated between the park's four walls.

'You don't have to stay, Ma Jian. Go home.' Guoping's face was glazed with sweat. The pink face powder creasing at the corners of her mouth masked her expression. The bare skin of her ears and neck made me think of her naked thighs.

At the bottom of the camera case I find a bar of foreign soap, still in its wrapper. Wang Ping, the *Hangzhou Daily* reporter, brought it back from her trip abroad. When our work unit sent a delegation to Norway she was chosen as translator. We met when she visited my department for a foreign propaganda training session. A photograph of a woman with long blonde hair is printed on both sides of the wrapper. When I hold it in my hand my thoughts turn to women.

The pawn shop pays me eighteen yuan: sixteen for the sheepskin camera case and two for the bar of soap. I buy one jin of pickled cabbage and two of sesame seed cakes, and blow the rest of the money on a bucket of beer. Then I create a makeshift table with an old canvas and a wooden crate and cover it with a sheet of newspaper. By the time I have set it with the food and glasses, it is almost dark outside.

I sink into my sofa and gaze at the bucket of beer. In fact, Li Tao was not the only one to remember my birthday. Last week I received a card from Lingling, a poetry editor at Guangzhou Press publishing house. It was a picture of Jesus. In tiny script at the bottom she wrote: 'Your expression reminds me of his.'

My mind drifts back to past birthdays.

Twenty-ninth. About ten of us went to Miyun Reservoir. I swam to the island with crippled Lu Desheng on my back. We nearly drowned. The tall poet Yang Ke came. He is an only child. After his mother was beaten to death in the Cultural Revolution he took over her job as gatekeeper of Beijing Workers' Hospital. He brought his new girlfriend, Weiwei. My heart sank when I saw her. She was the spitting image of Xi Ping.

In the twilight we all danced by the shore. The Taiwanese singer Su Rei sang from the cassette player, 'Speak to me in your soft voice and tell me what life is about . . .'

Our torch shone onto the rippling water. I swam into it, the light went out, and for a moment I felt as though I was floating in space.

In the evening, we sat on blankets in a cave and told stories to each other. Hu Sha rubbed his eyes and recited his new poem: 'Forgive me/ For when I lift my ideals to the sky/ I cannot help treading on the earth . . .' By day he teaches history at Beijing Steelworks University. Yang Ming, the buxom editor of Chengdu's *Star* magazine, read a verse she had just composed on the back of her hand.

Long after most of us had fallen asleep, Lu Desheng was sitting up, reciting his avant-garde poem by candlelight and glancing at the bodies around him.

'Hu Sha, stop messing around! I can see exactly what you're up to,' he said. Someone was fondling the girl on my right. I could hear her soft intakes of breath.

On the drive home, I turned to Weiwei and said, 'It was my birthday yesterday.'

Twenty-eighth. Had a drink with Li Tao and Hu Sha at Mimi's restaurant.

Twenty-seventh. Made red-bean dumplings at Zhou Zhen's house in Yanshan. After supper we pushed the sofa back and danced. Guoping did the rumba with He Nong and I waltzed to the *Blue Danube* with Zhou Zhen's wife. She was just back from work and still smelt of hospital corridors. I told her, 'I saw you last summer, queuing outside the cinema. You were wearing a black headscarf.'

Two years previously, the work unit informed us of Premier Deng Xiaoping's edict that anyone caught listening to the Taiwanese singer Deng Lijun would be sentenced to five years in jail. Guoping and I discussed the matter with Zhou Zhen as we had heard her tapes at his house. He advised us to stay away from him until the campaign was over.

Since we were not accustomed to the language of erotic love songs, when Deng Lijun sang 'Every day I wish you would take the loneliness from my heart' Guoping and I thought she said, 'Every day I wash, so that you will take the loneliness from my heart.' So when we returned from our weekly showers, Guoping and I would always jump straight under the bedcovers. It was only when a friend from Guangzhou sent me a copy of the tape last year that I discovered our mistake.

The party was to celebrate both my birthday and the end of the Campaign Against Deng Lijun.

Today, though, I am thirty years old. I open my notebook, and write a message to myself. Confucius said that at the age of thirty, a man should take a stand in life, but you still don't know who you are. Last year you lost your wife and your girlfriend and now you are about to lose your job. You have about twenty thousand days left before you die. Why are you wasting your life? You must focus your mind and do something.

Peng, peng! The door opens, Li Tao and Mimi walk in. Mimi always spreads a smile across her face.

'Cheer up,' she says. 'Look what we've brought you!'

Li Tao glances at the collection of his poems on my bookshelf and puts on Dvořák's *New World* symphony. He must have come straight from the office, he is still in his regulation white shirt. The bank where he works as a clerk is about a twenty-minute walk from here. 'Is that a new painting?' he says, slumping onto the sofa.

Mimi has a long cream dress, a gold necklace and a gold ring on the finger that is pointing to my canvas. 'Are those branches or stones?' she asks.

'Those are branches, and those are stones.'

'Why is the trunk twisted in a circle?'

I can't bring myself to answer that one.

'Have you finished your poem?' Li Tao asks.

'Not yet. My inspiration has dried. Maybe I really will have to go travelling. I'd like to visit the grasslands Fan Cheng wrote about.'

'You've poured all your poetry into your painting. You have nothing left to give.' Li Tao is my closest friend, he understands me better than anyone.

Mimi claps her hands. 'Enough chat. Let's eat! You can't paint on an empty stomach. Waa! Look at that bucket of beer! How many people did you invite, Ma Jian? Now tell me where you keep your kettle. I'll make us a pot of tea.' She swirls round and strides across the room, her leather sandals squeaking with each step.

Men in the Dark

'Chairman Mao was incontinent by the time Nixon came to China. During the state banquet, he crapped a turd onto the seat and it rolled onto the floor. Nixon asked, "What's that?" So Zhou Enlai rushed over and said, "This is a Chinese delicacy – it's the

Chairman's favourite. Waitress! Please remove the pickled gherkin that has fallen to the floor!" '

'That was last year's joke. Bet no one's heard this one . . .'

I am lying in bed, half drunk. Da Xian is sprawled beside me.
His breath reeks of alcohol. Last week, he drank so much he was
sick over his half-finished painting. He waited for it to dry then
hung it on his wall and called it a masterpiece of abstract art.
There are six or seven other men on the floor. Through the
darkness I can see red cigarette tips flicker above each face.

'Jiang Qing and Chairman Mao were having a screaming match.
She had just bought herself a bra, but Mao insisted bras were a
bourgeois vanity and refused to let her wear it. He snatched it
from her hands and threw it out of the window. Deng Xiaoping
was standing outside listening to their row, and the bra landed
on his head. When Mao saw him there he nearly blew his top, but
Zhou Enlai stepped in and said, "Look, Chairman! Comrade Deng
is training to be a fighter pilot!" '

'I don't get it. Why would a pilot wear a bra?'

'You fool. Haven't you seen those big goggles pilots used to
wear?'

'That's a terrible joke. Listen to this one. A kid asks his dad,
"Dad, why do we have a picture of Chairman Mao but no picture
of the Communist Party?" And his dad says, "Because the
Communist Party isn't human, stupid child." '

'The Communist Party isn't human! You're damn right there,
damn right.'

Fan Cheng and Hu Sha are mumbling on the sofa. They have
recently started publishing an underground literary journal
called *The New Era*. Fan Cheng works for the tax office and has
access to a mimeograph, so he is able to print copies on the sly.
'Chen Hong's written a poem about abortion. I think we should
put it in next month's edition . . . That American journalist said
the secret recording of Wei Jingsheng's trial was broadcast right
across the States . . .'

'Hey, Hu Sha! I heard the Wang brothers have set up a guerrilla force in Anhui.'

'Rubbish. They were caught ages ago on the railway outside Beijing and were clubbed to death.'

'You're both wrong. My neighbour works for the State Security. The brothers are still on the run, but they're not half as dangerous as everyone makes out.'

'Those gangsters are no worse than the communists. Our factory's Party secretary still can't read. At the study sessions, he gets his assistant to recite Deng Xiaoping's directives, then swings his bare feet onto the desk and starts picking at them with a penknife. It's disgusting.'

'That guy in glasses I saw in your room the other day – have you heard? He's latched on to a foreign student from the Language Institute and is moving to America with her.'

'Our finance department can send two people to Denmark this year. Everyone is fighting to go. Only Party members stand a chance, of course.'

'Wang Chong's girlfriend has left him. She's run off with that Swedish guy, apparently. He's old enough to be her grandfather, for God's sake!'

'It's all right for the girls. They just cuddle up to a foreigner and the next thing you know, they're married and living in America.'

'Ma Jian! Stop pretending to be asleep. It's your birthday. Have another drink!'

'I'm listening. My head's throbbing though. Turn the music down, Fan Cheng, or the night patrol will hear us.'

I know people need to huddle together to survive, but sometimes I long to run away and curl up on my own. I hate working for the Party, but how could I feed myself without this job? I wonder what Xi Ping did today. She is planning to denounce me to the police, apparently. Her father is helping her compile a report on me. So much for her undying love. Guoping collected Nannan yesterday for the summer holidays. She said my life is too precarious and insisted Nannan stay with her in Yanshan for the next school year.

'Ma Jian. Last month at the reservoir you shouted, "Where have all the women gone?" Well, it seems you had quite a few to choose from tonight, you rascal.'

'They're just friends. Go to sleep now, it's nearly morning.'

I try to remember the faces I have seen tonight. Mimi danced cheek to cheek with Da Xian, then stood in a corner on her own. Li Tao looked upset. Chen Hong arrived late in a white sun hat and heavy make-up. She had just completed the final exam of her medical degree. Fan Cheng shot her a disapproving look. I suspect he wants to break up with her. She stopped in the doorway and said, 'I feel out of place,' then went to the latrines to remove her make-up. After supper, Mimi announced she was thinking of moving to Shenzhen Special Economic Zone and Hu Sha accused her of being a capitalist roader. Then Lu Ping stood up and said, 'Come on, everyone, a toast for our friend, Ma Jian!'

My head is pounding. Li Tao's pig's liver and spicy chicken wings tasted good, but when they reached the fish and alcohol in my stomach I began to feel ill. I am glad Lu Ping came. She is now the prima ballerina of the Central Ballet Company. I used to photograph her regularly for calendars and product catalogues, until the police interrogated her last year and told her not to work with me again. She looked prettier than ever today, but my experiences with Guoping and Xi Ping have frightened me off women who are surrounded by crowds of male admirers.

'Who walked Lu Ping home tonight?' pipes a voice after a brief silence.

'Why are there so many damn mosquitoes in this room?'

'I killed two a minute ago.'

'I saw you in the corner, giving her your telephone number.'

'Her arms are so thin. I think she should dance Lin Daiyu in *A Dream of Red Mansions*.

'She has already. Gave three performances on 26 August at the Tianqiao Theatre. I went to them all.'

'Why did she wear those tight red jeans tonight? She looked like an Overseas Chinese.'

'She's got no tits.'

'Her second toe is too long.'

'Hey, Ma Jian. How come you're not chasing after her? She's much nicer than Guoping or Xi Ping.'

'You're wasting your time. Lu Ping has a boyfriend.' As the men discuss her, Lu Ping's image smiles down from the black ceiling. I presume the others are gazing at it too.

I remember sitting in the dark theatre last year, watching her dance in *A Dream of Red Mansions*. The second act ended with her twirling despairingly through the falling blossom having heard her lover Bao Yu was engaged to his cousin. Bao Yu had in fact been tricked by his family into thinking he was betrothed to Lin Daiyu. After the wedding ceremony he discovered the true identity of his bride, and he left his red mansion in horror and rushed to his lover's side. But it was too late. Lin Daiyu had died of heartbreak the very moment he was exchanging his vows. In a flash, Bao Yu saw through the red dust of illusion. He discarded his worldly ties and set off in search of enlightenment. Lu Ping is ideal for the part of Lin Daiyu. She has a frail, melancholy beauty.

'You pronounce your oath to the sun/ Let wild geese fly to the horizon and proclaim your chastity/ I believe you now/ So much so that teardrops drip from my passion/ It does not surprise me/ But I nearly die of laughter when you say the word: for ever . . .'

This is Hu Sha. He often interrupts conversations with a verse of poetry.

'No one is clapping, Hu Sha. You recited that one at Yang Ke's house last week.'

'Well, tell me who wrote it then, if you're so clever.'

'Wen Yiduo, as if I didn't know. Try me on the Tang poets, if you dare.'

'They're old hat. Let's see how well you fare on contemporary writers.'

'Shut up. It's nearly light outside. Can't you hear the muck carts driving down the lane?' No one is smoking any more, so I cannot see any faces. When the men stop talking a musty heat rises and spreads through the room. Hu Sha starts to snore. He always snores, even on the bus. He can sleep anywhere now. His father was rectified so severely during the Cultural Revolution that the old man lost his mind. He used to stay up all night wandering about the house, scratching counter-revolutionary slogans on the wall with household objects and shouting, 'Evil bastards, bloody communists!' So Hu Sha learned to sleep standing up. His father passed away last year, and the following day Hu Sha had a black band on his left arm and a few more wrinkles on his face.

I start to nod off. In my daze the house transforms into a large empty cardboard box, as light as a feather, hovering below the tall red apartment blocks. What was it that Saul Bellow wrote in *Humboldt's Gift*? Plump women with big breasts. No – fine breasts, big nipples. Damn, that can't be right. Big nipples . . . big breasts . . .

Writing my Self-Criticism

In early September, I turn up for another day at work under the crowd's watchful gaze. As I step into my office the secretary walks in and says, 'Ma Jian, Deputy Qian would like a talk with you. You're to wait for him in the conference room.'

There is a mountain of post on my desk. I am compiling a photography book entitled *Spare Time Activities of Chinese Workers*, and have written to trade unions around the country asking for submissions from their members. The book will be presented to foreign delegations as a souvenir of their trip to China. I have received thousands of photographs, but not one is fit for publication. I have pictures of everything from a mother bathing her child, to forty people huddled around a television set; from a family taking a group photograph in the park, to a man building a chicken coop in his backyard. None of these activities would meet with the leaders' approval. And besides, most of the pictures are either out of focus or underexposed.

It would be quicker to establish exactly what the leaders want and then take the photographs myself. I know how things work now. I have learned the hard way. When I first joined the foreign propaganda department, I had to make two trips to the Wuhan Steel Works for just one photograph. In the first batch the pictures were too dark and the workers' clothes were torn. Director Zhang, the department chief, was not pleased. On my second visit, I told the workers to change into clean uniforms and jab their pokers into the flaming furnace with beaming smiles on their faces. The factory chairman walked up to me and whispered, 'If they do that any longer the pokers will melt.'

'Be quiet!' I snapped. 'This is a political assignment!'

I was still angry that he had forbidden me to photograph the worker who was tending the furnace when I walked in. When I asked the man to pose for me, the chairman muttered, 'You can't use him, he's not a Party member, and he asked for sick leave last month.' He presented me with three model workers to photograph instead. By the time I had finished with them, their faces were blistered from the sparks of molten steel. When you work for the Party, you have to learn to falsify reality.

I enter the conference room and am joined shortly by Chairman Liu, the office supervisor, and Deputy Qian, the section head. As we sit down, Director Zhang walks in holding copies of *Workers of China* and *Chinese Trade Unions: Questions and Answers*. When I see where he sits, I know it is serious. The last time he sat there he accused me of being 'dangerously irresponsible'. I had photographed Yangzi Bridge in Nanjing and failed to notice a patch of flaking paint in the foreground. Before I returned to Nanjing I told the bridge leaders to ensure that all areas visible in the photograph were given a fresh coat of paint.

Director Zhang is a slippery Henanese. He has the face of a hippopotamus and shirt collars that are always too tight. The only time I saw him unbutton his collar was the night he came to warn me of my imminent arrest. He looked at my glass and said, 'What's that you're drinking? I'll take a swig if you don't mind.' I said it was Erguotou wine, and he gulped it down with trembling hands. Anyone would have thought it was him the police were after, not me.

Now he says, 'Young Ma, we have called you here today for a very important reason. Deputy Qian always keeps a keen eye on our work, as you know. The propaganda we produce for foreign countries has a great impact on the image of Chinese socialism abroad . . .' I notice Deputy Qian's eyes darting impatiently, so I say, 'What is the problem, Director Zhang?'

Deputy Qian coughs loudly. He always gives the impression of being in imminent need of resuscitation. He clears his throat and says, 'You have been in the propaganda department for a long time now, and we still haven't had a serious talk. You are a painter – we understand that – so we have turned a blind eye to your sloppy dressing and tried to concentrate on your perform- ance at work. But please, when you attend events involving foreigners, you must shave your beard, wash your hair and wear a clean suit. You are representing your country after all. Today we have called you in to discuss your work. It is probably my fault for not noticing before . . .'

'Deputy Qian is a very busy man,' Chairman Liu interrupts. 'He meets with foreigners every day. At ten o'clock this morning, he has an appointment with a French trade union delegation.'

'Let's ask Director Zhang to talk us through this matter, shall we?' Deputy Qian says, coughing again.

'There are some problems, and Deputy Qian brought them to my attention some time ago, problems concerning Young Ma's way of thinking. In the past, I always thought we could differentiate between the lax way he conducts himself in his leisure time, and his behaviour at work. But now it seems it is not as simple as that, really not as simple as that . . .'

'Just tell me which aspect of my work you are not happy with.' I stare at Director Zhang's whitening face.

'You have some artistic talent, otherwise the authorities would not have transferred you to the capital. But you must separate your personal creative work from your political duties to Party propaganda. You have held exhibitions of your paintings and photographs. We always gave you our consent, we even allowed you to attend the Buddhist ceremonies at Jushilin Temple. As the higher authorities have said: that is your own business. But you must not let any of this affect your work.' Director Zhang's eyes redden as he speaks.

'Director Zhang, let Young Ma work out the problem for himself,' says Deputy Qian.

A secretary opens the door and peeps in. 'I think it's Old Wu, Deputy Qian. Shall I tell him to wait for you in the personnel office?'

Mock-ups of the magazines and book covers I've designed are spread over the wide table. I have to lean over to see them.

'This is a photograph of the water pipes at Beijing Number Two Car Factory,' I explain. 'The decision to photograph them was taken at an editorial meeting. The central authorities have told us the emphasis of propaganda work should be placed on heavy industry.'

'Young Ma, you work in propaganda now. It is surprising therefore that you did not attend the meeting last month in which we distributed the latest directives from the central authorities.'

Chairman Liu's chins roll into his neck. He wears brown-rimmed glasses. The sky outside the window is two squares of light dancing across his face.

'I was in Changzhou interviewing a science and technology model worker.'

'Young Ma, the photograph itself is not too serious. At most it is a case of having a sluggish mentality and failing to keep up with new trends. There are old comrades in charge here who can help you rectify this. I must inform you though, that for the second half of this year the emphasis of our propaganda is on light industry, not heavy industry. If you do not study the documents or read the newspapers, how can you hope to be a good journalist?' Then Deputy Qian turns to the director and asks, 'Is it too late to change the photograph?'

'I have been talking to the printers. We can only change the colour of the title,' he says, rising to his feet.

'Young Ma, take another look at the colour you have chosen here,' Deputy Qian says still sitting down. 'What is this colour trying to say?'

'It is yellow. I chose it to brighten things up.'

'Can't you see the problem?' His beady eyes dart up and down like a mouse. He gets up now, and Chairman Liu goes to stand behind him.

Four pairs of eyes stare at the cover. A telephone rings in the office next door – or further away perhaps.

'I can't see the problem.'

'If you can't see the problem, then that is an even greater problem!' Deputy Qian slaps his hands on the table. 'Such a large patch of yellow! You are trying to suggest that we are a federation of pornographic trade unions!'

The conference room falls quiet. The table in front of me looks very heavy. 'What is a pornographic trade union?' I ask quietly.

'It's bourgeois, young Comrade Ma. You have committed a

fundamental error, fundamental!' The deputy's lips are quivering.

'Then tell me, Deputy Qian – if I had printed the title in white letters on a black background, would you be accusing me of turning black into white?'

The chairman points to the sample cover for *Chinese Trade Unions: Questions and Answers.* 'And what is this you have painted here?'

'A question mark, or the outline of an ear.' My throat tightens.

They exchange knowing glances. I don't know which face to look at.

'Why have you put a question mark on the front cover?' I notice the director has not spoken for some time.

'It seems to fit the title of the book. These lines are sound waves entering the ear. What is wrong with that?'

'If there was nothing wrong what would we have called you in for?'

'If you ask me a proper question I will try to answer you.' I feel like swearing.

'You put a huge question mark on the cover and then say there's nothing wrong! We all know what you're trying to do. You are trying to imply that socialism doesn't know where it's going!'

'Don't put words in my mouth, Deputy Qian. Who am I to know where socialism is going? Wherever it decides to go, it won't be looking at my book cover for directions!'

'Young Ma, things will get very dangerous for you if you carry on like this.' Deputy Qian walks to the door and shouts, 'You have one month to write a self-criticism.'

Walking back to my office, I suddenly find it hard to breathe. The corridor is so empty it makes me think of the desert. My colleagues probably heard the shouting and are hiding in their rooms. Neat patches of light fall from each door. The cement floor has been scrubbed so much it appears to be glazed by a thin layer of water, at the same time it looks as heavy as the earth. It suddenly occurs to me I have not seen the date tree I planted outside my flat in Yanshan since Guoping and I divorced. Apparently it has grown quite tall now and is already bearing fruit.

Mixing Blood and Urine

With my back against the wall, I pull myself up, take two steps, then stumble and fall. The ground is cold. I am at the entrance to the latrines at the corner of Nanxiao Lane. The lid to the manhole is loose – I always trip over it on my way home. The ground feels wet. I wonder where the men who tore out my eyes have gone. I glance down at my watch but cannot see it. My hands touch a black wall. I scratch and shout, 'Let me through!' then discover the wall is not in front of me – I have moved inside its bricks. My body cramps and hardens. I try to move my head, but it slowly cements into the darkness. I remember my throat again and shout, 'Let me through, let me through!' ... My dream solidifies. I wake in a cold sweat, roll over and pull the quilt off the floor.

I hate mornings. They wrench me from my dreams and force me to gaze at my life's familiar props. Each object is bathed in memories that fill my mind the instant I open my eyes, and tell me I am still living in this crumbling old shack. The newspaper ceiling above my head looks the same as it did yesterday. The brown stain by the damp wall resembles a map of China. The Sino-Russian border protrudes like a woollen glove. Last month it looked like a woman with long hair, although if you viewed it upside down it became an Alsatian dog. Sometimes my eyes wander inland to Hubei where two knights in silk pyjamas fight in mortal combat. The wire holding the newspaper in place serves as their shining swords. When my gaze reaches Inner Mongolia, I remember the dirt road I walked at fourteen on my way to visit my brother who had been sent to work on the farms. It is a road that appears again and again in hundreds of my paintings. When it rained a few days ago, the ceiling changed colour and suddenly Einstein's face appeared. Each time I look at his face I think of Yanshan Petrochemical Plant and the hill behind, where steam from the central-heating pipes poured into the sun. At the foot of the hill was a station where fast trains never stopped. The ticket office only opened its window a few minutes before the local trains arrived.

I have painted the wall behind my desk three times now, but the paint keeps flaking off. A framed photograph of Nannan chewing the corner of her chiffon scarf leans against my lamp. My easel is in the corner. I pushed it there last night when Li Tao and Fan Cheng came round. We sat on the sofa and talked about *Waiting for Godot*. Fan Cheng spoke of his years breeding horses on the grasslands and of his dream to leave his job in the tax office and set up an artists' commune on a cattle ranch somewhere away from it all. I said I was tired of working on my self-criticism and would try to wangle a sick leave and go to Hubei Province to find a suitable location. Li Tao rhapsodised about life on the road. He said nomadism is the purest form of existence. We opened some beer and Li Tao recited Whitman's 'Song of the Open Road'.

The sunbeam falling through the gap in my curtains is so bright it almost cuts through the orange sofa. I didn't have to pay for that cloth. My sister's work unit gave it to her last Spring Festival and she made it into a cover for me. Enough of these rambling thoughts! Get up!

My ears start to ring. I sit on the chair, push my manuscript aside and jot down a plan for the day. Morning: go to Beijing Workers' Hospital. Afternoon: buy some nails to mend the door-lock. Evening: take my paintings to Zhang Wen's house and finish *A Portrait of the Artist as a Young Man*.

I scrunch up the plan, toss it in the bin and scratch my leg with the pencil. I take a sip of water from my cup, splash the rest over my face, then look at the cigarette butts on the floor, exactly as I did yesterday, and the day before. Enough! I can't take this any longer. I must leave, go away for good. But where should I go? Where can I go? Where do I want to go? One thing is sure: I can't stay here. What am I afraid of? No one is guarding my gate. I can walk out, leave these city walls and go to a place where no one knows me, walk along untrodden paths, sleep under the stars.

Well, let's just see if this trip to Hubei works out.

I hold out my cup and piss – too much! I pour some out of the window, carry the cup to the kitchen area, break an egg into a bowl, pour some urine into an empty jam jar, add the egg white, prick my finger with a pin, squeeze a drop of blood into the jar and screw on the lid. A red streak snakes through the yellow liquid. A quick shake and the mixture turns deep ochre – too dark! A few more drops of urine and the operation is complete.

Yang Ke is reading a newspaper in the hospital's entry lodge. The desk in front holds a stack of post, a jar of green tea, registration forms clipped to a piece of cardboard, a dirty Rubik cube and a large ring of keys.

'Hey, Ma Jian. Haven't seen you for a long time.' He lowers his *Beijing Standard*. The lock of white hair dangling over his face is brighter than his eyes.

'It's best no one else sees me here,' I say.

'Well, you better not go in then.' He forces a smile. Friends are always pestering him for help, he is probably sick of it. 'How many days do you want off?' he asks, getting straight to the point.

'I'd like a full week.'

'You had three months off during the Campaign Against Bourgeois Liberalisation. Wasn't that enough?'

'I need to go away for a few days. I can't seem to write or paint. You're lucky, you have Weiwei to egg you on. I heard you brought out a new volume of poems last month.'

'Oh, I wrote them off the top of my head. Passes the time though, doesn't it? How's your novel going?'

'I'm working on some short stories at the moment.'

'New Wind bookshop is selling *A Hundred Years of Solitude* and *The Sound and The Fury*. I hear they are quite good.'

'I bought them, and a new edition of *For Whom the Bell Tolls*. The stocks are running low though. I had to buy last year's *Household Electrical Repairs Manual* before they would sell me the novels.'

'We're having a poetry reading next week at the Old Summer Palace. Do you want to come? There will be some foreign students from the Language Institute, Hasi the Greek sinologist, a few secret police too, no doubt.' Yang Ke rocks back in his chair. A beam of sun shines into his eyes.

'The police broke up Hu Sha's poetry meeting last week. Did you hear? They arrested Li Zhi, the Guizhou poet. He's about to be sentenced apparently. Is the Dr Huang I saw last time still here?'

'He's on afternoon shift. But you can try Dr Sun, he's a friend of mine. Quite decent.'

We step into the hospital's entrance hall. Yang Ke stretches his arm through the crowd outside the reception window and bangs on the wooden frame. A pair of eyes looks up from the tiny hole. 'Hey, Sister Zhou,' he says, 'be a friend, give this man an appointment for internal medicine, will you?' He presses my shoulders down so the pair of eyes can see my face. I lean through the sea of hands and stuff my money in through the window. Once the notes have been snatched from my fingers and replaced by a thin piece of paper, Yang Ke pulls me free. 'I must leave you now,' he says. 'The afternoon papers are about to arrive.'

Everything goes as usual. I tell the doctor I feel feverish and nauseous, he hands me a bottle, I take it to the toilets, fill it with the potion I prepared at home, then deliver it to the lab and wait.

'You should be in hospital!' Dr Sun cries as he walks in with the results.

'No need. I've had hepatitis before. A week in bed, at home, and I'll be fine.'

He hands me a note for a seven-day sick leave. I carry it to the work unit and press it into Director Zhang's palm.

'Go home and rest,' he says. 'In a few days' time, Deputy Qian and I will come and see how you are doing. You still have ten days before your self-criticism is due. Now you must take care of yourself.'

Go to hell, Director Zhang, I mumble as I step onto the street. Never trust the wily fox who shows concern for the sick chicken, as the proverb goes. The crowds and buses are moving faster than usual. Hurry! One foot in front of the other. My legs move faster and faster.

Zhang Wen is the chairman of our art discussion group. He lives in Meiguang Lane. You can get off the bus at Drum Tower or Beihai Park, the distance is about the same. But I always get off at Drum Tower to avoid walking past the former residence of Guo Muoruo. When that giant of Maoist literature passed away, the Party installed a guard to protect the hallowed ground. The thick red walls that enclose his house spread such terror through the air that no one talks or smiles when they pass, even children fall silent. In fact, it is not the walls that terrify, but the soldiers and guns that lie behind. There are many such buildings in Beijing. These fine compound houses used to belong to rich merchants and aristocrats. When the communists came to power they butchered the owners and moved their cronies in.

Zhang Wen's house is even smaller than mine. His single bed fills half the room and his paintings fill the rest. There are no chairs, so visitors perch along the bed while he stands by the door. Sometimes he weaves his tall thin body through the room, pouring out tea, eyes fixed on his guests' every move, terrified they might touch a painting. 'Careful!' he says, 'That one's not dry yet' or 'Careful! That frame is loose!'

Yang Yu is in the corner at the far end of the bed. He is stout and thick-set, wears a red T-shirt, and looks nothing like his delicate, fragile paintings. By day he works at the Red Star Machinery Plant.

Ke Lu is perched in front. The light glinting on his thick glasses makes his lips seem even heavier than they are. At night he sells lamb kebabs and boiled tripe in the Dongsi Muslim Restaurant. When I go there to buy sesame seed cakes, he always gives me one fresh from the oven.

Skinny Chen Wen, a welder at Tiananmen Match Factory, is sitting on his left. He looks at objects, not people, especially not people's eyes. Yu Lei the set designer is seated next to him, sketching me. From time to time he glances up with a look of furious concentration.

Zhao Lan steps into the room, sweeps her hair back and squeezes in next to Yu Lei. She paints large watercolours of lush, mysterious rainforests. During the Cultural Revolution, she spent five years clearing the jungles of Yunnan.

I sit on a stool by the door. Zhang Wen's belly presses into my back as he breathes. He puts a hand on my shoulder and says, 'Today Ma Jian is going to talk about his paintings and show us his work, then everyone can make comments.' He leans over and passes Zhao Lan a cup of tea. His arm shakes. 'Careful, Zhao Lan, it's hot!'

'What do you mean make comments?' Yang Yu growls. 'This isn't a Party meeting, for God's sake. If you want to say something, say it. If you'd rather fart, then fart!'

'Look, we all decided we needed a chairman. I said comment – not criticise. Remember when Yu Lei discussed Toulouse-Lautrec? It was very informal, everyone said what they liked.' Zhang Wen's paintings are subtle and intricate. During the Cultural Revolution, when landscape painting was considered a counter-revolutionary crime, he wrapped his paint box in a brown paper bag and sneaked outside the city walls to paint fields and rivers and lakes. He painted the small picture by the light bulb during a performance conducted by Seiji Ozawa at the Beijing Concert Hall. The orchestra looks like a rock lashed by the stormy waves of the sea. Next to this picture is a portrait of his sick mother, crowned by a spray of deathly white hair.

'I have seven paintings here,' I begin. 'This one is winter – a cement house behind a cement wall. Even the windows seem to be made of cement. The only sign of man's existence is the red and yellow slogan on the wall.'

'Careful! Put it – there. No – there!'

'It's leaning against my leg, don't worry.'

'Can't see, lift it up a little.'

'You're holding it upside down.'

The painting is passed around the room, then placed face down at the far end of the bed.

'This is a branch in the snow – a black stroke across a sheet of white. I wanted to convey the noise that lies within silence . . . I painted this on the streets of Wuhan. It was a hot day, a crowd of people were standing in a doorway eating noodles. It looked like a stage set so I made the awning drape like stage curtains . . . This one I painted straight onto hardboard after a dream about being eaten alive. That's my family photograph in the middle. Some of the faces in the crowd are familiar to me, some not. The man gnawing my foot in the foreground is my neighbour. He runs a grave-clothes shop outside the Chinese Medicine Hospital, and is always telling me the dead are nicer than the living. The face on the left is mine.'

'The tones are very interesting . . . Careful! Look behind you!' Zhang Wen jumps as Zhao Lan's hand approaches her damp fringe and nearly knocks the tea cup perched on the wooden bedstead behind. She lowers her hand just in time, sticks out her jaw and puffs the wet strands away.

With so many people sitting inside, the room soon gets very hot. The naked bulb dangling before my eyes makes everyone's faces look dark. Zhang Wen's mother has been lying in bed in the shed across the yard for years. The door is always kept shut. Zhang Wen gave up his job at the post office last year to look after her. He is continually popping in to fetch her dirty bedpans and soiled cushions. When Nannan was living with me, I used to have to bring her along to the meetings. Sometimes she would fall asleep in my arms and Zhang Wen would carry her into the shed and lay her down next to his mother.

'I like this patch of blue. In winter, the night sky always seems frozen solid like that.'

'The style is very simple. It conveys the ordinariness of Beijing life. Too many artists ignore the life going on around them.'

'Who needs realism? If you want realism you would do better taking a photograph. Art should express one's subjective impressions.'

'What is there to express in this rotten society? Your nationalism? Your love for the proletariat? What bullshit!'

Zhang Wen leans over me again and says, 'Your paintings are very expressionist, Yang Yu. That picture of the Chinese vase you did expresses fears of annihilation, of good being brutalised by evil.'

'Men don't have an inner world, they're just walking lumps of flesh. This nightmare here – I like the way Ma Jian's used soft colours to paint a terrifying scene. I often dream of being strangled to death, or chased by wolves, and although I am afraid, I always sense a strange warmth, as if I was being held within the arms of a woman.'

'Ma Jian, these paintings are very different from your last batch. Why has your style become so cold and negative?'

'I still haven't found my style yet. Not one of my brush strokes seem to belong to me . . .'

'What have the Star Group been up to lately?' someone asks Zhao Lan.

'Searching for foreigners to buy their paintings. They're putting on a show at the US Embassy. None of my work has been chosen.'

'I heard you sold a painting to the Dutch Ambassador the other day for two hundred dollars.'

'Nonsense. I swear on Chairman Mao I have never sold one of my pictures! I bet that fucking Da Xian has been spreading rumours again.'

'That rascal is trading stamps on the black market now. He's latched on to some foreigners. Must have six pairs of jeans already.'

'Let's stick to the paintings. Our next meeting . . .'

The room is as hot and airless as a crowded bus. 'Open the window, someone!' I shout.

'No, don't. If the old woman on night patrol hears us she will call the police.' Zhang Wen is sitting on a wooden stool now, his legs splayed across the threshold. He leans his head on the doorframe with a look of calm resignation. 'Ma Jian,' he says, 'you have not found yourself yet. Half of you is still stuck outside. If you went in completely you wouldn't think about brush strokes. You wouldn't need a brush – you would be slapping the paint on with your hands.'

On September nights, an autumn breeze blows through the streets of Beijing. Everyone at the bus stop is looking straight ahead, apart from the old woman sitting on a suitcase who is gazing at the bundle of pictures under my arm. Red and white light from the revolving lamp of the hairdresser's salon behind flashes over the backs of the waiting crowd. In China, where politics is the only religion, people can only find their so-called way in life along narrow, prescribed paths. For me, art is an escape from this, it relieves the boredom and makes life seem slightly more bearable. What a joke! Hauling my paintings around town hoping for some recognition. My inspiration has deserted me this week, every brush stroke feels wooden. My painter friends think I am a diehard conservative, my writer friends think I am a man of loose morals. In Jushilin Temple I am a quiet disciple, in the propaganda department I am a decadent youth. Women call me a cynical artist, the police call me a hooligan. Well, they can think what they like. I only have twenty thousand days left to live. Why bother myself with them? As soon as they talk to me, I get caught and dragged to a place where my thoughts become meaningless and confused, and in order to answer their tedious questions, I have to enter their heads, sit in their brains and politely sip their tea. What a waste of time.

Launch of the Campaign Against Spiritual Pollution

When I step off the bus and approach the office along the line of rustling trees, I always glance up at the arm of sky caught between the branches and the high roof. In October the sky is so blue and clear it makes one think of the sea. The conference room is packed. The smokers are huddled by the window. When Old Song laughs you can see his yellow teeth. Liu Xiaofang is reading the self-criticism published in today's *Workers' Daily*. 'Zhang Haidi says she has lost her legs, but not her will to live. Says the further she travels down life's road the smoother it feels. Well, it would, wouldn't it, from the comfort of her wheelchair! Last month she said the writer Pan Xiao may have legs, but he's walked himself into a dead end. Now she apologises, says she spoke out of turn . . . What a boring story.'

Old Bao and Aunty Wang are sitting by the door knitting television covers. They glance at me through the corners of their eyes. This morning, Director Zhang told me that today's meeting will focus on my self-criticism. 'It will affect your entire political future,' he said blankly.

Director Zhang walks in and takes charge. 'This is a plenary meeting for both Party and non-Party comrades. We shall start by reading Comrade Deng Xiaoping's speech concerning the ideological struggle against Spiritual Pollution that was delivered at the Twelfth National People's Congress. Would you mind reading for us, Chairman Liu?'

The room goes quiet. Chairman Liu stands up and starts reciting the speech. 'Spiritual Pollution is not just a problem of morality. If pornographic culture is infiltrating our nation, if erotic books and lewd pictures are poisoning the minds of our youth and ruining the socialist atmosphere of our country, then Spiritual Pollution is not just a problem of morality, it is the very destroyer of morality, and a violation of our penal laws . . .'

I scan the faces surrounding me. Wang Hai'ou, the Italian translator, is reading a magazine. After the banquet for the Italian trade union delegation last week, I followed him to the minibus and he gave me a carton of Triple Five cigarettes. 'Let's consider this our tip for the night. I've put it down on expenses.' I asked for a few cans of beer too but he said, 'Sorry, Old Ma, those crates are for the driver. Next time, all right?'

'Some foreign news agencies have suggested that our struggle against Spiritual Pollution is a political campaign. This is not true. But when something is clearly harmful – poisonous even – and foreigners insist that we welcome it into our country with open arms, well, I am very sorry, but . . .'

Yao Chunjun's face is pressed against the wall. His eyes are shut. He has volunteered to work night shifts to give his son a better chance of getting into nursery school. Nannan starts her new school in Yanshan today. Guoping and He Nong are married now and have been allocated a two-bedroom apartment. When I went to see Nannan last week, Guoping said my visits disrupted the stability of her new family and told me to go away.

'. . . and purify the Party organs. The Party must be rectified from the central organs to the grass roots . . .'

Lin Zhenyu is standing opposite me. He wears a wig. His wife works for the housing department. Her purple dress has yellow chrysanthemums printed along the hem. Her neck and upper arms are saggy. One day she brought her son into the office. 'My boy is very artistic,' she said. 'He saw a panda on television this morning and drew a picture of it straight away.' When the little boy in the red neckscarf glanced up from his homework, he looked just like his father.

'We must extend the scope of our criticism and self-criticism. We must make a clear distinction between right and wrong, and redress our mistakes. The central authorities have emphasised . . .'

Guo Xiaomei is on my left. Two years ago she was chairman of the students' union at Nanjing Foreign Language Institute. Her boyfriend did not make it into the Party, so he was sent back to his home town after graduation. Wang Jiayang, the man next to her, has the best classical Chinese in the editorial department. When his father died, he asked me to make a print of him from an old family photograph. In the darkroom I enlarged the dead man's pea-sized face until it was the size of an orange.

'Spiritual Pollution encourages passivity, laxity, disunity, corrupts the mind and erodes the will. It leads to distrust of socialism, communism and the leadership of the Communist Party. We must rectify the Party, and transform it into a steadfast kernel of socialist modernism . . . Now let's turn to Ma Jian. Everyone knows that Young Ma is usually very conscientious about his work. But serious worries remain concerning his so-called spare time activities, and the way in which they seem to be affecting his work. Of special concern is his lax, free-wheeling lifestyle which shows all the signs of the Spiritual Pollution the central authorities have been telling us about. Today the Party is giving him a chance to explain himself.' When the chairman stops talking, every eye in the room is fixed on me.

'I am very happy the leaders have allowed me to report to you on my thinking and my work,' I begin. 'I have spent five years in the foreign propaganda department, editing and reporting for *Workers of China*. At present, I am also collaborating with Old Wu from the *Workers' Daily* on a book about the spare time activities of Chinese workers. I admit I have an easy-going temperament, but I do not accept that this has adversely affected my job. On the contrary, I have always worked with great diligence. I take photographs, conduct interviews, write articles and oversee the layout and printing. You could say I do the job of four or five people. This year, I gave up my Spring Festival break to write a feature on workers celebrating Chinese New Year. I often stay late to print commemorative photos for our foreign delegations. I have visited countless universities and factories to talk about art, photography and socialist ethics, and the exhibitions I take part in during my spare time bring glory to the work unit. In fact, if I were to nominate someone for the title of Beijing's Number-One Model Worker I would place myself at the top of the list.'

Silence.

Then Chairman Liu explodes. 'You know very well what you have been up to, Ma Jian! Your free-wheeling tendencies have gone far beyond the type of behaviour we expect from a healthy young socialist! Think of those cover designs and photographs — without the leaders' scrutiny and advice, imagine what the consequences could have been! You do not understand how deeply you have been poisoned by bourgeois Spiritual Pollution!'

Director Zhang's eyes are red with fury. 'Those furtive friends of yours, with their long hair and denim jeans, like toads in their dark glasses. They visited you during office hours and delivered a bucket of petrol. The security office knows all about it.'

'We were going to the reservoir that Sunday. One of us made dumpling soup, one of us borrowed a car, someone else bought the petrol. There was nothing sinister about it.'

'The bucket was placed in the basement.'

'Are you suggesting we were trying to blow up the building?'

'You know perfectly well what you were trying to do.'

'Of course I do. If he had brought the bucket to my house, would you accuse me of plotting to blow myself up?'

Lin Zhenyu catches Chairman Liu's eye. 'I would like to say a few words, chairman. I visited Young Ma's room when he lived in the dormitory block. There were paintings everywhere. Young Ma is certainly keen on art, but in my opinion, not one of his paintings conveys the joy and excitement of life under the Four Modernisations. I asked why a face in one of his paintings looked like the face of a corpse. He laughed and said everyone puts on a mask but underneath our souls are ugly shameful things. He said we are born in a daze and die in a dream. His decadent thoughts have cut him off from social realities. He sees life as a great blackness. I feel he should confront his disturbed psychology.'

Guo Xiaomei raises her hand. 'I will say something too. Young Ma works very hard. I often go to the printers with him to check proofs. But today we are here to offer him advice. I think he is too arrogant sometimes, and he doesn't like taking orders. Those photographs he took at Spring Festival – the pictures of dumpling-making were fine, but the exterior shots of workers drawing money from the bank or strolling through the park were of very poor quality. He insisted on using them though, and a week later our department received a written complaint from Deputy Qian.'

Another colleague pipes up. 'Ma Jian has told us how able he is, so perhaps he will find my suggestion superfluous. I do not understand his spare time activities, but I feel he should take care to distinguish between the greater duty he owes to the Party and the Motherland, and the lesser duty he owes to himself. Young Ma often reads modern novels. We were travelling on a minibus once with a group of foreign delegates, and I caught him reading *The Catcher in the Rye*. I told him we should stick to foreign affairs protocol but he said, "We're on a bus, the foreigners are snoring, so what are you afraid of?" Sometimes he talks to me about modern literature. He says that socialism has alienated people's minds. Of course we work in different departments, so I don't know him very well.'

The thick tobacco smoke slowly warms the air. No one dares look at me when they speak, but I feel their eyes bore into every inch of my flesh.

'Listen to me, Ma Jian. You are the only person in the entire federation to have been called into the Public Security Bureau. Chairman Liu fought hard to give you this chance today. We know you have talent for propaganda work, but the paintings in your room are in very poor taste. They have affected your work. We are still trying to save you from arrest, but . . .'

A sudden rage overtakes me. I clench my fists and shout, 'If you don't shut your mouth, Director Zhang, I will throw you out of the window!' I pause and try to compose myself. 'Please excuse me, I must go now. I have to fetch my mother from the train station. You can mark me down as absent today.'

Back in the Public Security Bureau

Slowly my world closes in. When I queue for lunch in the cafeteria, everybody looks away. There are a thousand employees in this building. I hear them crack jokes in the corridor, drop their children off at nursery, collect post from the mail room, but not one of them will talk to me. Just once, when I am waiting for the lift, a voice behind me whispers, 'You were right.' I turn round, and the man looks away. It is the graduate from Beijing University who has recently joined our English section.

One morning in late December, I step into the corridor and pin a notice to the wall. 'Open letter to the foreign propaganda department. The leaders do not support my work. They are trying to muzzle me.' The security office removes the notice and summons me in for a talk. They inform me that from now on I must turn up for work on time and not take any more sick leave.

After lunch, as I sit at my desk reading my post, Director Zhang walks in and says, 'You are wanted at the Public Security Bureau.' I look round and see two policemen standing in the doorway.

It is dawn three days later before I am finally released from the Western District Public Security Bureau. The officer who walks me to the gates says, 'Don't look so pleased with yourself. If we want to, we can make you slowly disappear.'

The sky is still dark. A horse-driven muck cart moves down the street leaving a foul stench in the cold air. Cyclists swish by on their way to work, their faces a blur. A road sweeper whisks his brush over the frozen asphalt. The noise echoes between the high walls and the black buildings behind. The morning buses have not started yet. I stand for a while at the bus stop, then walk on.

It is a long walk home. I will have to cross the entire city. My legs feel weak. A cold shiver runs down my spine. I see a truck parked in a side alley and walk towards it. There is no one inside, so I take a crowbar from the back, prize the cabin door open and lie down across the seats.

Scenes from last night flit through my mind. The interrogator put his legs on the table and stroked his cup of tea. He wore black-rimmed glasses. The table was laden with reports from my neighbours, my self-criticism, my keys, the contents of my pockets and the belt and buttons removed from my trousers to stop me from running away. He kept repeating, 'Think carefully. If you had done nothing wrong, why would you be here? Confess now and we will be lenient. Just stop playing the bloody fool.'

'I have nothing to confess.'

'Did you kiss Lu Ping or not?'

'No, she just came to my house to pose for the photographs.'

'And why did she take her clothes off?'

'I told you – my old work unit commissioned me to take the pictures last year for a product catalogue. It was all above board. Anyway, you couldn't see her body, only her hands and the candle were in focus.'

'Still, you don't need naked women to advertise candles. What happened after you took the pictures?'

'She put her clothes on and said, "That was quick." '

'And what did you do?'

'Nothing.'

'Wipe that smirk off your face, you smug bastard. You think you're something special with your long hair and denim jeans. Well, you can't get away with that here! If you were such an upstanding citizen, how come we have received so many reports on you? We released you two years ago to give you a chance to prove yourself. But look what I have here: "Long-haired man, about forty, visited him twice in his office . . . A woman seen sauntering in and out of his house all day." Can you explain why the people have chosen to pick on you in particular?'

'That was my sister they were talking about. She often stays with me. The neighbours must have seen her using the tap in my yard.'

'Stop lying! Stand straight! I don't want to lose any more sleep talking to a hooligan like you. Give me the names of every layabout who's walked through your door. Tell me who they are and where you met them.'

'My address book is in front of you – you can check the names yourself,' I said, still clutching my trousers. 'Why not ask me about the notice I pinned up at work. I have nothing to hide.'

'Don't try to play politics, young man. This isn't the work unit. It's where we lock criminals up.'

They gave me nothing to eat or drink, so when the interrogator stepped into the back room I took a quick gulp from his jar of tea. I hated to watch him drink from it because each time he finished a jar he would go for a piss and make me stand by the wall with my hands in the air. One time I rested my hands on the wall and got a sharp kick in the back as he walked through the door.

The truck's cabin is very cold, but the seats are more comfortable than the cement floor I slept on for the last three nights. The cell they locked me in had a double steel door and a small window that let some light in during the day and a faint breeze at night. There was a urine-streaked bucket in the corner, the walls above it were smeared with shit. In the daylight you could read the messages daubed in blood: 'Fuck you, Lili! ... The Party gave me a heart of steel ... Sorry, Mum ... The people's police kill the people ... On with the revolution!'

At one point the hatch of the inner door opened and two faces peered in. It was too dark for them to see me, so they shouted 'Stand up, Ma Jian!' I grabbed the metal bars and breathed onto their faces, and they quickly stepped back. 'They won't let you off so lightly this time. Your name is on the list. It's nothing to do with us though, we've just come to say hello. I'd own up though if I were you – they're bound to get you sooner or later.'

They closed the window, but the square of light still flashed before my eyes. I recognised them as the two policemen who arrested me two years ago. The short one, Officer Wu, liked to smoke and kick people about. I confessed to attending a dance party at a friend's house, and the next day he pushed me into a police van and drove me around Beijing demanding I direct him to the homes of every other guest at the party. I regretted my initial confession and was determined not to make the same mistake again, so I said I had forgotten the addresses. Officer Wu kicked me in the chest and shouted, 'So you want to play games do you? You little fuck!'

I can hear more and more bicycles go by. It must be getting light. I sit up, climb off the truck and resume my journey home.

I walk as slowly as possible, afraid that if I get home too early I will wake my mother up. When she heard I was in trouble at work, she packed her bags and caught the first train to Beijing.

She has been looking after me for nearly two months now. I feel bad for all the worry I have caused her.

Bicycle chains and bus brakes grind and screech. Two men shout outside a grocery store as they unload crates of beer and fizzy orange from the back of a tricycle. 'Their soya milk has gone up again, I won't buy it from them any more.' The man kicking the crates across the pavement has a piercing voice, the one bending over to open the door speaks more softly. 'Doesn't matter where you buy it, it all tastes the same. They make it from powder. In the old days they would stay up all night grinding beans for the morning.' The roar of a pneumatic drill a few streets away pounds through the soot in the air.

The sky ahead begins to redden. It is caught between the walls of a long narrow lane. Through the criss-cross of branches and telephone wires it looks like a pane of broken glass. The clock tower on the left is still dark. As I draw closer, I notice the thick layer of dust on its eaves. Crows flit back and forth between the treetops and the roof.

When I reach my gate I stop and walk back to the latrines.

The men squatting over the holes puff steam into the air like warm teapots. My neighbour Old Liu shakes his dick dry. 'Eaten yet?' he says. 'Yes, thanks.' When I see his face I always think of his daughter's long teeth.

I stand at the urinal. The graffiti scribbled on the wall a few days ago – 'Mount the piece of flesh, squeeze into her thighs, up and down we go, it's just like paradise!' – is now hidden under a layer of whitewash. Outside the chicken-wire window a stack of wooden planks is propped against a wall. Women shout in the toilets next door. I can hear the clink of their metal buttons and belts. A song blares from a nearby street stall. 'Tibetans stop drinking barley wine and churning butter tea, and cry with tears of joy at the sight of the People's Liberation Army . . .'

I push through my gate. The yard is strewn with fallen leaves and pigeon shit. I open the front door and see my mother sitting up in bed smoking. Her eyes seem to want to nail me to the spot.

'So they've let you out then?' She frowns and flattens the quilt.

'For the time being.'

I sit down. My desk is piled with the upturned contents of my drawers: letters, newspapers, photo albums, negatives, note-books. The paintings have been ripped from the walls and flung to the ground. The little watercolour I gave my mother is perched on the top of the heap.

'I'll start sorting this out.' My mother turns away to clean her glasses. I notice her wipe a tear from her eyes. 'This is what comes of talking back to your leaders. I told you it would end badly. Did they hit you?'

'No. Stop smoking so much. It's not good for you.'

She pokes the fire. There is a kettle on the stove and some sesame cakes she brought from Qingdao. Her back is more hunched than ever. 'What do you want to eat? There's some pork jelly, if you like.'

'I'm not hungry, I'll just have some tea.' There are holes in my paper ceiling, I can see through to the beams. Mice love to scuttle across them. I imagine one now, running along, then falling through a hole with a petrified look on its face.

'Why did they tear the ceiling?'

'Don't ask me. They emptied the drawers. Four of them came in the night. One was quite nice, said she knew you – tall woman. Said, "Don't worry old lady, we've just come to check things out. I'm from Ma Jian's work unit. If he's done nothing wrong, he'll be out in no time." '

I remember the policeman taking the door keys from my pocket.

'What did they take?'

'Don't know – some documents, I think.'

'What about the envelope I gave you?'

'It's still here in my pocket. Do you want it?'

'No.'

'What is it?'

'Don't ask. I told you — you're only to open it if I die.'

'Must be a will then.'

'Did Li Tao come round?'

'No, but these letters came for you. I hid them.' She pulls the letters from her quilted jacket.

At school, my art teacher told me paintings can be dangerous, especially paintings of people. He advised me to stick to landscapes. But even these can get you into trouble. I paint as the mood takes me — it is an emotional release. But in this society moods and images can incriminate you. Writing is much safer for me. I can hide myself behind a maze of words and the details of people's lives.

There is no will in the envelope I gave my mother, just a message I wrote to Nannan when I was missing her. The first letter is from Lu Ping. She says she has been caught up in a stream of rehearsals these last couple of months and has had no time to come and see me. The second letter is from my sister. She tells me to take care. 'If the fish bites the bait then they both die, if it swims away, they both live . . .'

'You have been here long enough, Mother. There is nothing to worry about any more. You should go back to Qingdao.'

'You're my flesh and blood, I can't help worrying.' My mother's back is almost bent double.

Last Saturday, I lay tossing and turning in bed unable to sleep, so I got up and went for a stroll. My mother put on her coat and followed me out. She trailed behind me all the way from Chaowai Avenue to Tuanjie Lake, and from Red Flag Plastic Products Factory to Hujia Tower. I walked faster and faster. My mother caught up with me at last and said, 'It's the middle of the night, let's go home.' We turned back through a narrow lane. The dark walls pressed so tight it was hard to breathe, I felt as though I was sinking into a pothole. At the turning into Nanxiao Lane a street lamp glowed through the leaves of a tree. I stopped and looked up. The leaves were transparent in the light, the branches stretched into the black night like a silent dream. Back in my room, I started to paint it, and finished just as my mother was falling asleep. I dragged her out of bed and asked her to have a look. She said, 'That's the tree we stood under just now,' so I gave it to her. Looking at it now perched on top of the heap, the greens seem too bright.

Beams of sunlight slant through the window, slicing the room to pieces. Coal dust puffs from the narrow vents of the stove. My mother opens the door, walks into the yard, and takes some charcoal briquettes from the sill. Through the window I see her white hair splayed in the sun. A pigeon perching on the roof behind ruffles its wings and takes flight.

Leaving Nanxiao Lane

' "An autumn wind blows through a red pear tree/ And dries the dew from your skin/ You wake, dragging the night behind you (a strand of hair stuck to your chest)/ The plains empty: the pear tree has gone/ The sunlight trembles through the grass and whispers: Are you happy? Are you happy? . . ." That's enough for now, you can read the rest yourself.'

It was the first Sunday of October, the day before my self-criticism was due. I handed the draft to Lu Ping and poured another beer. My desk lamp shone on her long calves, smooth knees. I could see her thighs touch under her tight red skirt.

She leafed through the pages, then put them down and said, 'Let's have that fish before it gets cold.'

'The fish, yes!' I smiled and looked away. I was afraid to look into her eyes.

Lu Ping had been visiting me every Sunday since my thirtieth birthday. Sometimes she stayed over. I never touched her though – perhaps because she had a boyfriend, or because I was still not over Xi Ping, or because her graceful movements reminded me of Guoping.

Later that night she lay asleep on my bed. I stood beside her. Through the darkness I saw the curve of her breast, her stomach, the fingers resting on her thigh. Gradually I could see her feet too, pointing into the dark. Her still toes woke memories of her ballet shoes spinning across the stage. I sat on the bed for hours yearning to touch her and kiss her, but terrified of breaking the dream.

The next morning she leaned over the sofa and shook me from my sleep. 'Wake up, Ma Jian! Someone could have murdered me last night and you would have slept right through it.'

I rolled over and saw her eyes, neck, the buttons that ran down her shirt. A strand of hair had fallen onto her chest. I stretched over and plucked it off.

After breakfast she sat down beside me and said, 'If you do decide to give up your job and go travelling, let me know. When the police catch you, I will make dumplings and bring them to you in prison.' Then she said goodbye and left. I rose from the sofa, looked out of the window and sat down at my desk. Suddenly she rushed back, flung her arms around me and rubbed her lips across my face. Then she ran away without a word, and never came to see me again.

I missed her for a while, but tried to push her to the back of my mind. Then, after my release from the Public Security Bureau two months ago, my life began to change. I took the lay Buddhist vows at Jushilin Temple and found spiritual comfort and a new perspective on life. The desires and fears that used to complicate my life seemed to drift away. The belief that there were other realms beyond the hell in which I was living gave me the strength to carry on. Guoping said I was a dangerous political criminal and refused to let me see Nannan again. She demanded I leave her family in peace and sever all contact with my child. I had nothing left and no one to hang on to. I started running circuits around Beijing every day, in a vague preparation for the journey I longed to make. Then last week I plucked up my courage and resigned from my job. I have bought a train ticket to Urumqi and am ready to set off into the wilds. I had planned to leave Beijing without telling Lu Ping. It is too easy to get caught. But when I phoned Chen Hong this morning to say goodbye, she told me Lu Ping was stabbed in the back last week and is lying in bed in hospital.

I decide to buy some flowers and pay her a visit.

I scour every crafts shop and art store in the district, but none of them sell flowers. There was an article in the newspaper about a florist opening in Beijing, but I cannot remember the address. Jianguomen Hotel has a flower shop for foreign guests, but as soon as I walk into the lobby the security guard notices I am Chinese and throws me out again.

I comb the shops outside Friendship Hospital hoping to buy some fruit, then remember she cannot eat solid food. A man broke into her room and knifed her in the back, the blade slipped between her heart and liver, she was unconscious by the time she reached the emergency ward. She woke from her coma yesterday, but her life is still hanging on a thread. I don't want her to die. At least she can see. I must get her some flowers.

At the Temple of Heaven's north gate I find a small nursery that is filled with rows of potted chrysanthemums. I buy two pots, snap the stems off in the doorway, buy a sheet of wrapping paper from a stationary shop across the road and run back to the hospital.

She has had two operations and is still in intensive care. 'Her body was swimming in blood when she arrived, we couldn't hold on to her. You can have a couple of minutes, no more. The police will be here soon, they are waiting for her to speak,' the nurse says, pointing at the clock.

Lu Ping is bandaged from the shoulders down and suspended

in a cage of appliances. She looks like a model aeroplane. Her ashen face is immobilised by the oxygen pipe fixed to her nose and the metal clamp around her head. I wave the white chrysanthemums in front of her eyes, and she moves her cracked lips.

'I only found out this morning. Fortune is on your side, you will be up in no time . . . I am going away for a while. When I get back we can eat some more fish together.' She blinks her vacant eyes. I remember the expression on her face when I recited my poem to her. I had told her she was the inspiration, and she'd smiled and said, 'Give me a copy when you are finished.' No one would imagine this pale thin face belonged to the same girl.

'You must get strong, Pingping. I want to see you dance again. The police are investigating the case, I am sure they will find your attacker. It is a miracle you survived. The nurse said the knife scraped past your spinal cord, one millimetre to the left and you would have been an invalid for the rest or your life.'

A plump nurse walks in. I ask if she can help me find a vase for the flowers.

'Have a look in the rubbish bins in the backyard.' She unhooks the empty blood bag and replaces it with a new one.

I poke through the bins with a long wooden stick. They are filled with rotten fruit peel, soiled dressings, pill bottles, broken strip lights. At last I find an empty fruit jar, but the lid is stuck firm. I borrow some pliers from the shoe menders across the road and manage to prize it off.

I stuff the flowers into the jar and place it on the bedside table, but she cannot see it there, so I pull out a stem and balance it on the oxygen canister, and slowly her eyes redden. I watch her gaze pass through the wires and machines. Five months ago she fixed the same gaze on me and asked, 'Are you happy? Are you happy?'

What could I say? I wanted to say, 'No, I am not happy, I am tired of life.' I wanted to say, 'I don't know whether I am happy or not.' And I wanted to say: 'You, Lu Ping, sitting here on my sofa, the way you speak, the way you move – you are happiness, a happiness I can reach out and touch. But I don't believe in love, I don't believe in myself. I can only touch you in my poem, from a far distance.'

I leave the hospital and take off down the large noisy street. I run from Yongan Road to Temple of Heaven. At Chongwai Boulevard I turn left and run to the drink store underneath Jianguomen flyover. The cement road overhead drones under the weight of moving trucks. A song blares from a cassette player resting on a biscuit tin. 'Have I changed the world, or has the world changed me? Same old yesterday, same old yesterday . . .'

Lu Ping was born in the south, grew up in the Beijing Dance School and became the star of the Central Ballet Company. There was always a crowd of young men waiting for her outside the stage door. She was too beautiful for this world, so someone stabbed her in the back. Even if she survives, she will never dance again. I put down the bottle of fizzy orange and set off down Chaoyangmen Boulevard. The road seems to soften underfoot, the lines of buses and pedestrians begin to thin. I run to the corner of Dongsi Tenth, pause at the crossing, then race down Nanxiao Lane. Coal dust hovers in the evening air, it clings to my throat as I breathe. I usually wear a cotton face mask on my morning jogs. The only place where the air is clean is in the Sanlitun embassy district.

I don't know if I love Lu Ping or what I could do for her. I see the knife enter her back. I see her weak and helpless face. Then I see myself standing beside her, blank and numb.

I turn round and run towards the Workers' Stadium. Ahead of me the evening sky is trapped between two red walls. The road stretches towards it. This time tomorrow, I will have left this city behind.

2.

Dust Storm

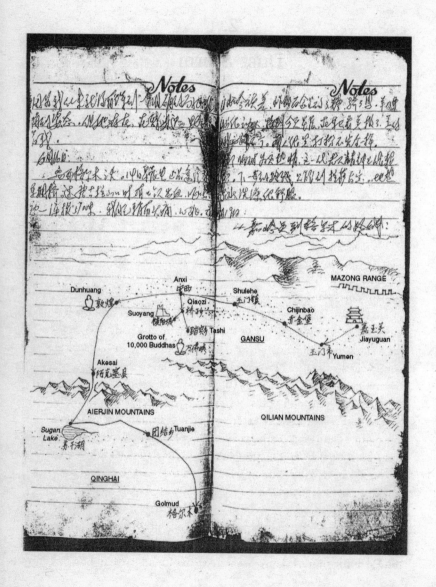

Emerging from the Gate of Hell

I board the steam train to Urumqi and watch the red walls of Beijing slip away. This time I am not travelling as a Party journalist on assignment to the provinces. I have left my job and packed a change of clothes, a notebook, two bars of soap, a water bottle, a torch, a compass, two hundred yuan, a wad of rice coupons, my camera and Walt Whitman's *Leaves of Grass*. My old life recedes into the distance and my heart races with the train as we rattle towards China's far west.

The map of China on my lap resembles a chicken, its head pointing east and its feet in the south. The train departed from the neck and will travel six thousand kilometres to the tail. I want to go as far away as possible, right to the western border. The neat fields outside the window flick past like pages of a book.

The man sitting opposite waves a cigarette at me. 'Want a smoke, comrade?'

'No thanks.' I don't want to speak to him. I hate the way his left hand keeps tapping the lid of the ashtray on the wall. His teeth are as grey as his shirt collar. The little girl beside him is cracking sunflower seeds with her teeth and staring out of the window on the other side. I look over too. The wheat fields on that side seem greener. The telegraph poles lining the track skip past to a steady beat. The bespectacled man on my right has nodded off. I am sitting in a hard-seat carriage with a hundred strangers, swaying from side to side as the train clatters along. It feels nice. My nerves begin to calm. I don't want to read, or speak, or move, or think . . . Live your own life . . . Sky beyond the sky . . . Empty, everything is empty . . .

For three days the train crosses the plains of Shanxi and Inner Mongolia, then swerves down along the Yellow River and enters the Hexi Corridor of Gansu – a long strip of land bordered by the

Qilian mountains to the south and the fringes of the Gobi Desert to the north. Two thousand years ago this was China's main escape route to the West.

At dawn on the fourth day I open my eyes and see the green fields have given way to a barren waste. Rays of morning sun beat on the Qilian mountains that stretch along the gravel corridor like a huge spread-eagled beast. The fierce rays heat the train windows and make the dust on the floor sparkle like snow. Everything bathes in their light: the gold-and-red banner emblazoned with the message LOVE THE PEOPLE that hangs above the door, the folded quilts at the end of each bench, even the cardboard boxes on the luggage rack. This is the sun of the high plateau that bakes the land dry and leaves one nowhere to hide. Distant snowcaps dangling in the sky gleam enticingly. I decide to make a break in my journey and get off at the next stop.

An hour later, the train pulls up at Jiayuguan. The station is huge, because the town stands at the western limit of the Great Wall, and the Wall is China's most prized cultural relic. Four years ago, when Deng Xiaoping first welcomed foreign tourists back to China, Jiayuguan was one of just twenty-eight towns he allowed them to visit.

So, smelling of tobacco, jasmine tea, dirty nylon socks and the vomit of my fellow passengers, I step off the train and take a deep breath of March air. After a last glance at the dusty carriage, I swing my bag onto my back and make for the exit.

A brand-new Japanese minibus is parked in the forecourt. Children and adults have gathered around it. Some study the foreign letters printed on the door, others peer through to the leather seats inside. The driver is smoking, his eyes fixed on the exit. He watches me approach.

'Excuse me, comrade, do you know if there's a hotel around here?' I ask, gulping the cold air.

'You can try the guesthouse run by the town's revolution

62

committee. Walk straight ahead and take the first on your left,' he says, pointing the way with his cigarette.

A long-distance bus pulls up in front of me. Two peasants clamber onto the roof to tie a sheep to the rack. As they pin it down, it kicks its legs in the air and stares into the sky. A boy with a runny nose sees me pass and yells, 'Big American! Big American!'

I walk to the centre of town along a wide empty street. Apart from the occasional concrete building, most of the houses are of pale adobe and crammed into a confusion of heights. Sunlight bounces off a propaganda picture on a whitewashed wall. It is a painting of a little girl in a red skirt standing between a man and a woman. The slogan beneath says CARRY OUT FAMILY PLANNING. CONTRIBUTE TO THE FOUR MODERNISATIONS. The sky in the picture is as blue as the sky above the roofs.

Smells of charcoal and grilled mutton waft through the air. A house is being built on the right. Mounds of cement blocks, bricks and sand encroach on the road. Wooden planks laid out for pedestrians lie soaking in a stream of whitewash. Horse-drawn carts, tractors, bicycles and shopping trolleys collide as they jostle past.

At last I reach the committee guesthouse. As I put my bag down half a girl's face peeps above the counter. 'We're full!' Her eyes linger on me for a while then return to the jumper she is knitting.

'I'm a journalist. Go and tell your leader to fix me up with a room.' Then I remember that the introduction letter I forged states that I am travelling to Xinjiang Province. 'Wait, don't bother, I'm in a hurry. Tell me, is there another hotel near here?'

'Yes, there's the Mighty Fort Hostel on Jianshe Road.' She is plump with big rosy cheeks. Her yellow padded jacket has a red collar attached.

On my way to the hostel, I take out the introduction letter and replace 'Xinjiang' with 'Gansu'. A cold shiver runs down my spine. If the police find out I have forged Director Zhang's signature and am travelling under false pretences, they will send me back to Beijing. Last week, when I transferred my registration from my work unit to the local Public Security Bureau, an officer called me in for a talk. He said, 'The Western District have sent us your personal file. I've skimmed through it and in my opinion, you're not such a bad sort. But we're not finished with you yet. We could summon you for further interrogation at any time. And don't think about running away – you wouldn't last a week.'

The Mighty Fort Hostel has no counter, just a window printed with the words RECEPTION DESK. I knock, twice. A girl emerges from the back room. I don't believe it. She looks identical to the plump girl I saw just now in the committee guesthouse – only she has a cup of tea in her hand.

'You look just like the girl in the committee hostel.'

'Which girl?'

'I don't know her name.'

'Oh, you mean Wang Shuyun.' A blush rises to her cheeks. I hand her my introduction letter and she buries her head in the registration form. Through the window, I watch her carefully copy out my address and employment registration number. She has forgotten the carbon paper, so she fills the second form by hand. The room has just been swept. Smells of dust and soot drift through the window. The certificates of merit and posters of Chairman Mao stuck on the wall have baked dry in the sun.

'I expect you don't get many tourists coming to Jiayuguan.'

'Tourists come here every day, don't you know – foreigners too.' She speaks in a local dialect, it is a little hard to understand.

'I don't have time to go to my room, can you look after my bag? I would like to see the fort before dark.'

'There's a two yuan deposit,' she says, putting down a thermos flask and a large ring of keys.

'Deposit for what?'

'The room comes with pillow covers, tea cups and a thermos flask.'

'I've never had to pay a deposit before.'

'We've joined the Contract System now. If a guest steals from the rooms, it's deducted from our salaries.'

'And what if they don't steal?' I smile, but her expression remains wooden.

'It's only two yuan, you'll get it back. You city folk are so tight-fisted.' She looks upset. As I walk out I notice the plaque on the door says, 'Mighty Fort Hostel, Contractors: Big World Tourist Company, Subdivision of Jiayuguan Transport Department.'

The fort is closed by the time I arrive. It rises from the stony plain, guarding a pass between the Qilian mountains and the Mazong range. In the late sun the pale yellow ramparts look as though they have just sprouted from the ground. I look east and see the dry bricks of the Great Wall snake along a bare valley and disappear over the faint hills at the horizon. From there it will continue five thousand kilometres to Beijing and finally plunge into the Yellow Sea at Shanhaiguan, sealing China from the outside world. When my friend the explorer Liu Yu heard a group of foreigners were planning to follow the Wall from end to end, he resolved to beat them to it. 'We must not let foreigners be the first to walk the Great Wall. It would bring disgrace to the entire Chinese race,' he wrote to me in a letter from Xinjiang. Last year, just as the foreigners' preparatory team landed in Beijing, Liu Yu set off from this fort, determined to march to Shanhaiguan for the greater glory of the Chinese people. Occasionally I see articles in the newspapers reporting on his progress.

My home lies in that direction. I turn round and look the other way.

The fort marks an ancient limit of the Chinese Empire. Everything west of here was called 'Guanwai', the land beyond the fort. Silk Road merchants travelling from the imperial court of Xian had to cross this forbidding waste on their journeys to Persia and Rome. Even today, the west is a place of banishment, populated by political prisoners, descendants of Turkic migrants, and the ghosts of buried cities. As I pass through the fort's western Gate of Hell, the poem of a Tang Dynasty exile comes to mind:

> Leaving Jiayuguan fort, tears rolling from my eyes,
> The stony desert ahead, the Gate of Hell behind.

Unlike the poet, I do not feel sad standing here. In fact, I feel strangely at peace. Perhaps because the fort is dry and weather-beaten, or because it stands on an empty plain, its walls do not seem as oppressive as the ones that surrounded me in Beijing. On the contrary, they look gentle and reassuring.

I climb to the top of a bare mound and see the gravel desert project endlessly into the west. On my right, the Great Wall crumbles to its end in the foothills of the Mazong. On my left, the silver Qilian peaks are still hooked to the blue sky. As the sun shimmers across them, specks of light scatter the waste like notes of a heavenly score. A marsh spreads to the south, its waters and reeds rippling in the wind. I lie flat on my back. A cool wind blows a white cloud away to reveal a thin strip of moon. I dig my fingers into the cold earth and whisper: I'm here, at last, and everything is beautiful.

When the sky turns red, I stand up and glance at my watch. Nine o'clock. The hotel doors close at eleven. An eagle cries out as it cuts through the sunset. Back at the fort I see an old couple painting the sky. They have white hair. The old man's wispy beard blows in the wind. I take out my camera to photograph the pink clouds. A girl walks over from Swallow Cry Wall. She too has a camera in her hand.

'Are you a photographer?' she asks.

'Yes.'

'How interesting! My name is Su Jin. The couple over there are painters. They're from Japan.' I look at the old man with the white beard and the picture on the easel in front of him: fort on one side, eagles on the other, a blood-red sunset in between.

'Are you their tour guide?' I ask.

'Yes, how can you tell?'

'You look like one, that's all.' I hesitate between continuing the conversation and walking away, then I think of the long walk back to the hotel. 'You came by car, I suppose?'

'Yes, it will be here in a minute. We'll give you a lift if you like.'

We walk back to Swallow Cry Wall. I stretch out my hand and stroke the rough surface. It is as hard and dry as tree bark.

'Give it a slap. Go on – hit it, hit it!' she shouts, smacking the stone. 'Does it sound like a shrieking swallow to you?'

I look up and the wall turns black, as it does in the legend when the father swallow crashes into it on his flight home. The story goes that the mother swallow waiting for him in the nest high above cries out day and night, yearning for his return, until one day her breath gives out and she falls to her death.

'No. But you do.'

'You have quite a sense of humour, it seems.' She smiles, and I look at her a little closer.

Men are like swallows, when autumn arrives they long to fly away. Life moves with the same rhythm as the sky and the earth. It changes as sun changes into moon and day into night. If they told me to return to Beijing now, I would charge straight into those ramparts. I would rather crack my skull and die than go back to moulder in that dank city.

A Japanese minibus pulls up in a cloud of yellow dust. A resistance song from the 1930s booms from the radio: 'Eyes of hate, raging fires, rivers of hot blood. The evil invaders perish in the mud while our dead martyrs shine like gold stars . . .'

The driver jumps out. It is the man I spoke to this afternoon outside the train station.

'So, what's up, Su Jin?' he shouts. 'It's dark already. Haven't those bloody Japs finished yet?'

First Steps

I seldom write in my notebook, for fear the police might read it. But at night, when I lie in a hostel bed with nothing to do, I cannot resist jotting down some thoughts.

5 March. Left Jiayuguan three days ago, and have walked nearly 100 kms already. Tonight I'm staying at the Peasant, Worker, Soldier Hostel in Yumen town. There is hot water in the bathroom and a television in the conference room downstairs. I went down a minute ago, but there were so many people watching, I couldn't squeeze in.

Managed to buy some biscuits this evening before the shops shut. The street lamps were very bright, but they pointed to the sky and left the roads in complete darkness. All the cyclists wore face masks to protect them from the pollution. There are so many factories here, the town is shrouded in soot. The Qilian snow peaks in the distance looked pure and other-worldly. I must walk faster tomorrow.

8 March. Third night at Guangming Hostel in Chijinbao. No central heating. The water in the enamel washbowl has frozen solid. Cigarette butts and chicken bones litter the floor. Went to warm up in the staff dormitory. Two young men were having a beer and a game of poker. One was

wearing a nylon jacket. Each time he threw his hand in the air you could see the large tear along the armpit.

Flicked through *Leaves of Grass* this morning. I like this verse:

Camerado, I give you my hand!
I give you my love more precious than money,
I give you myself before preaching or law;
Will you give me yourself? will you come travel with me?
Shall we stick by each other as long as we live?

Tried reaching the mountains this afternoon. Walked 10 kms, but didn't get near. Saw trucks stream from a quarry in the foothills. The clouds of dust behind them looked like yellow sails moving across the sea. Picked up some stones engraved with delicate fossils of primitive insects. Sat by a marsh for a while and thought of Xi Ping. Don't know why. Perhaps because she appeared in my dreams last night. Lost my sunglasses. Never mind – I suppose I can live without them.

On my way back, a boy gave me a lift on his tractor. From the moment I jumped on to the moment I got off, he never looked at me once.

The man in the next bed is snoring loudly. It's driving me mad. He's a long-distance truck driver. He was afraid someone might steal his petrol tonight, so he rolled the barrels into the dorm. The fumes are asphyxiating. I'm leaving first thing tomorrow.

9 March. Walked 30 kms today. It feels good to lie down. The gravel is hard on the ankles. My feet ache and are covered in blisters.

The stony plain continued endlessly, not a tree in sight. The only spots of colour were the green mountains in the south.

At noon I passed through a village market. A new restaurant was opening. Firecrackers exploded as the sign was hung, it was very festive. I went in and ordered a bowl of mutton noodles. They were quite filling, but I kept thinking of the sheep's head I saw bubbling in the pot. It seemed to have a smile on its face.

Reached Shulehe before sunset. Moon cakes are 8 mao a jin here, much cheaper than Beijing. They're very hard though. Perhaps they're left over from last year.

It is only when you take control of your life that you know you are alive.

Someone in a Yellow River truck tossed a bottle out of his window today and it smashed on my shoulders. Bastard.

The desert spreads to my left and right. I walk forward, continuing west along a hard black road that is sewn to the sky at the horizon. When I set out in the morning, the light on the Qilian mountains is a slant of pale green. At noon it is a straight beam of emerald. By the afternoon it scatters and becomes the same colour as the sky. White peaks follows me on the left. Sometimes I feel I am standing still. But I can't be, because there is a new telegraph pole every three kilometres and a new number on the post every two thousand steps.

The road never ends. Sometimes, tractors pass and leave trails of fumes that hang in the air for hours. When long-distance buses approach, children lean out from open windows and gawk back at me for as long as their necks will hold. When trucks go by, I hear radio music and smell tobacco smoke.

I am used to the bag on my back – it is my new home, all twenty jin of it. The straw hat on my head is a souvenir from Jiayuguan. Its brim is printed with a line of Chairman Mao's poetry: 'Grim pass, hard as iron.' Never mind. At least I can't see it.

Last night in Shulehe I met the leader of a fireworks factory who makes regular visits to Shenzhen. He said Deng Xiaoping decided to turn it into a Special Economic Zone in 1980 because of its proximity to Guangzhou. It was just a sleepy fishing town at the time, but in four years it has overtaken its prosperous neighbour, and now has the fastest growing economy in the country. Thousands of foreign companies have opened businesses there, enticed by the low taxes and relaxed bureaucracy. He said high-rises go up in ten days and business licences are issued overnight. Factory leaders are called 'managers', employees wear suits and ties to work and are provided with free lunch. He gave me his name card. 'Look after it,' he said. 'They cost me one mao each. It's Japanese paper. If you drop it in water you can still read the print.'

A tractor has stopped on the side of the road. Two peasants are wedging a plank of wood under the back wheel. A hundred chickens stacked in cages in the back poke their heads out and stare at me. The smells of straw and chicken shit remind me of Yellow, the cockerel I kept as a child. After school each day I would scour the streets for scraps of food to feed it. When I took it to a cock fight we always came home the champions. I would carry it around in my arms and when I opened my mouth it would stick its head inside and drink my saliva. Then, one year, on the eve of Family Reunion Festival, my father chopped its head off. When I smelt the chicken soup simmering in the kitchen the next day, I burst into tears.

'Bad luck, brothers,' I say, passing as quickly as I can. Four human eyes and two hundred chicken eyes blur into a single gaze.

The road stretches on. Occasionally I see a roadworker's shack or, at the end of a dirt track, a small settlement under a line of trees where the gravel plain meets the sand dunes. From the map, I notice the road ahead loops round to the north. I decide to take a short cut across the desert and head straight for Anxi. I want to get there as soon as possible and visit the Gorge of Ten Thousand Buddhas in the desert nearby.

I leave the asphalt road and turn left down a dusty track that takes me through rolling sand dunes. A few hours later, the sun starts to sink and I realise I might not make it to Anxi before dark. I see a water tower near the horizon, and a ragged line of roofs. Trucks move like boats across the heat haze behind. As the sun sinks lower, everything glows with a golden light. I drop my bag and lie down on my back in the sand. No wonder horses roll to the ground when they are tired. I feel better with my hooves in the air. I kick off my shoes and let my steaming toes suck the wind. Then I open my bottle, drink some water and splash some onto my face. My mind turns yellow. I hear a ringing in my ears – perhaps it is the noise of the sunlight, or the desert wind blowing through the telegraph wire. The water I swallowed charges through my veins. Eighty per cent of my body is water. My cells float in a sea. I am floating too, but my ocean is larger than theirs. I have the sky. I have freedom.

I jump to my feet, check my compass and continue west, chanting a verse from *Leaves of Grass*.

> Allons! To that which is endless as it was beginningless,
> To undergo much, tramps of days, rests of nights,
> To merge all in the travel they tend to, and the days
>   and nights they tend to,
> Again to merge them in the start of superior journeys ...

Allons, Ma Jian, allons.

Living in the Night

A warm sunset glimmers at the horizon, then the sky slams shut. I keep walking for a while but soon the track vanishes into the night. I switch on my torch and proceed, but find it hard to distinguish the track from the desert stones. A broken trail of bottle tops, soot and horse-dung helps keep me on course.

A biting wind starts to blow. At noon today it was so hot I had to strip to my vest, but now when I put on my down jacket, the collar freezes to my neck. If I lose my way tonight I could die of cold. Occasionally I hear a truck pass in the distance and the sky lights up for a while, but when it leaves, everything goes black again. I remember the water tower at sunset and the ragged line of roofs, and decide they looked no more than four kilometres away. As my nerves calm I hear hooves trotting towards me. The noise gets louder and soon my torchlight falls on a horse-drawn cart filled with spikes of maize. The driver has a white skullcap and a heavy coat draped over his shoulders. Panic flashes through his eyes and the eyes of his horse. As he approaches I shout, 'Is this the way to Anxi, my friend?' My torch is no longer shining on his face so I cannot see his expression. He drives past without stopping.

'Lost your fucking tongue, have you?' I mumble as he disappears.

Then I remind myself of the Silk Road travellers who passed through here a thousand years ago – Chinese monks on camel-back bound for the holy cities of India; Romans, Persians, Turks riding to the imperial capital laden with goods and ideas, and I press on into the night as the hoofbeats slowly fade. How is it that animals can see their way so easily through the dark?

A little further, and I hear the rumble of a tractor behind. The noise grows louder and the ground starts to shake. I hate it when vehicles pass during the day and cover me with dust, but it is nice to hear them approach at night. As the track lights up the desert opens again, and my long shadow stretches before me. I stand still and wave at the lights. The tractor stops. Through the dust and the roar of the engine a voice shouts, 'Where are you going?'

'Anxi, grandfather!'

'This is Anxi!'

I grope towards his voice, grab a metal bar and climb up beside him. 'This is Anxi,' he repeats as we drive off. I shuffle about, trying to find my balance. The cold wind blasts across my face. 'I want to go into town.'

'We'll be there in a minute.' His breath reeks of tobacco. I watch his headlamps illuminate the track and notice a few small lights shining in the distance. The lights grow larger. I can see windows now and the outlines of houses.

'We're here.' He stops the tractor and I jump off. When I glance back I see he is a young man after all. 'Thanks for the ride, brother!'

There are no street lamps, just patches of wall lit by the light from half-drawn curtains or half-shut doors, or candles in an open courtyard, perhaps. I remember Su Jin, the tour guide I met in Jiayuguan. On our ride back to town in the Japanese minibus, I told her of my plan to visit the Gorge of Ten Thousand Buddhas and she said, 'Well, you must look up my friend Zhang Shengli when you get to Anxi. We were at university together. He works for the cultural centre now. You will need an introduction letter from him if you want to see the Gorge.'

I wave my torch along a row of houses and see a window with a light on. I knock on the door. It opens and a middle-aged man peeps out and says, 'What do you want?'

A woman steps up behind him and glances at me, her forehead is smooth and shiny. I lower my torch and say, 'I wonder if you can help me, comrade. I'm looking for Zhang Shengli. He works for the cultural centre.'

'Go to the committee house then.'

'How do I get there?'

He points his chin into the black night and says, 'It's the big building at the crossroads over there, next to the post office.'

As he closes the door I say thank you and walk away into the pitch dark. My pack seems to weigh heavier and heavier.

At last I reach a tall gate. The sign on the concrete pillar reads, 'Revolution Committee House of Anxi County, Gansu Province'. I shine my torch over the two-storeyed house inside, then rattle the padlocked gate hoping to wake the gatekeeper. A light comes on in the lodge. I shout. A man steps out and points a torch ten times stronger than mine onto my face. I bow my head and he waves the torch down my body. 'Who are you?' he says.

'I'm a Beijing reporter. I've come to write an article.' I am not dressed like a cadre, but there is nothing else I can say.

'Where is your car then?' Whenever I have travelled before, there has always been an official car waiting for me at the station.

'I was posted here at the last minute. There was no time to send a telegram.'

He shines the torch on my face again. I attempt a smile, but know that my skin is dirty and chapped and my mouth is full of ulcers. He steps forward and says, 'Where's the introduction letter?'

'Let me see Zhang Shengli. I will sort out the formalities tomorrow. Can you show me where he lives?'

'I'll need the introduction letter first.' From his voice I guess he is over fifty. His throat sounds clogged with phlegm.

I put down my bag, take out my forged introduction letter and pass it to him through the iron bars. He peers at it and carries it into the building. I am tempted to call him back, but stop myself. A moment later, a light comes on and he walks out jangling a ring of keys.

He wraps the lock and chain around the gate and asks, 'What are you doing coming here on your own?'

'The colleagues I left with were called back to Beijing for an important meeting. I didn't want to proceed alone, but there was no choice.' I follow him round to the staff barracks at the back. Each room has a light on and a radio playing. He takes me to the farthest room and knocks on the door. A man in a woollen jumper steps out. His shirt collar is rucked around his neck.

'Someone here looking for you.' The gatekeeper has thick glasses and is much older than I thought.

'I will show you my papers tomorrow, grandfather.' I wish he would go. 'Hello, you must be Zhang Shengli. I'm a friend of Su Jin. She told me to pay you a visit.'

'Go back to bed, grandad. I will sort out the documents in the morning.'

'What about the form?'

'All right, I'll come and sign it in a minute,' Zhang Shengli says, and I breathe a sigh of relief.

He shuts the door. I put my bag down, sink into an armchair and glance around his room. His desk is piled with books, photographs, empty negative tubes. The table by the door holds a stack of bowls, chopsticks, half a cabbage on a wooden board, a wooden spoon, bottles of peanut oil, soya sauce and vinegar, a bowl of noodles, and a few paper bags.

'Where are you from? You look like a traveller. Most of Su Jin's friends are artistic types. Would you like some tea?'

'Beijing . . . Just passing through . . . Yes please.'

As he heats up the noodles I tell him I have come to visit the Gorge of Ten Thousand Buddhas.

'There's no road, I'm afraid. Just dirt tracks left by delivery trucks that drive to the electricity plant nearby.'

'How far is it?'

'Over seventy kilometres. I've been several times myself, but only in the committee car.'

'Could I walk it in two days?'

'It's stony desert all the way. If you miss the tracks it is easy to get lost.'

'I have a compass and a water filter.' I hand him a cigarette.

'Try one of mine – they're a Gansu brand. If you really want to go, I'll lend you my bicycle.'

'How come the Japanese documentary on the Silk Road that was shown last year never mentioned the Gorge? I only found out about it myself when I was leafing through a book on the Mogao Caves of Dunhuang. The Gorge has fewer cave temples than

Dunhuang, but from the photographs, the frescoes seemed much more interesting.'

'The Japs only visit famous places. They won't go anywhere their cars can't reach.'

'Su Jin said you've taken many pictures of the Gorge.'

'I was born in Anxi. I've photographed all the local sites.'

'What camera do you use?'

'A Minolta, and a Shanghai Reflex – nothing special. I applied for a Nikon once but the provincial cultural office turned me down. They allotted one to the cultural artefacts department instead.'

'No more thanks, I'm full.' I have swallowed several cloves of garlic and my stomach and face are burning.

'Could I spend the night here? I'll sleep on the floor. I have a raincoat.'

'Of course. You can share my bed.'

We lie across his single bed, our feet propped on chairs. He tells me he visited Beijing once as a student, and that his ambition is to own a Nikon camera and three lenses. He says the Gorge of Ten Thousand Buddhas is much more important than Dunhuang. He wants to organise an exhibition about it in the provincial museum. He thinks that in five years' time the Gorge will attract more tourists than the Terracotta Army in Xian. He asks me where I met Su Jin. He says at university she used to sneak off into the woods with her boyfriend and listen to Deng Lijun tapes. As he chatters away, I close my eyes and see the photograph he showed me of a Buddhist master who died in the lotus position: flesh fallen from his face, red robes fraying to dust. I see the gatekeeper and his forms, the wife with the shiny forehead, then my mind goes black and I fall asleep.

When he wakes me in the morning, the room smells of fried eggs and kerosene. He removes the noodles from the stove and starts frying some peanuts.

'Don't go to so much trouble. I can't eat that much, really.' As I search my mind for his name, I spot his identity card lying on the table: Zhang Shengli, male, 27 years old, Party member, single, cadre.

'Shengli, the gatekeeper still has my introduction letter. I will need it for the rest of my time in Gansu.'

'Don't worry, I'll pop over in a minute and fetch it for you.'

He is crouched down, stirring the peanuts with one hand and holding a cigarette in the other. 'A letter from our centre will open more doors though. People always prefer a local recommendation.'

He slurps the noodles and pulls out a blank introduction letter from his drawer. 'I'll sign this for you. It should get you into the Gorge. There's no need to ask the centre's head for his permission, he would pass you on to the county propaganda department. You must promise not to take any photographs though. If they got published one day the authorities would trace it back to me. The gatekeeper at the Gorge is called Wang Zhenglin. He's a good friend of mine. I'll write him a note. Sorry, what's your name again?'

The Gold-Digger

I leave town on Shengli's bicycle, along a road that passes through a succession of small villages. The young poplar trees planted along the sides are just starting to bud. Peasants ride into town on horse-drawn carts. The men wear Muslim skullcaps, the women wear scarves tied over their mouths. When I cycle out of the last village the desert opens again. Apart from the snow peaks of the distant Qilian range, everything is flat and grey.

For three hours, I alternate between riding my bike and pushing it. The tracks are too smooth and sandy for my wheels to grip. I try cycling over the stones by the side, but it is too bumpy and I hate having to keep my eyes on the ground. My throat feels sore. It occurs to me that perhaps the local women tie scarves around their mouths to retain the moisture of their breath. I pull up my face mask, and my mouth soon feels less dry. I regret bringing the bike. It would have been simpler to walk.

When the sun rises overhead the desert becomes a sheet of burning red iron. I strip to my vest and finish half the water in my bottle. I dare not drink any more. I am not a camel after all. One day without water and I would die.

At the banks of a dry riverbed the track forks. It is not clear which is the main path. I check the map Zhang Shengli drew for me, but there is no sign of the riverbed.

I decide to bury the bike and walk the rest of the way. I push it along the riverbed looking for a place to hide it, and suddenly notice a wooden cart parked on the crest of a sand dune. From this angle it looks like a wrecked boat lying at the bottom of a river. I examine it through the zoom of my camera, but still cannot make out what it is doing there. Then I spot someone seated in the shade underneath. He is looking at me. I walk towards him.

An old man with a white beard is sitting under the cart. He has boarded up the sides to make a nest sheltered from the desert sun. I step forward. He has a rifle on his lap, he is rubbing it. I drop my bicycle and say, 'You look tired, my friend.'

He looks away, his face is blank. I long to sit under his cart. It must be the only patch of shade in this entire desert. I move a little closer.

'Do you mind if I rest here, old man? I'm walking to the Gorge of Ten Thousand Buddhas. I seem to have lost my way.' I squat down and stretch my head under the cart. It is like plunging my face in cold water. The old man keeps silent, but watches my every move.

He obviously sleeps here. There is a sheepskin on the ground and a leather hat on the heap of quilts at the back. I turn and see an axe by his feet. His hand is no longer rubbing the rifle. I remain still for a while then slowly crane my neck into the cool behind his shoulders.

The man must be over sixty. He has short-cropped hair and, judging by the size of him sitting down, he is not much taller than me. If we were to come to blows, I could look after myself. But there is a glint in his eyes. Perhaps he practises martial arts. He has the air of an ancient swordsman. I play things by ear, and keep my eyes on the rifle. After a while, he moves a little as though to make room for me.

Then he turns and stares at me, and says, 'You won't make it there today.'

I slide in beside him, pull my legs up and gaze at the sunlight beating on the dry riverbed. I wonder when a river last ran through it. The stony channel cuts through the desert like an open wound.

I offer him a drink from my water bottle to repay him for his hospitality.

My temperature falls. I swallow the steam in my mouth, then – Peng! The bicycle tyres explode.

'It was stupid of me to leave it in the sun,' I say, and imagine my body exploding with the bike, my innards splayed over the hot sand.

'So you are walking to the Gorge on your own, then?' he says.

'Yes, just want to see what it's like. Where are you heading?'

'There's nothing but ruins there now. All the valuables have been pillaged.' The old man twists a piece of wire around his hand.

'I heard that when the Gorge temples were abandoned five centuries ago, a sage went to meditate in a cave and died in the lotus position.' I picture the sage's spirit floating through the cool breeze of Nirvana. The stony desert is a dazzling white now,

waves of heat tremble in the sun. 'If it wasn't for you, I'd be dried
to a bone.'

'You should cross the desert in the morning or evening, and
sleep in the middle of the day. If you were to ride a horse through
the desert now, its hooves would burn to a cinder. You are not
from these parts, it seems.'

'I come from Beijing. This is my first time in the desert. Were
you born in Gansu?' I run my fingers through the burning gravel.

'I'll be going back in a few days.'

'Where to?' The question sounds impertinent, so I add, 'It must
be hard living here.'

'Are you a piss-drinker or a shit-eater?' he asks, eyeing me
sternly.

'I have never drunk piss myself, or . . .'

He taps my leg with the twisted wire. 'So you're not one of us,
it seems.' I stare at the wrinkles at the corners of his eyes, trying
to guess his meaning.

'You don't seem like a gold-digger. You have no tools.'

'So you're a gold-digger?'

'Yes, I thought you were too at the beginning. There are many
robbers wandering these parts, asking questions, trying to discover who has struck gold.'

'Don't worry, old man, I'm not interested in your gold.'

'Sometimes I meet other diggers. They stop and chat for a
while, and if they think I have gold they stand perfectly still,
waiting for me to turn round so they can shoot me in the back.'

'Did you suspect me just now, then?'

'You can't trust anybody here. When you have seen gold you
will understand.' The old man turns his face away and looks into
the distance. 'I've hit on some gold, but there is not enough
water. I will wait for the winter snows and come back with my
son.'

'So there really is gold here?'

'Don't ask, young man. The less you know the better. You

should go now. Head east and spend the night in Qiaozi. You can continue your journey tomorrow.'

I realise I will not make it to the Gorge tonight, so I follow his advice and walk east. As the sun sinks to the west, the air cools and gusts of cold wind blow sand into my face. I reach the village before dark.

Stuck in Suoyang

Qiaozi consists of mud-brick houses surrounded by green vegetable fields. As I approach I hear a propaganda song blasting from the village speaker. 'Every village, every hamlet, beat your drums and strike your gongs! Chairman Mao's splendour shines throughout the land. Mountains smile, rivers smile, everyone smiles: Socialism is Good . . .' Old Mao has been dead for eight years now and they're still bloody smiling! I mutter as I follow the loudspeaker's cable back to a small adobe house.

I knock on the door, but no one answers. A crowd of children gathers behind me. When I look round they all run away, except for the smallest boy who falls over and starts to cry. Before I have time to pick him up, a woman appears at the front door. From her neat black hair I can tell she is a cadre.

'Are you the village announcer?' I ask. She says yes, so I pull out Zhang Shengli's introduction letter.

'Beijing journalist . . . reporting on the cultural sites of Gansu . . . The village head would have looked after you, Comrade Ma, but I am afraid he is not here today.' The hands that fold the letter smell of soap, she must have just washed them.

'We both work in propaganda. I am sure the authorities would be happy for you to organise my stay in the village instead. I would like to wash my face. Do you have water in your room?' I picture a washstand behind her door, and a thermos of hot water on the ground.

She opens the door for me, turns on the light and shouts to the children, 'Go home now, it's supper time!'

I tell her I am travelling to the Gorge of Ten Thousand Buddhas and would like a bed for the night.

'There's no hostel in the village. The militia headquarters have some spare beds though. I will have a word with their leader.' She fills the basin with hot water, hands me a flannel, then goes to pour me a cup of tea. The wall is hung with a framed certificate that reads 'Annual Prize for Advanced Workers, Awarded to Comrade Li Anmei, public announcer of Qiaozi village.'

A few minutes later, her husband, Tang Weiguo, returns from the fields. When he hears I am a Beijing journalist, he shakes my hand and invites me to stay for dinner. Li Anmei serves us bowls of noodle soup sprinkled with chopped spring onions, and sets the table with a plate of fried peanuts and a saucer of garlic cloves.

Tang Weiguo graduated three years ago from Anxi high school. Li Anmei was his classmate. Her family live in a small hamlet two hundred kilometres away. She moved here with Tang Weiguo when they married last year.

Their home is simply furnished. The adobe walls are freshly whitewashed, you can still smell the powder. The ceiling is neatly pasted with sheets of newspaper. A small pink curtain hangs over the one window. A brightly polished bicycle stands propped up against the door. The single bulb hanging from the ceiling is slightly brighter than the candle on the desk. Stacked on the bedside table are twelve volumes of *A Hundred Thousand Whys and Wherefores*, a new edition of *Deng Xiaoping's Collected Works*, and some old military magazines. The plastic flowers in the red vase are not too dusty.

After supper a girl called Mili walks in and sits next to Tang Weiguo. She lives next door with her uncle, and visits every night, apparently. Her mother is Kazak, her father Han Chinese. They live a hundred kilometres away in the Kazak Autonomous Prefecture.

Mili pours herself a cup of tea, then pulls out a bag of pumpkin seeds and proceeds to stuff them, one by one, into her mouth.

The scene takes me back to my childhood in Qingdao, when our neighbour Aunty Liu would come round every night, plonk herself onto my parents' bed and gossip for hours. Her husband was a cook on the trains. He travelled all over the country and saw many strange things. My parents were always eager for his news. Sometimes Aunty Liu brought a cup of tea or a newspaper, sometimes she delved into her pocket and pulled out exotic sweets for my sister and me. Those wrappers emblazoned with the names Beijing, Shanghai, Nanjing, or Dalian Sweet Factory were my most valuable possessions. I cannot remember what the grown-ups talked about exactly, but most of my knowledge about the world was picked up from fragments of their conversations. For example:

Shanghai women wear high-heeled shoes to work and paint their lips red. Their mouths look like giant prawns.

The train to Guangzhou takes three days and three nights. In winter you board the train in a leather coat and leave it in a cotton vest. The carriages have toilets and beds.

Children should not talk when grown-ups are speaking.

Xia Wanping's daughter is an air stewardess. At the end of each flight, she walks off the plane with a bag of leftover cakes.

In Hunan people eat a jar of chilli paste with every meal.

Two foreigners wanted to have their photo taken with Uncle Liu. He was in his work clothes at the time. Fortunately the head attendant was around to put a stop to it, otherwise he might have got into serious trouble. Foreigners print those photographs in their newspapers to humiliate the Chinese people.

I listened to the conversations, pretending to understand, never daring to ask a question. We had no radio then, no newspapers. The only things to look at were the New Year posters on the wall and the empty lane outside. I didn't see a map of China until my first day at primary school. The teacher pointed her wooden cane to Beijing then waved it around the national borders. Before I had time to read any place names the lesson was over. But I could sense that the people and places Aunty Liu told us about were hidden somewhere on that map, and on the world map I saw a few years later in the Qingdao Bookstore.

The door keeps swinging open. Villagers walk in, eager to listen to the 'Beijing journalist'. They stand at the threshold for a while, then move to the dark corners of the room and sit down to smoke. I only see their faces when they lean over for a refill of Anmei's tea.

I remember the song that blared as I walked into the village and say, 'Chairman Mao has been dead for years. You don't have to play those songs any more.'

Anmei frowns. 'Those tapes are very old, I know, but we cannot afford new ones. I hear in Beijing you can buy tapes of last year's Spring Festival television special.'

'That's not all. You can buy tapes from Taiwan and Hong Kong, the songs of Deng Lijun and Su Rei – even that French singer, Nana Mouskouri. In Beijing the cinemas are open every day. On Saturday nights, young people give parties at home. They play disco music and dance cheek to cheek.' The dark lives these people lead fill me with frustration, I cannot help my superior tone. Mili's eyes are the only bright things in the room.

'Some of my friends have moved to America,' I continue. 'They own cars and telephones now. Last September the government announced that Chinese citizens are allowed to marry foreigners. This country is changing, opening up. You can't just stay here like vegetables. You should travel, broaden your minds. Haven't you heard about Shenzhen Economic Zone? It's like a foreign country now. Employees are provided with free lunches. They can eat as much as they want . . .'

The men seated around me do not look up, but I can tell they are rapt by my talk. Everyone falls silent. Even Mili stops munching the pumpkin seeds. I try to keep talking, but my voice tails off. I hate it when this happens. When people visit me at home in Beijing I always play a tape in the background so that if an awkward silence occurs we can pretend to be listening to the music.

At last I ask Tang Weiguo what books he likes to read.

'I haven't read much since I left school.'

'How about you, Anmei? Have you read Mauriac's *The Desert of Love*?' I say, deliberately choosing an obscure title.

'Uh, I read whatever is lying about really. I have a subscription to *Youth of China*.'

'And you, Mili? What do you like to read?' She is about to spit a husk onto the floor, but when I look at her she dribbles it into her hand instead.

'Tell us about Beijing,' Anmei says, adding some hot water to the teapot. 'The papers say that parents have to queue to send their children to nursery school. I don't understand.' She walks to the cupboard and comes back with a bottle. 'Try some of this.'

'I'm fine with the tea, thank you.'

'It's orange juice, there's half a bottle left. I bought it in the county town.'

I take a sip. It's flat fizzy orange.

'Go on, have some more.' I don't want to upset her, so I pretend to take another gulp, then pass the bottle to Mili.

'Family planning is strict in the cities,' I explain. 'Couples are only allowed one child. They all want to give them the best education. Good nurseries have pianos, the top ones teach English and give chocolate at break time.'

'How much do they cost?'

'Top nurseries charge forty yuan a term. They provide apples and sweets in the morning and a meal at noon. The fees are double if the children board.' I swallow some more tea. The conversation is getting tedious. 'Are there any interesting sites around here?'

'The lost city of Suoyang. There's an article about it here in the *Gansu Daily*.'

Tang Weiguo hands me the newspaper. A boy standing behind me switches his torch on and shines it onto the page.

'Gansu Province has a long and glorious history,' I read aloud. 'A land of mountains and rugged deserts dotted with oasis towns which in ancient times served as caravan stops on the legendary Silk Road ... Although the majority of the population is Han Chinese, the province is also home to a number of Muslim minorities including the Chinese-speaking Hui and the semi-nomadic Kazaks ... The Mogao Caves of Dunhuang hold China's most spectacular Buddhist art ... world-famous Singing Sand Hills and renowned Crescent Moon Lake ... awesome Jiayuguan Fort ... I can't see any mention of Suoyang.'

There are six faces surrounding me, and six torches shining on the page. Tang Weiguo points to the spot and reads, 'Suoyang city was originally called Kuyu. Legend relates that during the Tang Dynasty, General Xue Rengui led his army west to repel the nomadic hordes of the Central Asian steppes. But when the soldiers reached Kuyu, the enemy troops surrounded them. General Xue and his men barricaded themselves within the city walls waiting for reinforcements to arrive from the imperial capital. As the months went by, supplies ran out and the soldiers had to dig the ground for food. The suoyang roots they found saved their lives, and the city was renamed in their honour. The expression "Stuck in Suoyang" entered our vocabulary. After the sea route to India was discovered in the fourteenth century, trade along the Silk Road declined and, like many other caravanseries, Suoyang was abandoned to the desert sands. The city walls are ten metres high ...'

'I'll go there tomorrow. Maybe I can dig up some suoyang!' The men chuckle and the women frown. I say I am ready for bed, and Tang Weiguo picks up a thermos flask and leads me to the militia headquarters.

The mud houses look cold and grey under the moonlight. A gravel track stretches straight into the stony desert. It is hard to believe I was walking across golden sands today.

I wake up late. Warm sunlight moves down my face and quilt like a woman's hand. A group of peasants have come to sit at the end of my brick bed. They are smoking and discussing the man in the next village who has made a fortune breeding angora rabbits. 'He rakes in ten thousand yuan a year from those animals.'

A mule brays in the yard outside. I hide under the quilt. It smells of feet but is at least cleaner than the blankets in the hostels I have stayed in. I realise I have been travelling for a month now. I think about why I left Beijing, and wonder if I will ever return. I imagine spending the rest of my days drifting from place to place.

I sit up, say hello, and climb off the bed. Perhaps these are the men who sat in Li Anmei's room last night.

At four o'clock, I put away the poem I have been working on, take a gulp of tea and set off for Suoyang with Mili. She has offered to be my guide for the afternoon.

The ruins are only eight kilometres away. The sky is blue.

Before long we are walking through desert. The Qilian peaks in the distance remind me of Hemingway's *Hills Like White Elephants*. It is the story of a man taking a girl to a distant town to have an abortion.

Mili is neither fat nor thin. Her lips are thick and red. When I look at them I remember how they moved last night as she chewed the pumpkin seeds. Her hair is brushed back into a tight ponytail, a straight fringe bobs over her forehead. She walks beside me, head bowed.

I ask her how much suoyang fetches in the market. The roots are used in Chinese medicine. They are believed to cure male impotence.

'Locals go to Suoyang every summer to dig up the roots. They dry them at home and sell them for two yuan a jin.'

'Gansu people don't talk much, do they? The men who joined

us last night didn't say a word all evening. You didn't say much either.'

She looks up and smiles into the distance. 'Can you see it?'

I see a crumbling wall fringed by tufts of green weed.

'It's wonderful! It looks like a fossilised dinosaur.' Then I turn and look at her. 'I would like to sleep there tonight. Will you stay with me?' Walking through the dry desert with a moist girl by my side, I cannot help thinking about holding her after dark.

She panics and says, 'I must get back tonight.'

Our footsteps dart through the still air.

When we reach Suoyang, the sun is still watching me in the west.

I climb the ramparts. The stone desert continues to the south, sand dunes roll to the east, five or six pagodas rise in the west. Below me stand the weathered bricks of the rectangular city wall. The buildings within are buried under metres of sand and clumps of shrub and camel-thorn.

I climb down, take some water from my bottle then pass it to Mili.

I see a willow in a dip by the far corner of the wall. Its withered trunk arcs through the green branches like a long sigh.

'That must be where the well was,' I say.

'Yes. A hundred thousand soldiers drank from it for five years and its waters never ran dry.'

Fragments of Tang and Song pottery lie scattered on the sand. I pick one up and examine the intricate moulding.

I imagine the imperial warriors standing on these walls, hurling their spears and rocks at the enemy hordes. I picture women crouched by the willow, filling their jars from the well, then rushing home with heads bowed ... Apart from the sound of our breathing, everything is quiet.

I yell. The noise melts into the soft walls. I tell Mili to shout. She does, and her cry shatters the brittle air. We climb to the highest part of the wall and sit down. I open a packet of biscuits and gaze at the sun.

'Those pagodas are beautiful,' I say, viewing them through the lens of my camera.

'See the hollow in front of them? It's an ancient burial site. There are human bones everywhere.'

I put down my camera and watch the sun turn a deep red.

When it sinks out of view, a swarm of mosquitoes engulfs us. We whisk them away and run into the wind, but our hands and necks are soon swollen with bites. The thought of spending the night here no longer seems so appealing. I look at Mili. She wants me to take her home.

Just before we reach the village I see a porcupine below a sand dune. I chase after it, but realise I cannot pick it up, so I kick it back to where it was.

Li Anmei and Tang Weiguo are waiting for me at the village gates. 'The village head has just returned. He says he is very honoured that a Beijing journalist has come to write about Suoyang. He has invited the three of us to have dinner at his house tonight.'

Resting in the Gale

To avoid walking through the desert at noon, I go to Li Anmei's house the next morning and start work on a new story. Mili invites me to her uncle's for lunch. In the afternoon she comes to my room to darn the tear in my trousers. As the sun rolls to the west I leave Qiaozi at last, and before nightfall reach Tashi, the nearest village to the Gorge of Ten Thousand Buddhas. Kang Ben from the Tashi cultural centre skims through Zhang Shengli's introduction letter and asks me how many days I plan to stay. I tell him I will leave at dawn.

When I wake the next morning, my nose and throat are clogged with dust. I roll over and peer at the window. The sky outside is black. Squalls of sand blast through the poplar trees and billow the pigsty's tarpaulin. The wind thunders like a thousand cantering horses as it throws branches and stones against walls and tears through the sky. Grains of sand blow through gaps in the window frame and cover the pillows and bedside table. I am glad I am not crossing the desert now.

I watch the storm for a while, then pull on my clothes and venture outside. The air is so thick with sand I cannot see the toilet hut, so I piss against the wall quickly and rush back inside. My face and neck are caked with sand. I heard this region is famous for its gales, but never imagined that when the wind carries dust, it can attack with the force of a hailstorm.

I decide to take the day off and stay indoors. The room smells of garlic and old socks, but is preferable to the storm outside. I jump into bed, light a cigarette, pull the quilt up to my chin and look over the passage I wrote yesterday.

> We lean against the tree and embrace. I kiss her mouth and think of the day she lay beside me by the reservoir and touched my chin with her foot. In the sun her five toes were as clear as a slice of lemon.
>
> 'I'm not that special,' she snorts when I stand back to look at her. Suddenly my feelings for her seem ridiculous. I turn round and look at the line of trees. I stare at one tree after another until I forget what I am looking at . . .

Damn, this passage won't do. I know I am writing about Xi Ping to purge her from my memory, but I must detach myself and put the pain in perspective. Why am I always trapped in the past?

Four days later, the wind still shows no sign of dropping. I take a nap and dream of Mili. I stroke her forehead and move my thigh between her legs. At sunrise I wake up seeing her face. The day I left Qiaozi, I gave her a Hong Kong bookmark printed with the words TAKE CARE. She was so happy her face went bright red. I must stop thinking about women. All emotional ties lead to pain.

Kang Ben's room is decorated with two dusty goat horns and a poster of Zhou Enlai. He hands me a pile of newspapers to read and tells me his ambition is to write for the *Gansu Daily*. When I mention I have had stories published in literary magazines, he starts pestering me for advice. I tell him to keep his articles brief and concise and to avoid too much personal reflection. He shows me a report he wrote on the county secretary's visit to the countryside. Apart from a brief description of the secretary's genial smile, most of the article is a dull transcription of lectures he gave to peasants on the new agricultural reforms. I tell him there is no need to make the secretary's visit sound like Deng Xiaoping's tour of Sichuan. I finish a whole packet of cigarettes, and by the evening my head is pounding.

The next day I wake to the sound of the same raging storm. I have been here a week now. Kang Ben says this region has a hundred days a year of force seven gales. The locals claim there is just one wind: it lasts from spring until winter. I have stuffed wads of newspaper into the gaps of the window frame but the sand still gets between my teeth.

In the evening the power fails and my torch batteries run out. I put my notebook away and lie flat on the bed. The dark room feels like a large shell enclosing my beating heart. My body seems to have vanished. If I don't leave soon I am afraid I will never escape. I must forget about the Gorge. It is only twenty kilometres away, but I would have to walk across open desert to reach it, I would never find my way in this wind. The Ten Thousand Buddhas obviously want to be left alone. There is a paved road to Dunhuang. I will set off for there tomorrow whether the wind stops or not. If there is road in front of me, I will follow it. I don't mind where it goes, as long as it takes me forward. I must remember to return Zhang Shengli's bicycle.

Kang Ben takes out a melon and cuts me a slice. It is delicious. The air is so dry here, melons will keep under the bed for up to six months.

The Living and the Dead

On 7 April, I return to Anxi and catch a bus to Dunhuang. The town stands in a green oasis at the end of the Hexi Corridor. As I come out of the bus station I see a string of grey-brick houses and a crossroads like the one in Jiayuguan. A copse of young poplar trees outside a construction site is shrouded in ghostly dust. The shop windows along the street are crammed with scrolls of calligraphy, brass buddhas, porcelain figurines of Guanyin, the Goddess of Mercy, and posters of the Mogao murals. Garish signs painted on the grey walls read: Silk Road Hostel, Dunhuang Watchmenders, Flying Apsara Photo Studio, Moon Lake Dental Clinic, Singing Sand Snack Store. Only the shops at the intersection are busy. Occasionally a tall, brightly dressed foreigner passes through the blue sea of peasants. Centuries ago, this town was an important frontier post on the ancient Silk Road. Its streets were filled with envoys from the Middle East and Buddhist missionaries from India.

I sit down at a snack stall on the corner. The plastic-covered table is set with white bowls, vinegar and a greasy roast chicken that still has hairs on its bottom. After weeks of noodles, I could do with some meat.

'How old is this bird?' I ask.

'Killed it yesterday.'

I pick it up and sniff. Not bad – it smells like the chickens sold on station platforms. I pay the stallholder three yuan and tear off a thigh. As I bite into the meat my body comes alive. I order a large spring onion and dig in.

There is sand in the air but the sky is still blue. In the middle of the traffic island a statue of a flying apsara plays a lute behind her back. She twists round with a beatific smile, one leg in the air, as horse-drawn carts, bicycles and buses circle around her. Apsaras are Buddhist nymphs who float through the air trailing garlands of diaphanous silk. Unlike Christian angels, they do not need wings to fly. The bright banner suspended between two telegraph poles behind her says FIRST CHILD: COIL, SECOND CHILD: ABORTION, THIRD CHILD: HYSTERECTOMY. The blood-red characters turn my stomach.

The next morning my throat is so sore I can hardly speak. Fortunately, I am not in a mood to talk. My Hong Kong roommate is sitting upright on his bed waiting for me to open my eyes. Through his face mask he tells me in broken Chinese that he saw ghosts last night.

'Flying apsaras?' I croak.

'No, imperial warriors. Down there in the yard. Hundreds of them. Beating drums, marching in circles. Looked like they were preparing for battle.'

I look out of the window. Two hens scuttle in the sunlight. The wire tied from the basketball post to the brick building behind is hung with shirts, trousers and nappies. A woman in a red skirt bends over a tub of laundry. Her bottom looks huge.

'It's an ordinary yard,' I say.

'But it was full of soldiers last night.' He pulls down his mask. His girlish, innocent face is contorted with fear.

'Perhaps you were dreaming. Or maybe you have been reading too many travel books.' I remember the legend of the Singing Sand Hills. An army of imperial warriors camped in the desert one night and a sudden sandstorm buried them alive. They say that if the wind is blowing in the right direction, you can hear the soldiers' ghosts wailing from inside the dunes.

'I never have dreams, and I don't believe in ghosts either. When I heard the noise last night I thought they were making a movie.' He fixes me with his terrified eyes.

'How much are tickets for the Mogao Caves?'

'Ten yuan for foreigners, one yuan for Chinese.'

I slip into my shoes and make for the door. When I see he is still staring at me I say, 'Don't worry, ghosts are just like buddhas – they only exist if you believe in them.'

Although I have taken the lay Buddhist vows, I still feel confused. I often wonder if the Buddha exists or where his Pure Land is. I question whether I am searching for faith or merely a sense of security. But now that I am a rootless vagabond, perhaps the Buddha is guiding my way. Perhaps it was he who told me to leave my family, friends, desires, ambitions, and to abandon myself to fate. Where would I have found the courage otherwise? Dunhuang is an important place of pilgrimage. It marks the entry point of Buddhism into China. I am here now. Maybe there is something waiting for me.

Before me stands the cliff face of the Singing Sand Hills, honeycombed with the famous Mogao Caves. From the fourth to the tenth centuries, communities of Buddhist monks hewed these cave shrines into the cliff and decorated them with murals and painted statues. I have seen countless pictures of them in art history books. I know the walls are painted with graceful apsaras, scenes from the life of the first Buddha, Shakyamuni, and portraits of the Silk Road merchants who sponsored the building of the caves to ensure a safe journey across the desert. I know that one cave holds a thirty-three-metre-high statue of Amitabha, the disciple of Shakyamuni, whose radiant wisdom transforms cravings into infinite light. I have seen a photograph of the huge reclining buddha who waits for death with a smile on his face. His tranquil expression touched me more than the tortured look I have seen on images of Christ. Buddhism teaches man to transcend the material world and view life and death as trivial. Christianity urges man to cherish life and fear death.

I buy a Chinese entrance ticket and turn right. Foreigners take the path to the left. I follow the stream of tourists, ticking off each cave as we pass. Most of the caves are locked and it is forbidden to peep over the railings. People in front and behind are talking and eating. Some carry cassette players and play tapes of revolutionary anthems, those who have run out of batteries tune their radios to a programme on the Yellow River. Four caves are open to the public, but there are no lights inside, so I cannot see the frescoes. Over the centuries, the temple caves have been eroded by the wind and stained by the woodsmoke of generations of squatters. It is hard to sense their sanctity. All I see are crumbling walls. The statue of wrathful Vajrapani glowers with rage, but his broken lips give him a ridiculous air. When we reach the cave of the nine-storey-high seated Amitabha, the crowds converge. Men and women from the Japanese tour group wear white hats and hold red flags. Blond Americans with cameras hanging from their shoulders circle the buddha and peer up with open mouths.

I look at Amitabha too: delicate brows, almond eyes, an air of sublime compassion, and I feel tiny and insignificant. When I chanted his name in Jushilin Temple, I sometimes felt my spirit rise from my body and enter another realm. The sense of calm and emptiness was liberating.

I must sit down. I am a Buddhist. My mind should be focused at this point. I have read the scriptures, and understand the concept of reincarnation and the law of just retribution. I have come here to still my heart and rid myself of worldly concerns. I glance at the mural of Amitabha's Western Paradise, but the scenes of clothes growing from trees and apples flying into mouths do not fill me with a wish to be reborn there. Tourists babble like monkeys as they climb the steps, gawking at the buddha who sits still and oblivious. I look at his face again and suddenly it reminds me of Mao Zedong. I drew the Chairman's portrait hundreds of times from primary school to middle school. The more I study Amitabha the more he resembles Old Mao.

I walk out in a daze. That was the largest buddha I have seen in my life, but my mind is blank. I am more confused than when I went in. Perhaps I should buy a foreigner's ticket and go round again. They are bound to get shown the better caves. Not today though. Remembering the Hong Kong boy's bewildered eyes, I leave the caves behind me and walk towards the empty dunes.

Lure of the Distance

Early next morning I pack my belongings, tie my damp socks to the straps of my bag, and set off for the road that runs north to Xinjiang and south to the empty wastes of Qinghai.

Trucks pass in a constant stream. The warm breeze is laced with petrol fumes – it smells like the breath of the modern world. My money is running out. I do not mind much where I go, I just hope I can get a lift to the next province.

After an hour of waving a one-yuan note in the air, a truck finally pulls up. When I climb inside the driver grumbles that he thought it was a tenner I was holding. I tell him it's all I've got.

Six, seven hours later, the truck stops at Akesai, the capital of the Kazak Autonomous Prefecture, close to the Gansu–Qinghai border. I step down and look up at the icy Aierjin mountains. The jagged peaks seem to have been hacked by a mad knifeman. The slopes look bare.

The committee hostel is the tallest building in town. Its three storeys jut above the low stone houses like a large solitary matchbox. The streets have no trees. A mountain wind sweeps up spirals of dust as it scurries through town. The Kazak faces under white skullcaps and white scarves echo the colour of the mountains. I remember Mili saying her mother was born in this town.

I suddenly regret not catching a lift north instead. Xinjiang is

China's largest and most desolate province, and is scattered with ancient Buddhist sites. In my pocket, I still have my half-used train ticket to the capital, Urumqi, but it expired a week ago. My only choice now is to cross the Aierjin mountains and proceed to Qinghai. At least I will see the Chaidam Basin once I am over the Dangjin Pass. It is a vast saline depression, apparently, dotted with clear blue lakes.

I hitch a ride in the morning and reach the pass at noon. A cleft opens in the mountain. The road enters, snakes down the other side, and pushes into the eerie waste of Chaidam.

I ask the driver to stop. Then I jump off, leave the road and climb a high scree. Halfway up I feel that I am floating in mid-air. The view to the west is blocked by a high mountain, but to the east I see a line of white peaks run far into the distance. A thousand years ago, when troops from the Jin Kingdom marched through here on their way to attack the central plains, a storm broke and buried the soldiers in snow. From that day forth the pass was known as 'Dangjin' – shield against the Jin advance. Apparently the ghosts of the dead soldiers still haunt the area. No one dares drive through at night.

Below me, the gravel basin stretches under the midday sun. I see a blue lake glisten in the distance, dangling in the desert like a jewel on a woman's neck. It must be Sugan, the lake that inspires so many local folk songs.

'It's beautiful, beautiful.' My hands clench.

I pull out my camera and look through the lens. The lake instantly shrinks to a spot in the landscape – a tiny sapphire no one notices on the finger of a beautiful woman. No photograph could capture its beauty. I put the camera away, finish the instant noodles I bought yesterday, take a swig of water and set off for the lake.

After an hour's descent I reach the desert. Sweat pours from my body and evaporates in seconds. My water is half-finished, and the lake has sunk from view. I must rely on my compass from now on.

The sun is still overhead. As I breathe the hot air in and out my mouth becomes as dry as dust. The compass in my hand burns like the gravel underfoot. The dry noodles have reached my stomach and seem to be sucking the moisture from my blood. I long to reach the shore of the lake and plunge my head in its cool water. For brief moments, refracted through the heat waves on the right, I see villages, moving trucks, or a sweep of marsh. If I didn't have a compass, I might be tempted to walk straight into the mirage.

Four or five hours go by. At last I see clumps of weed rise from the gravel. The land starts to dip. I check the compass. Sugan should be right in front of me now, but all I see is the wide stony plain.

Suddenly it dawns on me that distances can be deceptive in the transparent atmosphere of the desert. The lake that seemed so near from the pass could be a hundred kilometres away. After all, what looked like a tiny blue spot is in fact a huge lake. It is too late to turn back now though – my bottle is empty. I have no choice but to keep walking towards the water. Where there is water there are people, and where there are people there is life. There is no other path I can take.

As the sun sinks to the west, the lake reappears at last. It is not a lake exactly, just a line of grey slightly brighter than the desert stones, not wavering in the heat haze this time, but lying still at the edge of the sky. I am on course, but my legs can barely hold. There is camel-thorn underfoot now and the earth is covered with a thick saline crust. The sun sinks slowly below me, then reddens and disappears.

When my feet tread onto damp grass the sky is almost black. I move forward in a daze. The ground gets wetter and wetter. Through the green weeds ahead I glimpse a cold sweep of water. Hurriedly I drop my pack and wade down through the marsh towards the lake. I have arrived at last. Let me plunge into your waters! I stamp to the shore, throw myself down and scoop the water into my mouth. The taste is foul and brackish. A fire burns down my chest and my stomach explodes. I roll over and retch and my mind goes black.

A while later I wake up shivering with cold. Instinctively I start moving away from the lake. A briny taste rises from my stomach and sticks to the vomit on my tongue. I long for a sip of clean water to rinse my mouth and throat. My body and mind are frazzled but if I don't leave now I will die here on the shore. I try to crawl, but my hands give way. I fall and sink into the mud.

When I left Beijing I thought to myself, it doesn't matter where I go because I can dig my grave anywhere in China's yellow soil. But now that my life hangs on a thread, my only thought is of survival. I force my eyes open and try to see what lies ahead. A soft light falls on my brow. I crawl out of the marsh and see a full moon at the horizon, clear and round. I can almost touch it. I want to walk towards it, but stop myself. Its beauty is as beguiling as the lake's, and would prove just as murderous.

I scramble to my pack, pull everything out and rummage through the mess, ripping bags open, tossing things aside. At last I find a sachet of coffee granules in a small plastic bag. I stuff the bag into my mouth and chew through the plastic and foil. The granules are hard and dry. I swallow a few, and spit out the rest.

My mind begins to clear. I sense the need to pass water, so I hold out my bottle and wait. A few drops fall to the bottom. I swig them back and feel my blood start to flow again.

In the moonlight I sort through my belongings and discard everything unnecessary: books, magazines, clothes, socks. Then I swing on my pack and struggle to my feet.

I check my compass and decide to walk ten degrees north. That should take me back to the Qinghai road. Li Anmei, the Qiaozi announcer, told me her parents live in Tuanjie village on the road between Gansu and Qinghai.

Apart from the echo of my dragging footsteps, the desert is silent. The full moon rises into the night sky. After a few hours of slow march I see a light in the distance. At first I suspect I am imagining it. I walk for a while with my eyes closed, but when I open them again the light is still there. I walk towards it. The light grows larger. It appears to be a lamp. I stop and rest, still gazing at the light, afraid that if I blink it will vanish. Now that I have a goal to walk to, I feel my body being pulled towards it.

Soon I can see it is a truck. A lamp hangs over the boot. I hear noises. My legs move excitedly.

Getting closer, I see a man hammering at the wheel. The sound bangs through the night air. It is a comforting noise. I do not shout, in case it startles him.

Then I spot the lid of a thermos flask set on the path ahead. I pounce on it and empty the water into my throat. My body trembles with life. Moisture seeps into my eyes.

I crouch down and look at the driver. He is ten metres away, sitting in front of his truck, staring right back at me.

'Thank you, brother,' I say, putting the lid down.

He had placed the cup as far away as possible, it is clear he is nervous of me. He probably thinks I am an escaped prisoner. Why else would I be crossing the desert on my own? Still, his cup of water has saved my life.

'I'm going to Tuanjie to stay with the Li family. I seem to have lost my way.'

His hands move. 'Follow those wheel tracks up to the road. A truck will pass at dawn.'

I skirt around his truck. When it falls out of sight, I stop and collapse on the ground.

I shine the torch onto my watch. Four in the morning. Two hours to go before dawn. I lie down to sleep, but am woken before long by the wind.

In the moonlight the desert looks cold and empty. The only noise I hear is the ringing in my ears. For a moment it feels like a dream. Sometimes I dream of cantering under the moon on the hooves of a deer, my body as light as paper. But my bones feel pinned to the ground now and as heavy as death. My lips and throat are painfully dry. I dare not turn on my torch for fear of attracting wolves. As long as I keep still, I can melt into the darkness. When the cold becomes unbearable I jump up, stamp my feet and see the morning light tear the sky from the earth. Then I lie down and fall into a doze.

I am woken again by the faint rumble of a truck. I roll over, sit up, and look west to where the noise is coming from. From yesterday's experience I know that the truck could be a hundred kilometres away. The sky is clear now. The low horizon makes me feel very tall. The Aierjin mountains look less severe than they did yesterday from Akesai. The lines are softer, the slopes are bathed in a blue-green light and the peaks are rinsed in gold.

I plant myself in the middle of the track. The dawn air is moist, but my throat is still dry. There is no sign of the driver or the truck I saw last night.

A sheet of yellow dust lifts from the horizon, the rumble gets closer and closer. An hour later, the cloud of dust has grown. It looks like a wave of a stormy sea pushing the truck forward. I stand up, glance at the track and realise it is wide enough for the truck to drive right past me. I will just have to hope for the best.

I wave my hands in the air. The truck passes. I close my eyes. Then it stops, and a voice shouts, 'Want to fucking kill yourself, do you?'

I look up. There is sand everywhere. I grope my way to the front seat and cry, 'Help me out, brother, please! I need to go to Tuanjie. Thank you, thank you.' I climb into the back and sit on a heap of cement bags.

He pushes on the accelerator and we drive off. I look at the shaking desert and receding mountain range, and just as it did yesterday when I first saw Sugan, my heart begins to soar.

3.

Drifting through the West

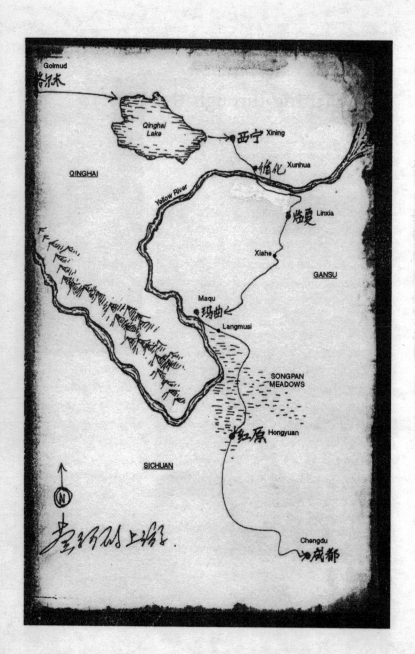

Hairdressing in Golmud

> Detonated mountains, untouched places
> Crawl with dry veins.
> As summer's phosphorescence drifts to its end
> Another kind heart squeezes from the
> Same simple spawn.
> The traveller's spine trembles . . .

I read through my poem. It is very long and still needs a lot of
work. I wrote it in Tuanjie after two days of solid sleep – it felt
like pulling out a dirty rag that had lodged at the back of my
throat. I can't make any changes to it now though. I will send it
off as it is and see if I can get some money for it. My bed is strewn
with letters ready to be posted. I have written a long letter to
Nannan which her mother will no doubt keep from her. The
letter to Lingling at Guangzhou Press contains grains of desert
sand, and the one to Wang Ping pressed flowers from the Kazak
pastures. In my letter to Yang Ming, the editor of Chengdu's *Star*
magazine, I have enclosed a short story called 'Escarpment'.

My letter to Li Tao is five pages long. I tell him my money is
running out, and ask him to find a publisher for my poem. 'Send
my fee to Yang Ming. I might pass through Chengdu in a few
months. First, though, I will travel to Tibet. I want to cleanse
myself in pure mountain air and undergo the privations of
spiritual pilgrimage.'

I recount my thoughts after leaving the desert. 'Walking
through the wilds freed me from worries and fears, but this is not
real freedom. You need money to be free.' Then I write:

Golmud is a grey dusty town on the Qinghai plateau that
serves as a staging post for Tibet. The railway from Xining

ends here, and migrant workers pour off the trains and wander the streets with desperation in their eyes, like the gold-diggers in American westerns. Trucks line the streets. As soon as a truck arrives back from Lhasa, yak skins and frozen meat are unloaded from its back and replaced with Chinese carpets and tinned vegetables. Tibetans with knives dangling from their waists stride through the traffic as though they were roving the empty plains.

In the long-distance bus station, passengers sit crammed in the morning bus waiting for it to leave for Tibet. Some lean out of the windows to buy dumplings and hard-boiled eggs. Others jump off to search for the driver, go for a piss, or look for a piece of string to tie up their broken bags. Late passengers push through the crowded forecourt, dodging pickpockets, horse-and-carts and puddles of urine. I have spent the last week working at this station, suffocating in the stench of dung and petrol, lugging bags around for just one yuan a day.

I have also written to Li Anmei to thank her for her parents' hospitality. I spent a month with them in Tuanjie, resting and writing, and making excursions into the surrounding pastures. I tell her:

A family of Kazak nomads put me up in their tent for a few days. I ate fresh yoghurt and learned to ride a horse bareback. The wife spent all day cooking while the husband sat watching his sheep. I lost all sense of time. They told me the government want them to give up their nomadic life and move to a concrete house in the city.

It is nice to spend a day writing letters. It feels like travelling through space.

It is June. I am sitting on my bed in a farmers' hostel in the dingy outskirts of Golmud. Smells of oil, diesel and horse urine waft through the open window. The dormitory's broken door rattles in the wind and two hens peek their heads through the crack in the wood. I get up to fetch some hot water and catch sight of my reflection in the mirror above the washstand. I look hideous – worse even than the day I arrived in Tuanjie. My skin is peeling, and the new layer underneath is still pale and raw. My hair and beard are excessively long. It is time I had a haircut. As I stare at the gruesome apparition I suddenly forget who I am looking at. That frowning face looks nothing like me. I realise my standards have been slipping. Last night I felt no compunction about squeezing my fleas in front of the Tianjin tiger-skin trader. I even got used to him spitting sunflower-seed husks onto the floor. I have taken to squatting on street corners munching raw tomatoes and ambling through town with my trouser legs rolled up, just like all the other peasants drifting through China trying to pick up work.

Before dark I stroll to the kebab stalls outside the workers' club in the centre of town. The Muslim boys in white caps shout at each other through clouds of charcoal smoke. In a corner behind them I see a man cutting hair, so I walk over and ask how much he charges. He says two and a half mao, no wash. I ask him where he is from, and he says Kaifeng, Henan Province. I remember reading about the Israelites who settled there generations ago, and look at him with keener interest. I ask how much he makes in a day, he says nine, ten yuan on average. I could do that, I think to myself. So I hurry to a department store and buy clippers, scissors, a comb and a metre of white cloth. Then I position myself by a lamp outside a video hall and cry, 'Haircuts, two mao a go!'

A Hong Kong action film called *Beyond Forbearance* is playing on the video machine inside. Men and children who cannot afford tickets gather under the speakers by the door to listen to the shrieks and punches. I spot a man with shoulder-length hair and ask if he wants a cut.

'How much?' he says, flicking back his fringe.

'Two mao, no wash.'

'I can watch the video for that.'

'One and a half, then,' I say, pulling him over to the lamp and draping the cloth over his shoulders.

'You don't even have a stool.' His breath stinks of tobacco, and his neck looks even dirtier against the whiteness of the cloth.

I make nine mao that night. It is much easier work than humping heavy bags around the bus station.

The next day I sneak out of my dormitory window with a borrowed stool and mirror, and set up business in a busy market street. I give crew-cuts to six peasants from Gansu and ten long-distance truck drivers. After lunch, I cut the hair of two boys from Jilin who have just graduated in Chinese literature and are off to Lhasa to start editorial jobs at Tibet Press. They say they want to experience 'life on the frontiers' and collect material for their novels. They tell me to look them up when I get to Lhasa.

By the afternoon of the third day, I can barely hold my scissors up, so I break off early, find myself a restaurant and order beef noodles, stir-fried pork and two shots of rice wine. After settling the bill, I light a cigarette and count the remains of my earnings. Six yuan. Enough for a new pair of plimsolls. A few more weeks of this and I will have sufficient funds for my journey to Tibet. I order a beer and feel the alcohol rush to my legs. The young man at the next table looks unhappy. I smile and say hello.

'Have a cigarette. It's no fun sitting on your own. Come and join me,' I say, pouring some beer into an empty tea cup.

'No, no, thank you. I'm fine, really.' His eyes are bloodshot. He looks like he could do with a good night's sleep, and a haircut too for that matter.

'Where do you work?' I ask, handing him a cigarette.

'At the State Building Commission.' He takes a puff and studies the table.

'Which department?' I presume he is based in Beijing.

'Sichuan engineering department,' he says, still looking at the table.

'The engineering department? You must have been to university then.' He probably lives in Chengdu.

'I work in the construction section.' He bows his head. All I see is his army cap.

'You haven't been there long, have you?' Now I suspect he is a labourer.

'I joined the team two years ago.' He looks at the floor.

'Which team?'

'The bricklayer team of Luding Number Two Construction Brigade,' he mumbles, turning a deep red. I can't help smiling. 'Don't worry. We all have to bluff a bit when we're away from home. You've come here looking for work, haven't you? I'll tell you what, come to the market tomorrow and I'll give you a free haircut.' I swig some beer and gaze at the waitress's bottom as she passes through the room.

'I'm looking for someone,' he says, puffing his cigarette.

'Who?'

'My sister. She was abducted from our village six months ago, and brought here to be sold as a bride.'

I remember Director Zhang reading out a report entitled 'The Resolute Fight Against the Abduction of Women and Children'. When he recited 'Due to high levels of Spiritual Pollution, cases of female trafficking have risen dramatically in recent years', he gave me a knowing look, as if it was all my fault. In fact, the rise in female trafficking has nothing to do with Spiritual Pollution. In remote backwaters that have yet to see the benefits of Deng Xiaoping's economic reforms, peasants are having increasing difficulty finding wives. It is often cheaper to buy one from a trader than to pay the marriage price that some families now demand before they agree to condemn their daughters to a life of rural poverty.

'Got a letter from her last week. The local police say the village is too far away. They can't afford a car. Told me to sort it out myself.'

'You can't rescue her on your own.' I look at his pale face and long white teeth and imagine what his sister looks like.

'She's my only sister. She said the man chains her to the bedroom door when he goes to the fields to stop her running away. He treats her worse than a dog.'

I also remember a journalist for the *Farmers' Daily* telling me of the time he accompanied a police team on a mission to rescue a student who had been kidnapped from a train station and sold to a farmer in the mountains. He said that when the police tried to wrest her from the husband, the entire village turned on them with wooden clubs and they were lucky to get out alive.

'If I were you, I would bring a Sichuan officer here to talk to the Qinghai police. That's the only way to get them on your side. You'll have to grease a few palms though.' I see his eyes welling up, so I raise my glass to him and we drain our cups in one.

The dusk deepens as I walk back to the farmers' hostel. A magazine article I read recently said that of the ten thousand women abducted last year, only a hundred have been rescued. It seems there is not much hope for his sister. Most women have a child to lull their husbands into a false sense of security, then pack their bags and make their escape.

I turn a corner and find two young men standing in front of me blocking my way. They tell me to open my bag. There is no money inside, so they take my camera instead. I run after them, hoping to grab it back. Serves me right for staying in the outskirts. I was bound to get robbed sooner or later.

The tall one turns round and gives me a punch in the face. I fall down.

'Leave us alone or we'll cut your throat.'

He has a northern accent, so I get up and pursue them.

'Hey, brothers,' I say, 'I'm a northerner too, just trying to get by. Nicked that camera this afternoon. Keep it if you like. More friends I have the better. Come on, I'll buy you a drink. We could be a team. What do you say? Divide the loot between us.' I cup my wounded ear, my head is pounding. I must have said something right though, because they are both standing still.

'How long have you been out?' the short one asks. I can't see his expression.

'Two months. I was in a Xinjiang labour camp.' I try to articulate each syllable, but my lips are numb with pain.

'What do you do?' His tone has softened. At least he won't punch me again.

'Break locks. We could make a good team. I respect a man who can fight.'

They take me to a small restaurant. As we sit down I remember I only have six yuan to spend.

'Order whatever you like,' I say. 'It's on me. We are brothers now. I'll stick by you through thick and thin.'

I can see their faces clearly now. The tall one wears a denim jacket, and a red vest printed with five gold stars. He has a round Mongolian face and cold narrow eyes. He rests his large folded hands on the table. The short one has jet-black hair and is taller than me. His eyes only close when he sucks at his cigarette. Their faces are familiar. I must have seen them in the bus station, or walking down the street perhaps.

'You look like a painter with that beard,' the short one says, spitting his stub onto the floor.

'I painted a bit when I was young.' I pour them some beer.

'How old are you?' they ask.

'Twenty-six.'

'Where are you from?'

'Place called Baodian in Hebei Province.'

'Been in Golmud long?'

'Just a week.'

'Do the pigs know about you?'

'No, haven't done much yet – just the camera. Stole it from a guest in the committee hotel. He's probably halfway to Tibet by now . . .'

They tell me everything, from their life in the Yingkou Farm Machinery Plant to the leather bag they stole last week from a Guangzhou businessman. They found a postcard of a woman inside – 'If you look at it sideways you can see her bare arse.' We finish two bottles of rice wine. I secretly let the alcohol dribble down my beard, though. My vest is soaking wet. I ask the waiter to bring us more drink, and they tell me they've had enough. 'No, my friends. I insist. If you hadn't beaten me up tonight, who knows, we might never have met.' I walk to the counter to fetch the beer. 'Quick,' I whisper to the waiter, 'call the police. Those men are dangerous criminals.'

But the waiter assumes I am drunk and takes no notice.

I turn round. They are talking to each other, and don't suspect a thing. I walk to the table with a bottle in each hand and smash them on their heads. As the tall one lurches back I pull the stool from under him and thrash it across his face, then swing it round and knock the short one to the ground. They are both lying on the floor now, completely rigid. I drop the blood-stained stool, open their bag and retrieve my camera.

Everyone in the restaurant has risen to their feet. 'What are you staring at?' I shout at the waiter. 'Why haven't you called the police yet? Don't just stand there!' I march out of the door. Back in the hostel, I pack in the dark, then slip out through the back door, run to the station and catch the first train out.

The train sets off for Xining. The carriage is so full, there is no room to stand, so I crawl under a seat and stretch out next to some clucking hens and a pile of dirty socks. I forget how far this six yuan ticket will take me. Never mind, I can sort that out later. I wonder if those guys are dead or not. They will kill me if they ever see me again. Tibet will have to wait. This train will pass Qinghai Lake in a few hours. There is an island in the middle inhabited by wild birds. A tangle of thoughts races through my mind, then everything becomes a blur.

Fishing on Qinghai Lake

Two stops before Qinghai Lake the train comes to a halt. I decide it would be wise to leave now before the conductor comes to check the tickets, so I push my way to the window, fling my bag out and jump. A fresh breeze wipes the stale smells from my face, the night is cold and clear. I follow the tracks for a while, but when the train pulls away I am plunged into a well of darkness.

The lake lies south of the railway. I strike a match, check my compass and glance at my watch. It is three in the morning. I can't sit here all night. I grit my teeth, step off the tracks and head into the night.

The soft ground underfoot dips and rises. I can tell it is grass – my plimsolls are wet through. I stagger forward, pivoting my body back and forth, trying to keep my balance. My arms are probably stretched in front of me, but I can't be sure, my mind has scattered into the dark. I try to walk in a straight line, but the constant fear of falling into a pit drains my energy. After an hour or so, I am too tired to know whether my eyes are open or shut. My legs grow weak, and slowly, just as I did as a child when my father walked me home from the beach at night, I walk myself to sleep. My next step treads through thin air. I fall and feel my shoulder and pelvis ram into damp earth. I pat the ground, discover I have landed in a pit, then close my eyes and sleep.

At dawn, I wake to a monotonous landscape of grass mounds and sandy pits. Along the side of a dirt track an electric cable coils feebly from one pole to the next. The sweep of water in the south must be Qinghai Lake. I strain my eyes but cannot see the further shore. It looks like an ocean. With a glad heart I leap to my feet and head down to the lake.

The sun reddens on the left and transforms the surface of the lake into a vast mirror. I see a tent by the shore and walk towards it. A dog charges out. There is no time to look for sticks or stones, so I swing off my pack and use it as a shield. The dog stops at my feet and barks wildly until someone leans out of the tent and shouts.

There is a fire in the middle of the tent. An old man lives here with his son. Steam from a pot of freshly cooked noodles rises into the thick woodsmoke. The old man pulls on a pair of waterproof trousers. His son whistles to the dog and walks in with a bundle of kindling. I tell them I have come to see Qinghai Lake.

'Not many people visit this side. We've been fishing here since spring, and in six months we have only seen two other people.'

I tell the old man I got off the train last night at Shatasi station.

'That's a thirty-kilometre walk away,' he says. 'You were lucky you didn't fall into a pit.' We laugh. He serves me a bowl of hot noodles and a piece of fish left over from their supper.

After the meal, they go out to prepare the raft and nets. I lift the door curtain and walk outside. The morning clouds have flooded the air with a yellow light, the margin of the lake is a band of rippling gold.

The old man says, 'Our home is simple, but you are welcome to stay if you like. No one will disturb you. You should rest a while before you continue your journey.'

'Thank you, it would be nice to get some sleep. He doesn't bite does he?' I ask, pointing to the dog. 'What's his name?'

'No name, just call her yellow dog. My son here doesn't speak Mandarin but he can understand a little.'

The boy looks about twenty. I smile at him and then call out to yellow dog. She walks over and sniffs my trousers. The horse tied outside the tent throws its head back and shudders.

After they leave, I decide to walk around the lake for a while, and drink the calm of the open space.

When I return, the sun is overhead and the lake is the colour of the sky. I enter the tent and lie down. Yellow dog rubs her head across my thigh. I watch her for a while, then fall into a doze. In my dream she smiles at me.

The next day I ask to join them on the lake. I borrow some waterproof trousers. They weigh a ton. If I were to fall in the water they would pull me straight to the bottom. The raft consists of two rubber tyres and four wooden planks bound together with rope. We carry it to the shore and jump on. The raft is too small for the three of us, so the boy gets off and his father and I row into the middle of the lake. Even through the waterproof trousers the water feels ice cold. The old man casts the net and I help straighten it. Now and then I ladle water from the raft with a large wooden spoon. The surface of the lake is smooth and the air is perfectly still. A flock of bar-headed geese fly past in the distance.

'Is it easy to get to Bird Island?' I wait for the old man to dry his hands and pass him a cigarette.

'It's been open to tourists for some years now. The birds have been frightened away.'

'What goes through your mind when you are out here all day on the lake?' There is water as far as the eye can see. It would be nice to float here for a day or two, but a lifetime would be unbearable.

'I dream about the day I won't have to come here any more.' He crushes the cigarette with his large callused hand. 'I'll fish here a few more years, save some money, then find my son a good wife.'

I remember the young man from Sichuan who was looking for his sister, and I let the subject drop.

In the afternoon, when we haul the lines in for the second time, I see a large yellow carp trapped in the net. I tug it out and throw it down, and it jumps across my feet. 'We'll have that for dinner,' he says. I ask if there is any beer left and he says he has a few more bottles stashed away. I remember how we sat up in the tent last night without a care in the world, safe, warm, talking and drinking by the fire, and I feel a strange pang – the joy of entering their simple lives mixed with a sadness that I don't belong.

On the third day I tell them it is time for me to leave. The old man, the boy and yellow dog walk me to the main road. They stop a truck and offer the driver eighty jin of yellow carp for half the usual price on condition that he drive me to Xining. He agrees to this, but later, when I get down for a piss at the edge of a small town, he hurls my bag out of the window and drives off without me.

Racing down the Ravine

I leave Xining on the morning of 12 June and reach Xunhua, a small town high in the mountains, late in the afternoon. From here I plan to follow the Yellow River east for a while, then proceed south to Chengdu. The director of Xunhua cultural centre invites me to stay in his flat.

He tells me of the Muslim and Tibetan minorities who inhabit this area. He speaks of the history of Tibetan revolt and of the Xunhua Tibetan Uprising of 1958 in which five hundred monks were killed by the People's Liberation Army and over three thousand civilians were arrested. Before I came here, the only thing I knew about Xunhua was that it was the birthplace of the Panchen Lama. After a few days' browsing through the local records, I decide on a route that will take me to the Salar village of Mengda, the sacred Lake of Heaven, and onwards to the Tibetan pastures of northern Sichuan. The director tries to dissuade me from travelling through Tibetan regions alone, as there is still much hostility towards the Han. Nevertheless, when I say goodbye three days later he gives me a letter of introduction, and twenty yuan from his own pocket.

After leaving Xunhua, I walk five kilometres south to see the sacred stone camel of the Salar people. According to legend, the Muslim ancestors of the Salar left Samarkand in the fourteenth century in search of a new home, bringing a white camel to lead the way and a copy of the Koran. When they reached Xunhua the camel turned to stone. The statue of the stone camel now stands outside the Salar's oldest mosque, surrounded by an ugly cement wall.

The next day I climb higher into the mountains and reach a clear stream. If a local peasant had not informed me, I would never have guessed that it was the Yellow River. I follow it east through a deep ravine, taking photographs along the way. At one bend in the river, I see a long beach of silver shale curving like a woman's leg around the base of a grassy slope. It looks a nice place to take someone you love.

Later, I meet three men and a woman washing for gold. They scoop sand from the banks on a ribbed board, flush the dirt away with buckets of water, pour the residue into a basin then pick the grains out by hand. They tell me they can each make five yuan a day from this.

Twenty kilometres along I reach a mud village called Mengda. I wander through the narrow lanes and see six or seven cretins, a cripple, and a child with a squint.

'Where are all the grown-ups?' I ask a girl with a baby in her arms.

'Out in the fields.'

'And that baby's mother?'

'I'm her mother.'

'How old are you?'

'Fourteen.' She turns and carries the baby indoors.

The village head puts me up for the night. He says Mengda is so isolated, people marry young, often with members of their own family. 'Reforms don't mean much to us up here. A free economy won't make bicycles or sewing machines grow from the earth. We planted a small orchard last year. I don't know if it will produce any fruit. All the young men have left to find work in the cities. They come back at Spring Festival with new watches and big bags of clothes.'

'What about the family planning regulations?'

'The Salar are allowed three children. The soil is so thin, we need big families to help on the land or we would never grow anything on these mountains.'

Continuing east I pass a single cable bridge suspended high above the river. Apparently, a small Tibetan community lives behind the mountains on the opposite bank. It is hard to imagine how they survive in such isolation.

A further twenty kilometres along, there are a few mud huts clinging to the steep slopes. The people who live in them tell me the Lake of Heaven, worshipped by the Salars, is only a six-hour walk into the mountains behind. I stop and spend the night with a gruff peasant who lets me sleep on his mud floor.

I climb up the next day and reach the lake at noon. There is snow on the mountain peaks. The lake is so deep I cannot see the bottom. A band of woodcutters in a lodge nearby offer me a straw bed and a simple meal for a reasonable price. They tell me the lake is being developed as a tourist site and that poetic names have been assigned to each mountain, tree and cave. I have trouble sleeping at night. My nose is blocked, my voice has gone and the air is so thin I cannot think straight. I crave red apples and corn soup, and have flashbacks of my primary-school friend Rongrong selling hot rabbit heads outside the Red Flag Cinema in Qingdao. I see the heads steaming in her saucepan. You could buy four heads for a mao.

There are holes in my shoes. I patch them with sticky tape, but it falls off after a few steps. I come down from the lake and continue along the ravine to a village inhabited by the Baoan. These people are Muslim, and claim to be descended from Central Asian soldiers who intermarried, centuries ago, with local Tibetan tribes. I look at them closely, but apart from the white caps on their heads, they seem indistinguishable from the Han Chinese. A little boy strikes a pose in front of an old man with a wispy beard, and shouts, 'Take a picture,' as I pass. So I do.

Five kilometres downstream I reach Guanmen. A bull tethered to the village gates observes me through the corner of its eye. A child lugging a heavy basket of potatoes walks past and pauses to catch his breath. Further along I see two women washing spring onions by a well, and an old woman and a hen sleeping in a courtyard. The rest of the village is dead.

As the ravine veers north, I continue east to Dahe and book into a doss-house that charges one yuan a night. The sesame cakes in the village store look good but they cost eight mao a jin, so I buy some boiled sweets instead and a new pair of plimsolls. Back in the doss-house, I lie on the brick bed in the dark, pining for a hot shower and a soft mattress. The man lying next to me says the small market town, Linxia, is a two-hour bus drive away, and that tickets cost one yuan twenty. I calculate that I have just enough, and decide to take the morning bus. In the middle of the night the police storm in and demand to see my documents. They suspect I am a drug smuggler. The peasant next to me says the locals make small fortunes growing opium on their private plots.

Meeting Ma Youshan

In a backstreet of Linxia I see crates of tangerines stacked along the pavement. I would buy some if I had any money, and if I wasn't carrying a heavy bag, I would steal a few and run. Instead, I crouch down, rummage through my belongings and pull out a pair of socks. I look at the old woman and say, 'I'll swap you these socks, Aunty, for a few of your tangerines.'

She takes the socks from me and holds them to the sun. 'The heels are threadbare.'

'I've only worn them once. They're a Hong Kong designer label.'

She shakes her head and throws them back to me. I must make

some money, I say to myself as I turn down a side road. There are no tangerines for sale here, just tables, plastic buckets, washbowls, food racks. A calendar seller has tied a rope across the road, and it is blocking the way of a passing tractor. The peasant in the driving seat howls abuse as diesel fumes chug from his exhaust pipe. A boy in a blue cap sits on the pavement behind a green carpet heaped with medicinal herbs and fly-infested bones. The carpet trader beside him pins a leopard skin to the wall. The black and yellow markings still exhale the air of mountains and forests. I ask him how much it costs. 'Sixty yuan,' he says. Cantonese pop purrs from an imported tape recorder on a table outside a hardware store. Deng Lijun sings, 'If I forget him I'll lose my way, I'll sink into misery . . .' I remember playing that tape to Lu Ping. She sang the chorus 'Forget him, how can I forget him?' in a southern accent as soft as water.

I reach a busy crossroads and see people pushing barrows of beer, rice and cigarettes. Bicycles pass with racks carrying bundles of bean sprouts, women with bare arms or children with large staring eyes. Dusty long-distance buses, back from the mountains, splatter mud as they crawl to the terminus.

I feel ashamed of myself, traipsing through the streets like a stray dog, so I return to listen to Deng Lijun outside the hardware store. The tape is playing at double speed now. A man in a straw hat yells, 'New listening experience! Advanced technology! All the latest functions!' I walk straight past, stroll down a street lined with food stalls, cross a small bridge and turn into a quiet lane. Suddenly I notice a small brick house covered with bamboo scaffolding. I stop and stare. It reminds me of my house in Nanxiao Lane. In a flash I see my bed, the sketch of Lu Ping on the wall, the tea cup, orange sofa, cassette player, the jade seal I found on the beach as a child and keep in a box in a drawer next to the gramophone needle, divorce certificate and the paperweight engraved with a picture of an old man crossing a bridge . . . While I stand there daydreaming, a middle-aged man with a thick chin walks up and asks me who I am looking for. I tell him the house reminds me of my home in Beijing.

His face lights up. 'Beijing residences are built to very exacting standards, with taste and elegance. My home has not been renovated since the Liberation. It is a humble little brick affair, hardly in the same league as the splendid houses of the capital.'

'No, no. I can tell it will look wonderful once the work is completed, and besides, it has the best feng shui in the lane.' I picked up a geomantic handbook at a village fair, and the chapter on the four cardinals and five elements is still fresh in my mind. 'The house has a mountain to the back, a stream to the front and green hills to the east and west. Taking a cursory glance, the wood, fire, earth, metal and water elements of the site appear to be in harmonious balance.' Since I am only halfway through the book, I make a hasty retreat before I run out of things to say.

He drops his cigarette, grabs my arm and says, 'Brother, I could tell at once you were no ordinary man. Please, may I ask your name?'

'My surname is Lu,' I say.

'Brother Lu, would you give me the great honour of allowing me to buy you a meal?'

'Yes, yes,' I blurt, a little too eagerly.

We walk back to the food stalls and sit down at a small restaurant.

'Order whatever you like, Brother Lu, please. How lucky I am to have made your acquaintance. To think you have travelled all the way from Beijing!'

'It is too early in the day for me to eat,' I lie, attempting to sound less desperate. 'A beer will do fine.'

'Well, let us at least have some snacks,' he says, and orders pigs' trotters, sliced cucumber and a plate of sweet and sour ribs.

'Come, Brother Lu, drink, drink!' We raise our bowls and drain them in one. 'I am a common man,' he says, 'no education. I inherited the house from my father.'

121

'He was a herbal doctor, am I right?' When I peered through the windows earlier, I noticed what looked like an old-fashioned pharmacy.

'So,' he pauses to collect himself. 'So you really are a sage. You have received teachings from the holy men, I am sure.'

I smile to myself. 'I sought refuge in the Buddha last winter. Master Zhengguo ordained me and gave me the name Mighty Steel. I have left the red dust of samsara and resigned myself to my karmic destiny for the sake of all sentient beings.'

He gazes at me with admiration. It is a long time since anyone looked at me like that. 'What is your name, sir?' I ask.

'Ma – Ma Youshan.'

'An auspicious name. It will bring you fortune and good health for the rest of your days,' I say, reminding myself I have no money for a room tonight.

'I would like to receive your teachings, Mighty Steel. My family have been Buddhists for five generations. Please, come back to my home and stay with us for a while before you resume your journey.'

So I move in with Ma Youshan for a while. His father was deputy head of Linxia People's Hospital, but was attacked during the Cultural Revolution because Ma Youshan's grandfather ran a private pharmacy in the 1930s and treated a Guomindang general injured by the Eighth Route Army. He was forced to attend study sessions and confess his political crimes. One day they paraded him through the streets and someone hurled a stone at his ear. A few days later, the gash went septic and he died. Ma Youshan is an accountant for the local rice and oil depot. He has a wife and three sons. The youngest runs his own wholesale garment business and has been featured in the local papers.

Out of politeness, I give his house a rudimentary geomantic survey. I tell him it is unlucky to have the front door in direct line with the back door as it encourages the flow of malevolent currents. So he moves the front door a few metres to the right.

Then I draw up a five-year astrological chart for each member of his family, and paint a mountain landscape above the new front door. In the evenings I lie in bed and scribble a few lines in my notebook.

20 June. Ma Youshan is a good man. His hospitality has saved me. I feel bad for duping him. His wife lights incense every night and bows to the clay buddha on the family altar ... Nannan must have freckles again by now, and grown even taller. It hurts when I think about her. I keep remembering the piggy-back I gave her last summer, and how the ice cream I had bought her melted and dripped down my neck. Why was I allowed to bring her into this world, but am forbidden to be a father to her?

25 June. While painting the mural today I felt a stabbing pain in my chest. In the morning I sometimes forget about death, but by the afternoon the memory returns and tells me that however fast I run or high I climb, my body is pregnant with death ...

5 July. A friend of Ma Youshan's eldest son came round tonight and paid me 10 yuan to read his fortune. We had a drink and he told me about Shenzhen. He said the shops have automatic stairs – you step on at the bottom and they carry you to the next floor. He said if things go on like this, they will fix them to roads and we won't need bicycles any more.

7 July. Went to a bookshop to browse through some graphology manuals, and saw a girl in a long skirt. Her neck was milky white. Various thoughts came to mind. I have tried to renounce all attachments and desires, but it is hard to stop thinking about women. Love shields us from loneliness, but when it falls apart, the pain is even deeper. Ma Youshan's neighbour paid me 5 yuan to select an auspicious date for his son's wedding ... Man's sense of

well-being derives from thoughts of future gain. It is these that give him the will to live.

10 July. Saw two men wrestling on the street. A crowd gathered and watched like spectators at a dogfight. I pushed my way through and dragged the men apart. Ma Youshan said that during the Cultural Revolution nameless corpses lay strewn on the street for days.

After three weeks in Linxia, I tell Ma Youshan it is time for me pursue my search for enlightenment. His youngest son drives me to Xiahe and drops me at the gates of Labrang, the largest Buddhist monastery outside Tibet.

The Girl in the Red Blouse

It is not until I leave Labrang a few days later that I finally open the brown envelope Ma Youshan gave me as we said goodbye. There is a stick of ginseng inside and a one-hundred-yuan note.

If I keep to a budget of two yuan a day, I have enough money to last for seven weeks, and in less than a month I should be in Chengdu, where I hope Yang Ming will help me find some work. Before me lies the long road to Sichuan. I will follow it from Hezuo to Luqu, veer west to Maqu, then join it again at Langmusi. This region of Gansu used to be part of Tibet, and the grasslands near Maqu are still inhabited by Tibetan farmers and nomads.

For the first two days the road follows an icy stream down a steep mountain valley. Occasionally I pass a flock of sheep grazing on a mound beside a tumbled shack.

On the third day I reach Luqu, a small village consisting of a few mud houses scattered along a straight stretch of road. There are trucks parked on the verge and horses tied to posts. I step into the village shop, buy a fizzy orange and sit drinking it on a large sack of flour by the doorway. Tibetan herders stream in to buy chillies, tea, oil, cigarettes. When it comes to settling the bill they empty their money onto the counter, let the shopkeeper take what he needs, then stuff the remainder into their pockets.

'Mind he doesn't cheat you,' I say to the young Tibetan buying three bottles of rice wine. He doesn't understand but smiles anyway.

'I never take more than I should,' the shopkeeper says.

'Where do they get all that money from?' I ask.

'Wool. It fetches a good price in the market. They just need to sheer fifty sheep and they can make five hundred yuan in a day.'

I stock up on pineapple sherbet, malt biscuits, shoelaces and boiled sweets, then leave the village and continue south.

The weather is clear and the road is good. Sometimes it twists through mountain valleys, sometimes it climbs over green hills. I walk fifty kilometres a day. Late in the afternoon on the fourth day, I arrive at Maqu. The villagers are mostly Tibetan, there is hardly a Han in sight. I dump my bag in the committee guesthouse and go outside to take photographs.

Tibetan men in army caps haul a felled tree from the back of a truck.

A woman waiting for a lift sweeps back her finely plaited hair and smiles into my lens.

A girl in a sheepskin wrap crouched in a corner biting her nails watches a man haggle over a leg of beef.

Two monks in red robes sit on the pavement talking. They raise their arms in the air then cover their eyes and laugh.

The mud houses and cement path turn gold in the late sun. I come to the narrow door of a small shop and see a girl inside with a long silver headdress. She is wearing a red blouse under a heavy sheepskin coat that is swung over the left shoulder and tied at the waist with long leopard-trimmed sleeves. Her cheeks are flushed with meadow light. As she turns to leave, she catches sight of me and stares straight into my eyes. She studies my hair, mouth, clothes, shoes, then strides past me, unties her horse from the post outside and jumps into the saddle. My heart thumps as wildly as the horse's frantic hooves. She grabs her reigns, turns to glance back at me, then gallops into the evening sun. Yearnings buried deep inside me surge to the surface. I want to chase after her, I want to see her again.

And I didn't even have time to take her photograph.

Next morning I wake with the dawn. The streets are empty. A little puppy sits shivering where yesterday the girl tethered her horse. It looks no more than two days old. I pick it up and brush the straw from its back. Then I walk west out of the village and head into the wide grasslands.

At noon the sun grows warmer. I am walking through endless pasture, the scent of grass seeps into my skin. A few hours later the Yellow River appears again, lying flat on the grass ahead. It is as clear as before, but wider now, and almost motionless.

I follow its banks and soon I see a white tent in the distance and a woman outside, stripped to the waist rounding up a herd of sheep. She moves slowly, hips thrust forward, the folds of her sheepskin robe bulging over her rear. A dog barks at me. This is how I dreamed the grasslands would be. The puppy in my arms is trembling too.

Further along, a naked child canters past, clinging to his black steed like a little monkey.

At the crest of a hill I sit down to rest. There are sheep on the opposite bank, and behind them another white tent. Perhaps that is where the girl in the red blouse lives. I think of her breasts hidden under the sheepskin cloak, and imagine staring into her eyes as I touch her, just as she stared into mine. The words of a folk song play through my mind: 'Far away there's a shepherd girl with a face like the morning sun. I wish I were her little lamb, we would have such fun. She could beat me with her leather whip until the day was done . . .' North and south, white clouds pour from the seam where green hills touch the sky. A flock of white sheep spills over a distant hill and scatters like mist.

I put the puppy down, lie on my back, pull my jeans off and soak up the sun. I rub my stomach and tremble until the sky darts through the clouds. The puppy licks my thighs. I would like to curl up and sleep but I am too weak to move.

As the evening sun pulls the white clouds in and stains them a deep red, I come to a tent with a smoking chimney. It looks like a good place to spend the night. Before I know it two sheepdogs leap out and bite into my flesh. I howl and kick. By the time the owner looks out, my clothes are ripped and my arms are dripping in blood. I curse him and he curses back in Tibetan. My puppy sneaks under the sheepdogs' legs and snarls at me.

I turn round, flick the midges from my face, and decide to walk back to the main road as fast as I can.

As twilight falls I hear someone riding towards me, humming a tune. A young man on a horse stops by my side and waves his felt hat. 'Get on,' he shouts. So I hoist myself up and wrap my arms around him.

The wind brushes past my ears as we gallop away, but I can still hear him humming his tune. I bounce up and down as the horse plunges into a river and charges up a grass bank. The young man nearly slips off the neck, but manages to right himself just in time. At last we reach a dirt track and pass three houses with lighted windows. The horse stops. I lose my balance and topple to the ground. The young man dismounts and walks into a courtyard, motioning me to join him for a drink.

I slowly rise to my feet. My thighs feel raw and the dog bites are starting to hurt. I shuffle into the yard and find a sheep market inside. A Han in blue overalls is seated by the scales. He is here to buy sheep for the Gansu food authority. I ask how much he pays for the animals. He says, two yuan a jin, minimum weight twenty-five. When the sheep are placed on the scales, they stick out their chins and kick their bound legs in the air.

'What brings you to these parts?' he asks, eyeing me curiously.

'I went to the grasslands to interview some herders for a

newspaper article, but I got lost on the way back. That young man who walked in just now brought me here on his horse.'

'You mean Gyaltso. It's Tibetan custom that if a herder sees someone on the grasslands after dark he is obliged to ride them to safety. There are wolves out at there at night, you know.'

I ask him how far it is back to Maqu by road, and he says ten or twenty kilometres. I think for a while and say, 'Where are you sleeping tonight? I'll squeeze in with you if that's all right.'

'Fine, I'm staying in the room upstairs. Go and lie down now if you like. Gyaltso's up there playing cards,' he says, breaking off to speak to the herders in Tibetan.

I stay and chat for a while then climb up to bed.

Loud bleating wakes me at dawn. The army coat I have slept under reeks of mutton. I step through the dung in the courtyard and urinate against the wall. Half my body aches, the other half itches, my mind and legs are numb. I kick a few sheep out of the way and, feeling slightly better, walk out of the yard.

The houses in the village are small and squat, allowing clear views of the hills beyond. I make for the highest hill. There are prayer flags at the top, a temple too. An old woman spins a prayer wheel as she circles its white walls. I step into the temple courtyard. It is empty apart from a flagpole that carries one's gaze to the sky. I enter the prayer hall and see a gold buddha sitting on the altar above a sea of flickering butter lamps. The heat warms my face.

I hear a muffled chanting and trace the noise through a dark corridor to a chapel behind where thirty or forty child monks are sitting cross-legged on the floor. I quietly kneel in the doorway. The old lama leading the prayers is the first to see me. Then two child monks peer round and soon the whole room is staring in my direction. I stay where I am. After a while the chanting peters out. The little monks laugh and prod each other, then rush over and engulf me.

'What's this temple called?' I ask.

'Nyima Temple.'

'How old are you?'

'Ten.'

'And you?'

'Eleven.'

'And you?'

'Ten.'

'Twelve.'

The old lama storms over and barks in broken Chinese. I show him my identity card and explain I am a journalist from Beijing. His expression changes. He thinks for a second and asks, 'Where's your car?' When I tell him it is parked at the bottom of the hill, he relaxes at last and joins the crowd of little monks who are examining my camera and denim jeans. I ask to take their picture and they arrange themselves at once into three neat rows.

One of the novice monks speaks Chinese. He shows me the dormitories, dining room, printing room, even the wild-dog den on the other side of the hill. He says his father is Tibetan and his mother is Han Chinese. He spent six years in a Chinese school, before his father had a change of heart and sent him to the monastery. He does not like chanting sutras and wants to be a truck driver when he grows up. He has two little sisters and his father is a local government cadre. He tells me his Tibetan name is Sonam, his Chinese name is Xu Guanyuan, and he is not sure which one he likes best.

In the afternoon, I leave the monastery and return to the committee guesthouse in Maqu. The straw pillows are rough and noisy and stink of insect repellent. In my dreams that night I see a Tibetan butter pouch made of soft suede. When I squeeze it between my hands it gasps, and moans, 'Stop it, you're hurting me . . .'

The next day, I fill my water bottle and leave Maqu at dawn. Another dirt road stretches ahead, not a truck in sight. I scratch my flea bites with a twig and walk for hours until my head throbs. At last I reach Langmusi village – a few stone shacks clustered around a fork in the road. All the doors are padlocked. It looks like a roadworkers' camp. The tall mountain behind is dotted with sheep. A shepherd boy stares down at me from a rocky outcrop. The summit is a sheer stone cliff. I look at it for a while, then take the road that curls to the right.

On the other side of the mountain, I see the fertile basin of Sichuan sweep to the south. I stop and think back on my route through Gansu and Qinghai. I think about the puppy I carried in my arms, the girl in the red blouse, the monk called Sonam who dreams of being a truck driver, and I wonder what they are doing now.

I spend the night in a hostel attached to a petrol station outside the village of Redongba. The electricity is turned off at dusk. I fetch a basin of hot water and wash my feet and socks by candlelight. The bedcovers are filthy and full of fleas, so I douse myself with tiger lotion, lie on the bed fully clothed, and escape at the first light of dawn.

The road soon leaves the mountains and cuts into the Songpan meadows. In 1935 Mao Zedong led the Red Army through here in what proved the most arduous stretch of the Long March. The grass is green and lush, but beneath it lies treacherous swamp. I remember the pictures in my history textbook of soldiers and horses sinking into the mud. It is still not known how many died – hundreds, thousands, tens of thousands. The ones who survived the marsh are the founding fathers of today's communist tyranny. No one has thought to retrieve the bodies of the dead soldiers and give them a proper burial. All that disturbs the meadows now are the red poppies wavering in the wind.

As I scan the swathes of grass and inhale their perfume, my mind fills with images of death and misery. Under my breath I sing a song from the revolution: 'The Red Army climbs a thousand mountains and crosses ten thousand rivers, yearning for a moment of rest . . .'

I stay off the grass and tramp for hours on end, watching noon change slowly into dusk. After three days I lose interest in the scenery and keep my eyes on the road. On the fourth day, I reach Hongyuan as a cold rain begins to fall.

The guesthouse I book into is an old-fashioned two-storey building with wooden floorboards and a veranda at the back. The pillars flanking the front door are still marked with the peeling red slogans 'Long Live Chairman Mao' and 'Long Live the Communist Party'. I take a stool onto the veranda, light a cigarette and watch the raindrops burst bubbles on the puddles in the backyard. I remember as a child how excited I would get at the first glimpse of rain. I would run outside and build mud banks across the gutter so I could wade in the puddles behind. I never got very far though – someone would always cycle through my dam before I had finished building it. Now, as I stare at the rain and look at my muddy shoes and crinkled white feet soaking on the wet floorboards, I feel tired and a long way from home.

In the evening I have a beer and close my eyes. I have a whole room to myself and it costs just two mao a night. This must be the cheapest hotel in China. I decide to stay a few days and take things easy.

The first day I have a shower and wash my clothes.

The second day I stroll into the meadows and take photographs of Tibetan prayer flags. The Buddhist sutras printed on the cloth murmur in the breeze.

The third day, I take my blanket onto the veranda and shake out the dust. Then I walk through the village and buy a Tibetan knife.

The fourth day I walk to the next hill. Rain clouds fill half the sky while the other half bathes in sunlight.

The fifth day I write some poetry, mend my socks and drink a bowl of fresh oxblood bought from the local abattoir.

After two weeks I finally leave Hongyuan and catch the morning bus to Chengdu.

4.

A Country in Ferment

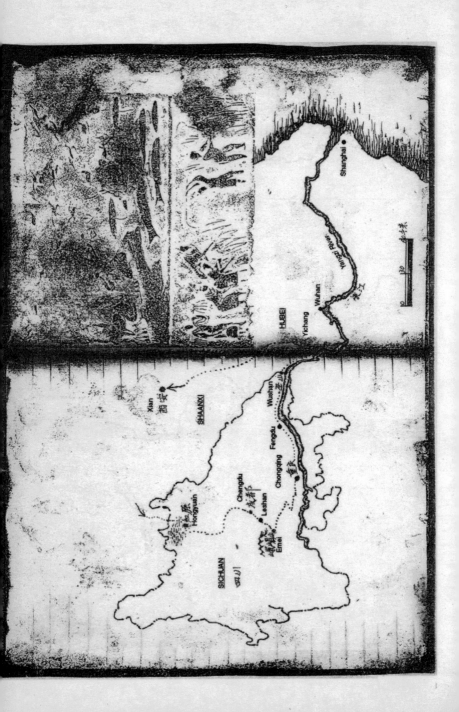

Back to the City

Yang Ming and I walk out of the concrete building that has baked all day in the Chengdu sun, and squeeze ourselves onto a bus that is even hotter than the editorial office we have just left. When the doors close I feel oppressed, not by the number of passengers, but by the stale stench of the noisy steam that rises from the city.

'It's easier to get on buses here than it is in Beijing,' I say.

'It is if you look as bad as you do.' Yang Ming has a voluptuous figure, but she speaks and moves like a man. She was the eight hundred metres racing champion one year at her university. We clutch the hot rail. My fingers look dark and chapped next to her delicate, white hands. 'My boss rejected "Escarpment", so I sent it to a literary journal published by Guizhou Press,' she says. 'It's got past the lower committee. The editor, Old Xu, is a friend of mine. He likes your style. I told him you are travelling the country and he said you should look him up if you visit Guiyang.'

The last time I saw Yang Ming was in Hu Sha's room. She had come to Beijing to recite her poetry at a literary conference.

She is wearing brown jeans today. Her large round eyes stare vacantly at my beard. I cannot connect her with the Yang Ming I saw last winter in the red knitted hat, so I resort to discussing mutual friends.

The road is packed, but the bus sways like a fish above the sea of faces and the silver light thrown from the metal handlebars. When we pass the main square the cyclists thin. Ahead, a huge statue of Chairman Mao, one arm raised in salute, towers above a smoking chimney stack behind and makes the pedestrians seem much smaller.

'In the Cultural Revolution, we came here to pledge devotion to the Party before we were sent to work on the farms,' she says. 'My classmates asked the teacher, "How long are we going away for?" And the teacher said, "Just look at the Chairman's hand: that's right, five years." '

I peer back at the statue. 'What about the hand behind his back?'

'There are only three fingers on that one!' She laughs and sweeps back her shoulder-length hair. A smell of damp feet moves through the bus. Outside the window, red banners advertise a raffle for holders of a fixed deposit account. A man in a white shirt yells into a microphone and points to a bicycle tied to the roof of a truck with red silk ribbons. In the sweltering evening, the people milling about him look like ducks drifting on a waterhole.

'Is it true you can buy bicycles on the free market now?' I ask, tugging at my shirt collar. The bag sticking to my back is soaked with sweat.

'Yes, but you still need coupons for Shanghai Golden Deer bikes. All the department stores have raffles now. Peasants flood in from the countryside and buy like mad. The hotels are full. Everyone is caught in the race to get rich. A ten-year-old wrote a letter to her neighbour threatening to kill his son unless he shared his prize with her. What do they buy? Anything as long as it comes with a raffle ticket. I've seen people buy a hundred boxes of matches, three hundred bars of soap, six alarm clocks . . .' She looks like a gypsy girl with her fresh face and heavy lips. I remember the rumour circulating Beijing poetry circles that she and Hu Sha are lovers.

We walk through a meat market that reeks of the scorched hairs on roasted pig heads. We climb a stairwell strewn with charcoal briquettes, bicycles, glass bottles, rotten vegetables, enter a room on the fourth floor and sit down on a double bed.

Yang Ming's husband Wu Jian is sitting on the sofa. He has the face of a student and the unkempt curls of an artist, or of someone who has just crawled out of bed. He speaks to me in a thick Sichuan accent. 'So what do you think of Chengdu?' I look into this stranger's face and say, 'Hot, crowded, polluted. Too many cars.'

We huddle around an electric fan that churns heat and sweat through the air. I think longingly of the meadows. This room is not even large enough for a horse to stand in. Wu Jian comments on the articles in the paper he is reading.

'Stupid farts. It's all very well telling us to put some elegance into our lives, but we don't even have room to wash our feet!'

I put out my cigarette and read the article he is pointing to. 'In the past, due to prevailing leftist ideologies, anyone paying attention to how they ate or dressed was accused of aspiring to a bourgeois lifestyle. But now that living standards have improved, we must be brave and encourage people to introduce some elegance into their lives. Elegance is a mark of socialist and spiritual civilisation . . .' As I read aloud, Wu Jian drums his fingers on the sofa's wooden armrest.

Yang Ming walks in with the soup that has simmered on the kerosene stove in the corridor, places it on the table and sprinkles coriander leaves over the top. She is wearing a long flowery dress now. She must have changed in the toilets, or in a neighbour's room, perhaps. Her breasts swing freely as she moves her arms. I imagine it feels good to take off one's bra after a long hot day.

'Try one of our Chengdu cigarettes, they're not bad.' Wu Jian is wearing a white vest. His soft, pale face is dripping with sweat. He looks as though he might jump up any moment and scream his head off.

'Did your work unit give you this room?' I ask. 'I lived in a dormitory block like this once. Nearly drove me mad.'

'At least it's just the two of us. Next door there are three generations living in one room. The women sleep on the bed and the men camp on the floor. I can't imagine how those babies were conceived.'

'Haven't they built you apartments yet?' I remember coming to

Chengdu a few years ago to interview a model worker. His room was so small I had to create a living room in a corner of his factory and take the pictures there.

'After thirty years of communism, our work unit has only just got round to building some decent homes. But there are five hundred families fighting for forty-five flats. The unit set up a committee to allocate them, but six months have gone by and nothing has been resolved. The clever ones get someone high up to put in a good word for them, the others snitch on their colleagues, accusing them of lying about pregnancies or dependent mothers. Last month the committee was about to announce the results of the third selection process, but two of the candidates got married, and a woman accused of faking pregnancy gave birth to a child – so they had to start all over again. I will be old and grey before I get on the list.' He waves his hands in the air as he speaks. There are thick tufts of hair under his arms.

'A child might help,' I say.

'Seniority counts more than children. In the communist world, the older you get the more you're worth.' I can see he is waiting for me to laugh.

'The electrician downstairs used to fight with his sister-in-law over the cooking and washing up,' Yang Ming says. 'Last month he punched her eyeball out. Now that she has lost an eye, her family have jumped to the top of the list. Seems a big price to pay for a flat.' She pulls her hair into a tight ponytail. The damp hair in her armpits is jet black.

I take a slug of beer. 'You're doing all right though,' I say. 'Got yourselves a television. How many stations can it receive?' As I glance at the screen, a soprano steps onto the stage and sings, 'Rock, rock, waves of the sea, cradle our warriors to sleep . . .' A huge cut-out moon dangles above her head.

'Everyone keeps teasing me at work about the letters that come for you. They say, "Your husband's called Wu Jian, isn't he? So who is this Ma Jian all of a sudden?" '

I laugh and look down at the table. 'You shouldn't have cooked so much, Yang Ming.'

'Least I could do.' She wipes a hand across her face and rubs a handkerchief down her cleavage. 'Our Party secretary looked worried today. I'm sure he read that piece in the papers,' she says, pausing to take a sip of soup. 'A labour exchange has just opened in Guangzhou. Skilled workers can resign from their posts and look for equivalent jobs elsewhere. Nine thousand workers signed up at the inaugural meeting, and the committee was able to find new jobs for two people there and then. Everything will change now. We'll all be able to switch jobs, move to other towns, other provinces.' She glances at Wu Jian. I sense they have a lot to talk about.

'Has Chengdu changed much in the last two years? I read that after Guangzhou and Shenzhen, Chengdu has the largest number of private businesses in the country.'

My eyes sweep over the room and fall on a life-size photograph of Yang Ming's face that is staring at me from the wall. Smells of fried chilli blow in from the corridor and mingle with the steam and cigarette smoke in the room. Sweat pours down my face. The fleas soaking in my hair burrow into my scalp. I am terrified they might start falling onto the clean bed I am sitting on.

'The country is starting to shake, like a kettle coming to the boil. People are buying televisions, cassette players, electric fans. Wang Qi has a foreign cassette player, cost him three hundred yuan, it has four speakers and stereophonic sound. I went over the other day to listen. You're staying with him tonight, it's all arranged.' She leans back and puts her wet handkerchief on top of the television.

'Sorry, which way is the bathroom?' I push the table towards Wu Jian and squeeze out. The elderly neighbours are chatting in the cool of the dark corridor. I find a relatively clean corner of the latrines, pull down my trousers and scratch my thighs. A lump of someone's fresh turd steams by my feet. I look at the city through the cracked window pane, and know that every room is crammed with bodies and each body is dripping with sweat. I feel a longing for the empty grasslands and the cruel deserts. At least the air was clean there. Now that I have sunk into this steaming city, everything seems familiar and ordinary.

'This city is a furnace,' I say, walking back into the room. 'The bed is too hot. I'll sit on the stool.'

'So tell us about your adventures. Everyone wants to travel now that things are loosening up. I've always longed to go to Tibet, just never had the time.' Wu Jian has a beer in one hand and a cigarette in the other. He works in the propaganda department of a heavy machinery plant. He joined five years ago, straight from university.

'Beijing felt like a prison. When I escaped I wanted to go as far away as possible, scatter myself across the wilds, spend all my new-found freedom. I didn't care where I went, as long as I hadn't been there before. I needed to empty my mind.' My words embarrass me. I turn to Yang Ming and say, 'How is your poetry going? Are there many writers in Chengdu? I hear there's an English Corner now in the People's Park.'

'Yes, hundreds of students visit to practise their English. They all want to go abroad.'

'There will be private English schools opening next.'

'Well, there is a private ballroom already. It's open for three hours every Saturday evening. Costs five mao to get in.'

'Really? We must go. The cities have changed so much in the last six months. When I left Beijing we weren't even allowed to dance in our own homes. They said things would change, but I didn't realise it would happen this fast.'

After supper, Wu Jian walks me to Wang Qi's flat in the staff compound of Sichuan University. Wang Qi edits the university newspaper, his wife is a nurse in the hospital's orthopaedic department. They look like brother and sister — even their expressions are the same. Their flat has two bedrooms and space enough in the sitting room for a table and four chairs. It is much cooler than Yang Ming's room.

Wang Qi and I talk late into the night. We keep popping to the bathroom. I go not to use the toilet, but to splash my face with water to keep myself awake. I am used to sleeping at dusk and waking at dawn. It is hard to readjust to the rhythm of the city. He reads me his poem ('My stranger's teeth/ Chewing at my soft tongue . . .') and talks about Chengdu poets and the underground journal they publish. He asks me about life on the road. I tell him about my trek to Sugan Lake. I must have romanticised it, because the story seems to excite him. 'Yes, yes,' he says, 'you have to reach despair before you can see any hope. Life should be dangerous and full of constant challenge.' Then he leans over and whispers, 'I can't stand this life any longer. I must leave . . .'

There is no need to whisper. Our voices are drowned by the whirr of the fan and his wife is sound asleep in the bedroom next door. She could not have heard his treacherous words. Each time I pass on the way to the bathroom, I glimpse the curve of her bare legs.

'Travelling is hard work,' I tell him. 'Danger is not exciting, it's just proof of your incompetence. Besides, the biggest danger anyone can face is a life behind the Iron Curtain. You have a nice home, a pretty wife. I had nothing. That's why I left. It was an admission of failure. But now I know that nature is as cruel and heartless as the cities I ran away from. It can eat you up from inside . . .'

I want to dissuade this man from leaving home, but I am drowsy with drink and can barely hear my words, and my body is sinking deeper and deeper into the sofa.

'No, I need to change my life. Always the same three men in the editorial department. We're proof-readers, not editors. The university vice-president makes all the decisions beforehand. I spend the mornings longing for lunch break, and the afternoons longing to go home. When I do get home I have supper and wonder what exactly I have done with the day, and realise the only thing I have done is fill my stomach with green tea. I wish I could do what you did – leave it all behind. That takes real courage.'

I watch his pale hands twirl the glass of beer and, thinking how those same hands can stroke the woman in the bedroom next door, I slowly drift into sleep.

When I wake it is morning already. I can hear the wife in the bathroom telling her son to lift his feet, and a spoon scraping against the wok in the kitchen. Smells of warm dofu milk waft into the stale air of the sitting room. I am not in the mood for polite conversation, so I keep my eyes shut and pretend to be asleep.

As soon as they close the front door, I crawl off the sofa, change into the trousers Wu Jian has lent me, dunk my dirty clothes into a bowl of boiling water, then return to the sofa to open my post.

The first letter has a Beijing postmark. It is dated 1 July. I recognise Li Tao's handwriting.

Had to wait four months for a letter from you, you bastard. I took out my map to try and get a sense of your journey but all I saw were some unfamiliar place names. It disturbs me to hear that children run away and cry at the sight of your haggard figure. But I am sure that your mind is calm and detached, and I envy you.

Life in Beijing is dull and uneventful. I've finished the novella I told you about. *Harvest* will run it in December. They rejected your poem – said it was too abstruse – so I passed it on to *Northern Literature* . . . Mimi has closed the restaurant and decided to go and try her luck in Shenzhen. She doesn't seem to need me any more. I have applied for a job at Shenzhen University, and am still waiting to hear back from them . . . Sometimes I want to give everything up – women included, but I know I can't of course . . . Why don't we meet up over Spring Festival? I need to get away.

I've been keeping an eye on Nanxiao Lane for you. I've paid your water and electricity bills. Sometimes when I sit by your easel and look at your paintings, strange thoughts come to mind, frightening even, but as soon as I pick up a pen my mind goes blank . . . It's your birthday again soon. I've enclosed 20 yuan. Go to a restaurant and have a good meal. This letter came for you. Take care of yourself, dear friend.

The letter he enclosed is from Wang Ping.

. . . Very upset to hear you've been targeted in the Campaign Against Spiritual Pollution. But this is your fate, accept it quietly and try to control your temper . . . One of the many men chasing me is a Party cadre who lectures on the evils of Spiritual Pollution, of all things. What a strange world . . . Anything exciting happening in Beijing? Hangzhou's cold and gloom deadens the soul . . . As you know, *Hangzhou Daily* was planning to send me abroad this year, but the head of the local tourist department demanded his daughter go instead, so that was the end of that. I'm not giving up though. I've applied to do an MA in the States. I'm taking the TOEFL exam in November. I'm bound to do well. I have a degree in English literature, after all. I will keep this to myself though for the time being, just in case . . .

I remember you saying you needed a break. Why not visit me in Hangzhou? I'll show you the sites. If you do come, make sure you bring a copy of *The Van Gogh Story*, or any other foreign book you can find in Beijing.

The letter is dated 19 February. Since her work unit is attached to mine I did not contact her before I left in case she would be compromised. Besides, I thought she had gone abroad. From the tone of the letter, it seems she likes me.

Hu Sha writes from Beijing.

> I warn you, Ma Jian, loneliness is inevitable, it hides within us like death. But art can transform our loneliness into a tree, and from its high branches we can study the crowds below . . . Don't forget, this is a ruthless society. We must unite and build a force for change . . . Fan Cheng and I are busy editing our next edition of *The New Era*. Your poem is too long, I can only use a few verses . . . Held another secret reading last month. That Czech girl came again, we get on very well. Problem is we're both trying to free ourselves from the yoke of political oppression, so it's clear from the start we have no future together . . .
>
> I talked to my students about Thomas Paine the other day, and I sense my leaders are about to turn on me. They haven't said anything yet, but I'm going to fake a hepatitis test, just in case . . . Remember to disseminate our ideas as you travel around the country – the future of China depends on our struggles . . .

His letter takes me back to our dissident circle in Beijing. We huddled together and cursed society but never came up with an alternative. I remember the fear in Hu Sha's bloodshot eyes when he recited his subversive poem to us one night. 'Because I sing for the sun/ I must follow in its wake/ I convene the oppressed and the abandoned . . .' It was the same look of panic he had the time we were attacked by some thugs in a dumpling restaurant.

The next letter is written on prescription paper, and is signed Chen Hong.

> I've been practising at Miyun Hospital since June. It's way out in the Beijing suburbs. I am often sent into the

countryside to perform vasectomies and ligations. When I return at night I cannot eat a thing. After a day's hard work, I read and write. On Sundays I am usually too tired to go home. My room is on the first floor of the doctors' dormitory block. My window looks out onto the mortuary and the wide fields beyond. The purity of sky and air reminds me of the poem you sent me. I like it. It is cleansing, full of vigour. You insert your scalpel at just the right point. But you must go more to the source of things, and for that you cannot rely entirely on your personal experiences. Have I spoken out of turn?

. . . I wrote the first lines of a new poem last night: 'Inside my reconstructed wooden house/ I try to forget the wood/ And the window/ And accept there is no road that will lead from my two hands/ To you . . .' Fan Cheng and I have broken up. I hear he's gone to Xinjiang. You men always have an escape route . . .

I sent a copy of your poem to Lu Ping as you asked. She was discharged from hospital in May, a shadow of her former self. She will never walk again. Don't worry though, her boyfriend is taking good care of her . . .

Chen Hong's delicate characters slant like blades of grass in the wind. I like her poetry. When a colleague of mine asked me to help his girlfriend get an abortion, I asked Chen Hong to sort it out, although she was still at medical school at the time. She must think I fathered the child because she has never mentioned it since.

There is a telegram from Guangzhou which reads: 'happy birthday loneliness is my water filter it nurtures me.' I guess it is from Lingling.

Another Hangzhou postmark. Wang Ping again.

Dear Ma Jian, I got your letter today. So you really have

gone! I can't believe it. I sent a letter to Nanxiao Lane a few months ago, but never heard back. I thought you were ignoring me ... The dried flowers are beautiful, I've stuck them into my notebook. To think you have spent the last six months roaming the Great North-West! I can picture you now, dragging your long shadow across the desert, the sun beating on your back. How exciting! I wish I could be with you ... My life is so dull, I would like to disappear and have done with it all ... I go running every morning. After work I write for an hour, study some English and go to sleep at twelve. On Saturdays I compere the Chinese acrobatic show at the Hangzhou Hotel ...

In your letter you wrote: 'Life must be nice when you are in love.' I was shocked. It is the first time I have heard you say anything remotely positive about life. It made me think of that windy day you took me to the Forbidden City. Do you remember? You wrapped my scarf a little tighter around my neck and said, 'How nice to have found a friend like you.' And they said it was the coldest day of the year ...

Stay off the cigarettes and liquor. I will buy you some brandy if you come to Hangzhou. Inside the parcel you will find a jar of King Bee honey and a bag of malt extract ... I kiss your evil claws.

I look at the carefully stitched parcel, and imagine the look of blank intent on Wang Ping's face as she sewed it together in the post office. Her face is not always blank. Sometimes it breaks into a smile and you can see her two little pointed canines. She has long straight hair, writes short stories and newspaper articles and knows the words to some American songs.

Lingling has sent me a parcel too. It contains five rolls of colour film, a bag of chocolate and a packet of crushed biscuits.

Fan Cheng writes to say he has given up his job at the tax office and run away to Xinjiang. I know he will be all right. When he was sent to breed horses in Inner Mongolia he managed to kill a rabid dog once with a single piece of wire. He says he is popping back to Beijing in October and asks whether he can stay at Nanxiao Lane. He does not mention the fact he has broken up with Chen Hong.

The last letter is from my father.

> Come home to Qingdao. You can visit my friend's lace factory and write an article on the success of his new management reforms. If you guarantee it will be published, his factory will pay you two thousand yuan for your expenses . . . Be humble and courteous during your travels. Look after yourself – remember: your body belongs to the revolution.

My parents do not know I have resigned from my job. When I left Beijing I told them I was going away for a while to conduct some research into Chinese society.

I have read twenty letters and finished a whole bag of chocolate. I feel happy and surrounded by friends. Wait for me, Wang Ping. I will visit you. Don't go off with any of those men just yet.

Night Sprinkler

The private ballroom is located in the cafeteria of a transport company. Music and steam pour from the four windows that open onto the street. Only two of the ceiling lights are on, but the room is still bright. Moths, paper chains and dust particles glow under the bulbs. Hundreds of people are seated around the room on folding stools. The dining tables, dustbins and crates of tomatoes have been pushed to the back. Three pretty girls are sitting on sacks of flour there, dressed in red, white and pale green. The lunchtime slops are turning rancid in a concrete sink along the wall. A Chinese version of 'Rhythm of the Rain' blares through the speakers. I wander around the room with Yang Ming, He Liu the poet, Du Chuan the painter and his girlfriend Xiao Juan, but there are no seats left so we go and stand near the dirty puddles by the sink. I glance back at the three pretty girls. The one in red is being accosted by a boy with his shirt stuffed into his trousers. She stands up and they get into position.

'Come on, Ma Jian, let's dance!' Yang Ming pushes me into the crowd. The music starts and we spin and twist through the sea of moving limbs. Everyone's hair is steaming. The women smell of soap and shampoo. Sweat drips into my eyes. I catch glimpses of the girl in red bobbing up and down and edge towards her until our shoulders rub. When the waltz comes on I ask her to dance, and we twirl around the room. She is as light as a feather. Through her thin dress I can feel her moist, soft waist.

'What's your name?'

'Ding Xue.'

'What do you do?'

'I am an actress in the theatre company. And you?'

'I'm from Beijing.'

'I could tell from your accent you weren't from Chengdu. Are you a painter?'

'No.'

'You look like one.'

'You're very pretty. Can I take some photographs of you?'

'Only if you give them to me afterwards.'

'I'll keep one and give you the rest.'

'All right then.'

'Let's go to the People's Park tomorrow. We can take the pictures there.'

'All right.'

'Are those boys with you?'

'No.'

'I'll come and join you then.'

'All right. How many people did you come with?'

'Five. And you?'

'Three. The girl in white is my sister . . .'

The room is like a bathhouse, everyone is streaming with sweat. The waltz comes to an end, but I don't want to let go of her. I squeeze her clammy hand all the way back to her seat. Deng Lijun sings, 'When you walked by and looked at me a flame burned through my heart. They say that where there is fire there will be love, I hope they are not wrong . . .'

Everyone is parched when we leave the ballroom, so we go to a small restaurant for a drink. It's called the Mousehole. The floor is littered with butts and snail shells but there are two electric fans on the wall so at least it is cooler than the ballroom.

We order beer, four colas and some Chengdu snacks: shoulder-pole noodles, osmanthus dumplings, and hot-sour tripe. 'Try some of our Sichuan beer! Cheers!' He Liu removes his sunglasses at last and raises his glass. He is smooth-faced and thin as a rake. He types speeches in the army camp by day, and in the evenings writes poetry and studies aesthetics. Ding Xue is on my left waving a fan, her right hand perspiring in my palm.

The sweat pours as we swig cold beer and slurp the oily noodles. Moths flit through the steam and crash into the naked light bulbs. 'That poet you invited from Beijing, he can fool the students but he can't fool me. That's not poetry, that's shit!'

Yang Ming pulls a face. 'No one invited you to the reading. Waiter! Get me some chopsticks!'

'All that songbird, rowing boat, moonlight, fountain, sunset pseudo-innocent crap! Stop anyone on the streets of Chengdu and they can write better poetry than that.' He Liu's stool squeaks as he rocks back and forth.

I keep quiet. He obviously has a grudge against Beijing poets. In his flat this afternoon he said how depressed he was at not being able to move to the capital. He put on Beethoven's Fifth Symphony while I examined his shelves. The books were identical to the ones you see on the shelves of Beijing intellectuals, but instead of the usual Beethoven bust and bottle of French brandy there were Buddhist figurines from Anhui and Wa bracelets from Yunnan. Despite this show of fine taste, he kept humming 'Every sha-la-la, every wo-o wo-o'. It drove me insane. Wang Ping sings that song so much better. Perhaps she is singing it now at the Hangzhou Hotel. She too has no idea that today is my birthday.

Du Chuan, on my right, has even longer hair than mine. Everyone looks round and stares at him as they enter the restaurant. I have not seen his paintings yet. He chain-smokes throughout the meal, resting the cigarette on the table before he picks up his chopsticks. I imagine his pillow cases at home are riddled with cigarette burns.

'How is the Campaign Against Spiritual Pollution affecting Chengdu?' I ask.

'Two painters have been arrested, both friends of mine.'

'Have they been sentenced yet?'

'Qu Wei has. Talented man, but a complete sex maniac of course. Had girls streaming in and out of his room all day. He went to Guangzhou to buy some cheap cigarettes but came back with nine packs of playing cards printed with pictures of naked women. He sold one pack for fifty yuan, and the man who bought it sold the cards on individually. By the time Qu Wei was arrested thirty people had seen the cards. The police retrieved them all except for two that were sold to a long-distance driver. Four officers were sent to Xinjiang but they never found him. If they had retrieved the full pack he might have got away with two years.'

'What did he get then?'

'Seven. It wasn't just the cards though. He was also accused of holding private parties, dancing cheek to cheek, watching obscene videos, performing foreign sexual acts and perverting an innocent policewoman.' Everyone laughs.

'I wouldn't mind perverting a policewoman,' He Liu says. He pops a clove of garlic in his mouth and slowly spits out the skin.

'There was a policewoman at the dance just now. She lives a few doors down from me on Huaishu Lane.' You can never tell who Ding Xue is looking at when she speaks. When I introduced her to my friends outside the ballroom they all started babbling away in Sichuanese about the friends they had in common, which spoiled the romance a little.

'The other guy printed photographs of a naked woman from negatives his father had hidden for twenty years. He sold the prints for two mao each, but only made a couple of yuan before the police put him in handcuffs.'

'You wouldn't go to prison for that in Beijing. At the most they would throw you out of the work unit.'

'He won't go to jail. His family are Overseas Chinese who moved back here from South-East Asia. He'll get off with a few years in a labour reform camp.'

'The woman was probably his father's Thai mistress. By the way, can you get colour film developed in Chengdu?'

'Yes, but if there are pictures of naked women you need to be an art teacher and show written permission from the college.'

The plates are empty. I finish the pieces of fat Ding Xue has left in her bowl.

Yang Ming is discussing contraband cigarettes. 'We're planning to go to Guangzhou and buy a hundred packs. Wu Jian is thinking of giving up his job. You know what they say – buy one pack and you're a fool, buy ten and you're smart, buy a hundred and you're rich, buy a thousand and you're behind bars!'

'I'll join you,' Du Chuan says. 'Benson and Hedges cost five yuan there and you can sell them here for eight.'

'I won't let you go,' says Xiao Juan, replenishing his cup of tea. 'The hotels are full of loose women.'

'You shouldn't fawn on him like that, Xiao Juan,' Yang Ming snaps. 'He should be pouring tea for you. In foreign countries, men open doors for women and help them off with their coats.'

'If I helped you off with your clothes you'd scream!'

Yang Ming leans over and slaps Du Chuan's hand. 'Behave yourself! Listen now, Ma Jian has been travelling for months and he needs some money. Can you find him some work?'

'I'll do anything,' I add.

'Du Chuan does sketches for a construction company. They pay him a fortune. He's nearly a millionaire.'

'Rubbish!' he says. I glance at his wrist and notice a gold Swiss watch. 'Some friends are producing an animation of *Journey to the West*. I can make enquiries for you, but I will need samples of your work. Come to my flat tomorrow and I'll lend you some paper and pens.'

'Have you been to Guangzhou?' I ask Ding Xue.

'No, but I'm planning to go to Shenzhen. You can see Hong Kong television there, and foreign films. Our dramatist lived there for six months and came back with a foreign motorbike and a colour television.'

'Had he given up his job?'

'No, he'd just spent three years in prison. No one would employ him when he got out so he went to Shenzhen to try his luck.'

'What was he in for?'

'Listening to enemy radio. He shouted "Down with the Communist Party!" in our backyard and was overheard by some neighbours doing their morning exercises.'

'He'd probably been hitting the bottle.' He Liu fiddles with the arm of his sunglasses.

'The police interrogated me.'

'So you were shouting too?' Du Chuan blows a puff of smoke into the air.

'No, but my window happened to be open. The neighbours

reported me. I was washing my hair at the time and didn't hear a thing.'

'What would they have done if you had?'

'Not much, just taken me to the Bureau and rectified my thinking. But because of him the entire company had to attend political study classes every day for a month, and no one was allowed a day off.'

As we say goodbye outside the restaurant I offer to walk Ding Xue home. Yang Ming looks cross and says, 'Make sure you return to the university in time, the gates shut at eleven. And don't forget, you have those sketches to do tomorrow.' Because she has come dancing tonight, there is a lump of amber dangling from her neck on a length of black cord.

I walk with Ding Xue to a large tree, we lean against it and embrace. I kiss her lips. People walk towards us, so we move on. Soon she says, 'This is Huaishu Lane, my home is over there.' And I say, 'Let's walk a little further, then.' In a lampless part of the road I pin her against the wall and kiss her neck, her face. Her legs shake, her body slackens. I hear someone coming, so I slip my arm around her waist and we walk on. 'What if the neighbours see me?' she says, bowing her head. We approach a street lamp and see people sitting on straw mats playing cards. From the back they look like hemp sacks. Old women sit in silent doorways, waving their paper fans. We turn into a dark lane. I hold her and brush my hand down her breast. She pushes me away, then pulls me back and kisses me. A voice shouts, 'Filthy buggers! Haven't you homes to go to?' We walk on and come to a busy road. Car horns shriek through the night sky. 'Let's find somewhere quiet,' I say. She takes my hand and leads me back through the long dark lanes until we reach the crowded forecourt of the train station. An announcement crackles over the speaker, 'If anyone has lost their child . . .'

We cross the road and sneak into a shady park. It is quieter here, people are sleeping on benches waiting for the morning trains. We crawl into the bushes and sit on a rock. I lift Ding Xue onto my lap and kiss her breasts. Someone wheels a suitcase past and she shrinks back in fear. I whisper, 'Don't worry, no one can see us,' and stretch my hand up her damp red skirt. She strokes my hair and blows into my ears. The roar of my blood drowns the noise of the traffic. I let go of myself and pound into her. The lamps flicker, everything clenches, and for a moment I forget the litter, the smell of urine, the mosquitoes. We drip into each other and sink to the ground and I say things to her again and again.

'I'll go and get some fizzy orange,' she says, standing up. I help buckle her sandals, then get to my feet, zip up my jeans and stare at the station lights through the branches. I would love to lie in bed now and have a cigarette. I smooth my hair back and sit down again. 'If anyone has lost a child, they should report at once to the attendant in the main waiting room. The night train to Beijing is about to depart from platform three . . .'

Ding Xue returns and jumps onto my lap. One of us has bad breath, but soon our mouths taste only of fizzy orange. We rub tiger lotion onto each other's mosquito bites, then lie down and close our eyes.

'Get up! Show us your documents!' I look up and see four torches shining on my face.

'I missed my train,' I say. 'This is my girlfriend, I am just off to change my ticket.' When Ding Xue is escorted away, they unzip my trousers and pull out my penis. 'What's that girl's name, where did you meet her?' I answer their questions and say, 'If you don't believe me, go and check with the photographers' union tomorrow. They are my host organisation for this trip.'

'You're no photographer. Look at the state of you! You've just travelled here to fool with our women.'

When I see their red armbands and realise they are just a division of the people's patrol, I breathe a sigh of relief. 'I'm sorry, I've made a fool of myself. Don't be angry. Here – have a cigarette. Do you have the time on you? That's a nice watch, I had one like that once. My dad pinched it of course . . .' The others bring Ding Xue back and say it is time to go. As we watch them march out of the park gates Ding Xue says, 'Don't worry, I know the officer in charge.'

We leave the park and stand on the pavement, waiting to cross the road. 'If they do make enquiries though I will be in terrible trouble,' she says, scraping her sandals across the lip of the curb as the petrol fumes gush into her face.

'Why is that?' I look at the traffic, still waiting for a chance to cross. A road sprinkler drives by and drenches us in water from the waist down.

'Because my husband works for the Public Security Bureau.' A gap opens in the traffic and she dashes across the road.

I look at my watch. It's three thirty. I wish I could shut my eyes and sleep inside my dreams.

River of Ghosts

A month later, having earned two hundred yuan for painting twenty-four cartoon characters, I post my Tibetan knife to Li Tao, leave Chengdu and head south to Leshan to see the largest carved buddha in the world. He is a mountain of stone, seventy-one metres high with trees sprouting from his ears and tourists clambering up between his toes to pose for souvenir photographs. The buddha looks down impassively at the white river below his feet, as he has done for the last thousand years.

On 10 September I visit Wulong Temple then proceed to Emei town. The two men sharing my hostel room are itinerant peddlers of plastic running shoes. They examine a photograph of Deng Xiaoping and argue about whether the cigarette in his mouth is a Panda or a Double Happiness. I lean over and read the caption. 'On 2 August, China and Great Britain agreed that Hong

Kong shall return to Chinese sovereignty in July 1997. The draft accord stipulates that laws presently in force in Hong Kong will remain basically unchanged for the next fifty years.' Mrs Thatcher's face scowls in the left-hand corner of the photograph.

'Deng Xiaoping employs a fellow Sichuanese to roll his cigarettes,' I tell them. 'He won't smoke anything else.'

'Will we be able to visit Hong Kong after 1997, like we can visit Shenzhen now? Will Hong Kong and Shenzhen merge into one huge city?'

'That depends how long your old compatriot lives.'

On the 11th I begin my ascent of Emei, the highest of China's four Buddhist mountains. It is believed that the Indian saint, Puxian, travelled here in the sixth century on the back of a white elephant to perform miracles and expound on Buddhist law. I visit the Temple of Eternity in the foothills and see the sixty-two-ton bronze statue of Puxian seated cross-legged on a white elephant. In my dreams that night, the white elephant stomps through a busy market street. Crowds stumble back in terror and watermelons roll to the ground.

For two days I scale the stone steps of the narrow mountain path. At noon on the third day, I look down from the Golden Summit and see three silver rivers snaking through the hills of Sichuan and a line of snowcaps piercing the sky in the west. The landscape looks primordial and untouched. It is hard to believe that Sichuan is the most densely populated province of China, and home to a hundred million people.

Down from the mountain, I walk east and see the hanging coffins of the Bo tribe on a cliff of the River Min. The coffins are suspended on wooden plinths halfway up the rock face, and are the only legacy of the vanished Bo. Historians are not sure how the Bo placed their coffins there, or why the tribe vanished so mysteriously. But local legend has it that when imperial troops invaded the area in the seventeenth century to quash restive tribes, the Bo retreated to the rim of the cliff and hurled themselves off the edge.

Further east, at Neijiang, 'City of Sweets', I buy half a jin of sugared plums and go to munch them by the banks of the River Tuo. A small crowd gathers beside me to watch an old man swallow a sword. When the blades bulge through the skin of his neck everyone claps, and a little boy of eight or nine holds a plate out and asks for money. The old man announces his next act is called 'Drawing Blood'. He raises his sword in the air and with one strike hacks right into the little boy's neck. The boy faints in a pool of blood. The old man panics for a second, then begs the crowd to donate some money for the emergency hospital treatment. I give him ten yuan. When I squeeze free from the crowd I discover someone has stolen my sunglasses.

The next day I reach Dazu and see the Buddhist rock sculptures of Mount Baoding. A thirty-one-metre reclining buddha protrudes from the rock face, flanked by shrines to Confucian precepts of filial piety and statues of Laozi, the Daoist sage. A cliff nearby is carved with a Wheel of Life showing scenes from the six states of existence into which man is destined to be reborn. Those who kept to Buddhist law are shown languishing in the comforts of paradise, while sinners condemned to hell writhe in agony as cruel demons rip their tendons and tear out their eyes. The barbaric tortures remind me of Zhang Zhixin, the idealistic high-school teacher who was executed in the Cultural Revolution for daring to question Mao Zedong's rule. The soldiers who walked her to the execution ground were afraid she would shout subversive slogans at the firing squad so they slashed a knife through her larynx, and in her agony she bit off her own tongue.

On the 19th I continue east, trudging for hours along a noisy dusty track. When I can bear it no longer, I jump onto a packed bus, buy a ticket, and breathe smells of dirty teeth and soiled nappies all the way to the city of Chongqing.

It is raining when I step off the bus. The air is cool and fresh. Below me, through the grey mist, I glimpse the brown waters of the mighty Yangzi converge with a muddy tributary. The river is so wide I cannot see the opposite bank. Boats float near and far, some moving, some not. I climb a steep, narrow street lined with small shops and food stalls. The man with wet hair wheeling his bike, the girl in black stilettos, the old woman riffling through the rubbish bin, the lady with a sagging bottom and a dainty leather bag, the children thrashing each other with their satchels, the rats scrambling up the gutters, all seem oblivious to the rain.

I reach the address He Liu gave me before I left Chengdu. It is an old wooden house. I creak up the narrow staircase and see a large rat on the landing. He watches me approach, and politely steps to the side. Our feet almost brush as I pass. I knock on the door but no one is there. I presume they are not back from work, so I walk outside and buy a fizzy orange. A bald shopkeeper is hurling abuse at a female stallholder across the road. 'I'll fuck your grandmother, bitch!' he shouts. 'I'll fuck your wife, bastard!' she retorts. 'Better stuff a cucumber in your knickers first!' he bellows triumphantly. The stallholder looks crestfallen and everyone laughs. The rainwater cuts small channels into the mud on the road and seeps through the holes of my shoes. It reminds me of the night I got drenched outside Chengdu train station.

The following day I visit White Palace Prison on a hill outside town. My school textbooks were full of stories of communist martyrs who were tortured here in the Second World War by the merciless Guomindang. The communists have now turned the prison into a propaganda museum. I expected to see a dark, sinister fortress, but instead find the building resembles a small country hotel. The cells inside are dark and musty, and strewn with mangles and iron chains.

On my way out I stop to read the notice pasted on the gates. My eyes skip past the first paragraph ('To commemorate the founding of the People's Republic and strengthen the dictatorship of the proletariat . . .') and focus on the list of criminals below. Each name is struck with a red cross.

Zhang, male, 23 years. Planned to incite insurrection by setting up an illegal 'China Youth Party'. Execution imminent.

Wang, male, 24 years. Listened to enemy radio stations and corrupted his friends with counter-revolutionary discourse. At 10:00 a.m., 10 October 1982, he stormed onto a tourist bus parked outside the Natural History Museum, claimed to be armed with explosives, and distributed leaflets on the benefits of plural democracy among the terrified foreign passengers. Fortunately, the driver was able to perform a brave citizen's arrest. Execution imminent.

Chen, male, 27 years. Since June 1979 made frequent plots to leave the country. On 2 October 1981 he stole a fishing boat and, when crossing into Japanese waters, he yelled 'I'm free!' at the top of his voice. A few hours later the tide pulled his boat back across the border into the capable hands of the Chinese naval police. Execution imminent.

Lu, male, 25 years. Held private parties and danced cheek to cheek in the dark, forcefully hugging his female dance partners and touching their breasts. Seduced a total of six young women and choreographed a sexually titillating dance which has spread like wildfire and caused serious levels of Spiritual Pollution. Execution imminent.

Yang, male, 31 years. Duped 25 women into marrying farmers in Anhui and Qinghai with empty promises of a better life. The police confiscated 16,000 yuan and four wristwatches from his room. Execution imminent . . .

The thirteen criminals listed above will be taken to the public execution ground and shot in accordance with the will of the people.

Public executions take place throughout China in the run-up to National Day. I have grown up reading these death notices and have attended several executions. I once watched an army truck stop, a young man called Lu Zhongjian come out, handcuffed, and two soldiers escort him away. When he started to scream, they slung a metal wire over his mouth and tugged it back, slicing through his face. Then they kicked him to the ground and shot three bullets into his head. His legs flailed and his shoe flew into the air. A year later I married his girlfriend. I only found out they had been lovers when I discovered his death notice hidden at the back of Guoping's drawer.

I wonder how many people have been executed so far in the Campaign Against Spiritual Pollution. As I leave the prison gates a taste of stale blood rises to my mouth.

A week later I say goodbye to my friends in the wooden house, post a few letters and embark on my journey down the Yangzi. As the boat steams away, Chongqing looms behind us, stranded between the confluence like a wet, storm-battered ship.

I get off that night at Fulin. Yang Ming's friend Liao Ye is waiting for me on the wharf. He reads me his long poem, 'City of Ghosts': 'Listen to the silent voice of the Han/ The sobbing of the dead in your heart/ Saying: Once you belonged to the state of Ba or the state of Chu/ But who do you belong to now?/ Bereft of home and country/ Are you still the person you were? . . .' We spend half the night discussing poetry and the other half talking about women. He tells me of a beautiful poetess called Ai Xin who lives downstream in Wushan. 'She is a river siren,' he says. 'Her beauty has lured many of my friends into the Wu Gorge and they have never been heard of again.'

The next morning, I take a boat to Fengdu, 'City of Ghosts', the legendary abode of the Son of Heaven who decides the fate of departed souls. The town's narrow streets are filled with hordes of peddlers screaming their wares. A man selling rosaries throws one around my neck and I start screaming too. The fishmonger slits a knife down a live eel and grabs his money with blood-drenched hands. In the Temple to the Son of Heaven at the top of the hill I see the Eighteen Levels of Hell depicted in clay friezes along the wall. Garishly painted demons torture miserable sinners with spears and boiling fat. The quiet temple is a welcome respite from the hell of the streets outside.

On the 29th I reach Wanxian. My throat feels sore, and by the afternoon I have a temperature of thirty-nine degrees. Xiong Gang, my host at the cultural centre, takes me to the local hospital. Sick people who cannot afford treatment lie sprawled outside the gates. Flies dart between their faces and the oranges on the fruit stall. Inside, the wards are filled with glazed-eyed patients and the corridors stream with young men selling ice cream, tangerines and stolen drugs. When someone in a white coat appears they are besieged by patients asking the way to the ear, nose and throat clinic or how much longer they will have to wait for an X-ray.

Xiong Gang's doctor sees me immediately and gives me a week's worth of pills. He tells me he is a poet, and is writing a poem about fish-eating fish. I tell him it sounds interesting, and take the opportunity to ask what happens during a ligation. I have always been curious to know.

'We constrict the Fallopian tubes with a piece of wire.'

'Do you still have to use contraception after that?'

'No. Unless it was a fake ligation.'

'What do you mean fake?'

'If you give the doctor some money he'll make a loose knot and you can go home and have another baby.'

The next day we cross the Yangzi and visit a New Stone Age burial site near Daxi. Local peasants make their living by selling fake Neolithic weapons. Xiong Gang takes me to one man's house where I am able to buy a real one.

On 1 October, I catch a steamer to Fengjie, a town a hundred kilometres downstream. When the poet Li Bai travelled down this stretch of the river during the Tang Dynasty, he wrote of coloured clouds above the Yangzi and monkeys wailing from the banks. Today the monkeys have been replaced by fertiliser plants and cement factories that pollute the river with yellow waste. Where the green slopes have been cut away, the earth shines like raw pigskin.

I lie awake all night, soaked to the bones in sweat. My fever is still raging. The river breeze is not strong enough to blow the flies from the greasy bunk-bed frames or dispel the stench of urine and rotten pickles from the waters that slop over the floorboards. At dawn, I see a young man standing on deck with a book in his hands, and I walk over for a chat. He tells me he has left the army after three years in service. He managed to secure Party member-ship but not a driver's licence, so he was unable to find employment in his home town. Now he is off to Wuhan to try his luck. An old army friend of his has found a job there as a driver for a factory chairman.

Fengjie is set high in the hills. Its tangle of narrow lanes wriggles up a steep slope. The only piece of flat land is a small basket-ball court, where villagers sit gazing at the Yangzi or at the boys who circle the perimeter of the court on battered bicycles. There are red flags everywhere and National Day banners which say CONTINUE THE STRUGGLE FOR MODERNISATION.

After touring the temples of Baidicheng, I take another boat to Wushan that passes through the first of the famous Three Gorges. I crane my head out of the window at the appropriate moment. No one else in the cabin can be bothered to look, they just sit on their bunks staring at me. I think back on the buddhas I saw at Leshan, Emei and Dazu. Although their size and beauty were impressive, they struck no chord within me, and I left each one as disappointed as I left the Buddhist caves at Dunhuang.

The Yangzi River cuts through the heart of China, dividing the country into north and south. The south is green and fertile but I prefer the wastes of the north. I will travel to Shaanxi Province next. There are too many people in Sichuan, everyone has to fight for attention. The men glower with bloodshot eyes. The govern-ment has liberated the economy, the country is moving, and the south is moving faster than the north. The waters of the Yangzi look tired and abused. When man's spirit is in chains, he loses all respect for nature.

A white cruise ship sails by laden with camera-toting foreigners. It is hard to believe they have to travel so far to see a river and some mountains. When we arrive in Wushan I go straight to the cultural centre to look for Ai Xin.

I knock on the door, Ai Xin is not there, but a boy leads me to her parents' home. When her father hears I am from his native Qingdao, he invites me to stay and have dumplings. I spot a photograph of Ai Xin pressed under the table's glass cover. Her mouth is pinched into a smile and there is sadness in her eyes. I can tell the moment I set eyes on her my heart will jump.

My temperature is still high when I wake in the hostel the next morning. I take some medicine, slip into my flip-flops and go for a stroll outside. Mountain peaks loom on all sides; I feel as though I have fallen into a deep crevasse. I find a copy of Hemingway's *The Old Man and the Sea* in a small bookshop, then return to Ai Xin's parents to say goodbye. I walk into the room and notice a chicken tied to a leg of the double bed. The mother says, 'My husband wants you to stay for supper, I've bought food in especially.' She brings out her daughter's photograph album and tells me to take a look.

About fifteen, wispy hair, tongue sticking out.

About eighteen, looking straight into the lens, blue skirt blowing in the wind, face framed by the clouds of the Wu Gorge.

Ballet tunic, one leg high in the air. 'She studied at Chengdu Academy of Dance,' her mother says proudly.

Hair in bunches, smiling at me, lips pressed together. On the back of the photograph: 'Chongqing, Aug '83.' I remember how Lu Ping was still beautiful then and full of life.

Her mother goes to the kitchen to kill the bird while I sit on Ai Xin's single bed. Her small desk is covered with a neat red and white cloth. There are notes scribbled on her calendar: 'Send poem to Huai Dong . . . Ask Old Wu for the libretto . . . 4 yuan 8 mao.' I take the comb from her pencil box and touch the wavy strands of hair. Variously shaped lipsticks and bottles of nail varnish stand next to her notebook. I flick it open and find it filled with her poetry. Many of the lines have been crossed out and rewritten in the margins. 'The sea breeze brushed through my heart and tossed it into the ocean' is struck through and replaced by: 'The sea breeze blew away my secrets/ My love became an ocean.'

Her parents' bed is pressed against the opposite wall, next to a sofa and two red thermos flasks. Her stilettos and gumboots peep from under a tall wardrobe. At the end of her bed are a pair of soft pink slippers that bear the dark imprints of her feet. I decide I have to see her.

So I stay another night in the hostel and move in with Ai Xin's parents the next day. I take a sampan up a tributary river through a smaller version of the Three Gorges. Steep flights of stone steps rise from the banks to villages high above. I close my eyes and think of the smell of her hair on the pillows, and imagine holding her in my arms.

Two days later her father says she will arrive by boat tomorrow. He pours me some beer and talks about his daughter. He says he doesn't want her to spend the rest of her life trapped in the Wu Gorge.

I wait for her at the wharf at the top of the stone stairway. A steamer comes into dock, all the passengers get off, but she is not among them. I sit down again and open my book. Two hours later another boat arrives. A woman emerges from the crowd and moves along the rickety wooden plank like a lotus rising from the mud. I stand up and feel myself getting smaller and smaller. She climbs the steps and peers up at me. In this sea of peasants heaving wicker baskets and cardboard boxes we are the only ones with empty hands. I call out her name. She smiles and asks who sent me.

'I've waited for you for five days,' I say pathetically.

'What on earth for?' she asks, as if she didn't know.

We stick to each other's side all day. When one of us goes to the toilet, the other stands outside and we continue our discussion about life and poetry. We go for a meal and talk about love and sacrifice. I tell her about the ocean and my childhood by the sea. We go shopping and she buys me food for my journey. In the evening we go to her office and sit together in the dark. She speaks of the men who are in love with her and the studies she longs to pursue in Beijing.

And she keeps asking me again and again, 'What is it you are looking for?'

And I say, 'I want to see my country, every river, every mountain. I want to see different people, different lives.'

'Why are you travelling?'

'China is a black hole, I want to dive into it. I don't know where I am going, I just know I had to leave. Everything I was I carry with me, everything I will be lies waiting on the road ahead. I want to think on my feet, live on the run. Never again can I endure to spend my life in one room.'

'Do you want to change this country?'

'I just want to know it, see it with my own eyes.'

'Do you hate this world?'

'Love and hate can drive you on, but hate can drive you further.'

'Do you believe in love?'

'No. But love plasters the wounds, it makes you feel better.'

She cries out and slumps back into her seat as if struck by a fatal bullet. 'You men are all the same!' she says. 'You need women but you don't need love.' I say nothing. All I can think about is the print of her feet in the soft pink slippers.

She switches the light on and makes a camp bed up beside her desk. 'Let's go to sleep, it's nearly morning. You can lie by my side if you promise not to touch.'

'Promise.' I try to repair the damage. 'When I say I don't believe in love it's because I can't trust myself. It doesn't mean I don't need love. Everything one says is a product of one's past experiences, it is not a true reflection of one's inner . . .'

'Shut up, will you.' She touches my hand. We hug each other and kiss. It is not until I suck her breast that I discover her heart is silent.

I step onto the boat and look at her standing at the top of the stone steps, exactly where I stood yesterday. Her long neck is still as lovely. I drift downstream over muddy, turbulent water. That night I dream my head is plunged into the river and I cannot breathe. I wake up screaming. My bag is still here, but the sleeping mat I hired for two and a half yuan has been nicked from right under me.

5.

The Wind-Blown Soil

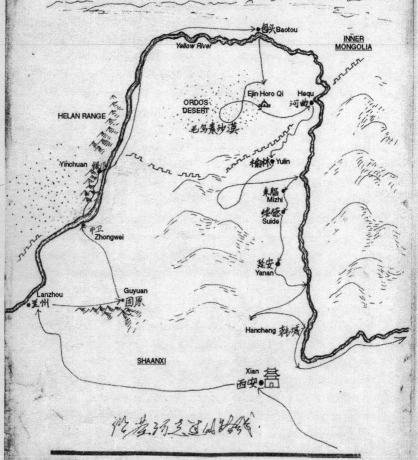

新 华 通 讯 社

INNER MONGOLIA

包头 Baotou

Yellow River

HELAN RANGE

ORDOS DESERT

Ejin Horo Qi

Hequ 河曲

毛乌素沙漠

Yinchuan

榆林 Yulin

米脂 Mizhi

绥德 Suide

中卫 Zhongwei

延安 Yanan

Lanzhou 兰州

Guyuan 固原

Hancheng 韩城

SHAANXI

Xian 西安

电报挂号：一六三一   电话总机：六六局八五二一

City of Tombs

I leave the Yangzi at Yichang, then walk north through Hubei Province from the Shennongjia mountains to the Wudang range. After a five-day rest in Shiyan town I press on into Shaanxi Province. It is only seventeen days since I left Sichuan but my money is almost gone.

In the evening of 23 October I arrive in Xian, exhausted and penniless.

24 October. Clear sky. Came straight to Shaanxi Press last night to find Yao Lu. Haven't seen him since he visited Beijing for the 1979 Democracy Wall Movement. He is editor of *Yellow River* magazine now, but looks as dishevelled as ever. He sleeps in his office during the week, and said I could stay with him. This morning he even found me some work. His leaders have contracted me to draw the illustrations for this month's magazine. They'll pay me 20 yuan a picture, so I should make 400 yuan all being well.

26 October. Fierce winds. Three of Yao Lu's friends came round last night, and we drank and talked for hours. One was a set designer at Xian Film Studio. He said there is nothing left in Xian but ancient buildings, if you want to see the real Shaanxi you must travel north. Another, Yang Qing, writes poetry. His favourite poet is Tagore. By day, he works at the Public Security Bureau as censor of post. He said all the city's mail passes through his hands before it reaches the post office. Yao Lu said Yang Qing's wife is the belle of the local song and dance troupe. She comes from Mizhi, a town in the north where the women are famed for their beauty.

I told Yang Qing about how the Qinghai police accused me of selling drugs, and when they found none on me, accused me of wanting to buy drugs instead. 'It's not funny,' he said. 'Drugs are rife in Qinghai. Some come from Xinjiang to be processed, some are grown locally. Many villages have been taken over by the army. When people start to make money, they experiment with drugs. It is considered one of the pleasures of modern life. One man I arrested said a puff of opium costs more than a policeman's wage. Our detoxification centre is filled to capacity.' We discussed the sensations that drugs induce, even though none of us had ever taken any, or seen any for that matter. I asked Yang Qing if I could visit the centre. He said he would take me next week on condition that I wash and shave and try to behave like a normal person.

The other visitor was Sun Xi, *Yellow River*'s literary editor. He said, 'I know every writer in Shaanxi. Just mention my name, and you will enjoy free meals and accommodation throughout the province.' He drank far too much, and is snoring on my bed as I write.

On the 28th I take Sun Xi's letter of recommendation to the Forest of Steles Museum and get in free of charge. The seven grey exhibition halls house 2,300 stone tablets inscribed with classical texts of Chinese history and philosophy. A total of 600,252 characters carved in stone. The earliest inscriptions are over a thousand years old. I wander breathlessly through the stone library, exhilarated and absorbed. Each tablet is a living testament to the past, each one deserves an exhibition room to itself.

On Saturday, Yao Lu takes me back to his home in Lintong. On the way he talks to me about a book he is reading on Daoist philosophy. I meet his wife who is six months pregnant. She and Yao Lu have just completed a translation of Ginsberg's poetry. They have not found a publisher yet, so I am their first reader. They live in the compound of the town revolution committee and must register with a soldier each time they enter the main gate. Their small room holds a pail of water, a bucket of coal, a shovel and a poker. A traditional Shaanxi embroidered waistcoat hangs from a nail on the wall. In the evening, the wife leaves to spend the night with her mother. She tells us to clean our feet in the red plastic washbowl under the bed. Yao Lu and I take turns to wash, then sit on the bed and talk.

He tells me his wife has a violent temper, and that she attacked him once with a fire poker and knocked his teeth out. We discuss the Xian literary scene, then I pick up the Ginsberg and read through it again.

'Listen to this,' I say. 'They "sang out of their windows in despair, fell out of/ the subway window, jumped in the filthy Pas-/ saic, leaped on negroes, cried all over the street,/ danced on broken wineglasses barefoot ..." It reminds me of a night in Beijing when our group of poets and painters took some empty beer bottles outside and smashed them into a metal rubbish bin. We hurled with all our strength. It was the loudest noise I had ever made. But Ginsberg can sing out of his window in despair, he can cry all over the street. That sounds like heaven to me. He implies his country is not fit for humans to live in. Well, he should live in China for a month, then see what he thinks. Everyone here dreams of the day we can sing out of our windows in despair.'

'No society is perfect. Freedom is only possible when the heart is in line with the Way. If the heart is tempered and the mind is clear then you will see there is no right or wrong.'

'I am more concerned with the outside world. I want to live in a country where people can cry all over the street.' I pause then say, 'Xian feels as though it is being crushed under the weight of tombstones. The air is as heavy as death.'

'The Chinese alive today are reincarnations of torturers. The wronged souls of the past will haunt us for ever. We must pay for the sins of our ancestors. Daoist scriptures say if you dig more than a metre into the ground you pierce the heart of Mother

Earth. But beneath the foundations of Xian, the earth is riddled with cavernous tombs.'

Yao Lu hands me a book of Xian legends. 'It might give you some ideas for a story. I admire you, you know, giving up your job, roaming the country alone. You will be a sage before long.'

'I am not looking for ideas. I just felt confused about life, and thought travel might clear my mind. I still know so little about this country. If you want to write about society, you need to see the whole picture.'

'It is hard to empty your mind. Desire is the root of all suffering. I write very little these days, I'm thinking of giving it up and going into academia.' He gives a bitter smile and rubs his glasses.

I read the four characters on the scroll hung above his desk: Sky, Man, Become, One. 'What martial arts are you practising these days?'

'An esoteric branch of qigong. I took it up three months ago. It is a form of deep meditation which helps redress the flow of one's inner energy. It has improved my concentration. You should try it. After years of practice one can heal the sick and change stone into gold.'

'I don't have the discipline. I long to enter a state of calm, but I am plagued by constant distractions. I planned to make a pilgrimage to Tibet a few months ago, but my mind was too clouded, I turned back halfway.' I am about to mention the fight I had with the thugs who stole my camera, but decide to keep it to myself.

'Shall we give it a go?' he asks.

We sit facing each other at opposite ends of the bed. The only sound in the room is the pan of water simmering on the stove. Yao Lu starts giving me instructions. 'Close your eyes, empty your mind, perceive the Celestial Eye.'

I lower my eyelids and picture the wife's bra dangling from the peg on the door and Yao Lu's face bashed to a pulp. I look up, and see Yao Lu, eyes shut, stroking an imaginary ball of air. I close my eyes again and see an open sky.

'Focus your mind on the pit of your abdomen and discover your vital energy. Breathe in through your mouth and let the energy rise to your hands. Are your palms starting to sweat? Breathe out and feel the heat rise to your forehead. The Celestial Eye sees the fire . . .' Half an hour later my limbs are swollen and my face is dripping with sweat.

'Good. You have the root of wisdom. Nourish it carefully and you will prolong your life.' I look up and see a halo of steam hovering above Yao Lu's head.

'Have you joined the Daoist Society?' I ask.

'No. I refuse to enter any organisation. But they have asked me to give a series of lectures on religious divination and the five elements.'

'I regret taking my Buddhist vows so soon,' I say, leaning back against the white wall.

'Daoists believe that Buddhism, Daoism and Confucianism are three paths to the same goal. No matter which path you choose through the clouds, they all lead to the same blue sky. Daoism is for me the most interesting, though. There are no gods to worship or rules to obey. It teaches us that man is part of nature, and is condemned to a life of constant change because the Yin and the Yang are inseparable, and follow each other as night follows day. It teaches us not to waste time fighting and grasping but to resign ourselves to fate and live at peace with the world. Every evil has its punishment.'

'Yes. People waste time fighting one other, when the real enemy is time itself.'

'There are no enemies in this life, Ma Jian. You have too much aggression inside you. You must learn to be as meek as a new-born child. Daoism tells us the belligerent are always the first to fall.'

'I don't approve of aggression, but everyone should know how

173

to defend themselves. I agree that weakness can be strength, but by advocating submission, I feel that Daoism sometimes encourages slothfulness and a sense of complacency.'

'The police have sunk their claws into me, Ma Jian,' Yao Lu says, suddenly changing the subject. 'They have not allowed me to leave Xian since I was arrested for writing that poem on the Beijing Democracy Wall. I feel trapped.'

'Run away to Shenzhen, then. It's a haven of free enterprise. You can buy yourself a fake identity card there and get a job with a foreign company. You could even buy a forged passport and make a new life for yourself in America.' My eyelids are drooping, I am struggling to keep awake.

'But I have a wife and a child on the way. I can't leave. Besides, there is no culture in the south.' His voice is quieter now that he is lying down.

'Your wife attacked you with a fire poker, for God's sake. What kind of woman would do that? Leave now before it's too late.'

'You cannot change the course of fate,' he whispers to himself.

With that stone in his heart I know that Yao Lu will never be free, no matter which path he chooses.

The next day I visit the Huaqing Hot Springs at the foot of Mount Lishan. Tourists peer at the empty pools trying to imagine emperors and their beautiful concubines taking their baths here a thousand years ago.

I go to the public bathhouse at the back of the complex and share a small pool with five strangers. The sides are green and slimy, and the water is very hot. My pores slowly open in the disinfectant steam. It feels good. This is my third bath this year. I don't like showers, but wallowing in warm water is very relaxing. No wonder all the expensive hotels are equipped with baths. The attendant knocks on the door again and shouts, 'Get washing, you lot. You're out in five minutes!'

In the afternoon I sit by the Pool of Nine Dragons reading the

legend of the stone tablets, then catch a bus to the Terracotta
Army. I buy a ticket for the museum, and enter the hall only to
find a crowd of peasants selling fake Neolithic tiles and
arrowheads. When I return to the ticket booth and ask for a
refund, two fat men walk over and shout, 'You bought your
ticket, so go in or shove off!' I walk away, fuming with rage, and
discover the real Terracotta Army Museum is on the other side of
the road. A group of southern tourists mill around me, grumbling
about the scam. Another tour bus pulls up outside the ticket
booth. I walk over to warn them but a tall man in an army coat
blocks my way and says, 'Breathe a word and you're dead.' So I
stand back and watch thirty people buy tickets, file into the hall
and come out seconds later looking disgruntled and confused. I
tell myself all sins have their punishment, then turn round and
cross the road.

The Terracotta Army vault is just a corner of the vast
necropolis of the first emperor of unified China, Qin Shihuang.
Like all Chinese emperors, he divided his time between con-
structing his lavish mausoleum and collecting beautiful women
for his harem. Historical records claim that in 246 BC, Qin
Shihuang conscripted seven hundred thousand workmen to
build his funerary compound which was only completed thirty-
seven years later, a year after his death. His son was afraid the
workmen might divulge the location of the buried treasures, so
he ordered the men to be buried alive, together with the emperor
and his concubines. This fifty square-kilometres of land is
packed with corpses.

In the cavity of the museum's main hall, five thousand life-size
clay soldiers stand poised for battle, their faces identical to the
tourists peering down at them. The vault next door is still under
excavation and the soldiers are not yet restored. Some are still
half-buried, others have crumbled onto mud walls or lie shat-
tered on the floor. I am reminded of the photographs of the mass
graves unearthed just west of Qin Shihuang's main tomb.

I study the ancient warriors. A layer of skin has been peeled from the earth, and China's cruel, ugly soul is exposed to the light of day. The emperors who followed in Qin Shihuang's wake restrained themselves slightly by stipulating that only a third of the national income should be spent on their mausoleums. But they continued to take their most precious possessions with them into the nether world, including jewels, gold and live concubines.

According to local legend the workmen who were buried with Qin Shihuang lived on beneath the soil. They engraved the story of their plight onto a large stone tablet which grew through the earth like a root. But when the tablet reached the surface no one could decipher the script. The tablet grew taller and taller, until one day it blotted out the sun.

'No photographs!' A policeman with a thick Shaanxi accent pounces on a foreign tourist, snatches the camera from her hand, flicks the back open and pulls out the film. The shiny grey strip coils down like a loose gut. The lady starts screaming at him, but no one understands what she is saying. A crowd of Chinese tourists gather to stare. 'We let you in to see our glorious past, but that's not enough for you! You want to take photos on the sly and sell them to magazines when you get home!' The policeman's self-righteous voice booms through the hangar.

The winds that blow through Xian carry a fine yellow dust. I take a sip of eight-treasure gruel, and a bite of stuffed persimmon roll, but there is sand in both of them. I pay the snack vendor and leave. Most of the pedestrians are dressed in blue overalls, peasants are only distinguishable by the mud on their sleeves. As I walk through the streets, the garish shop signs and Marlboro advertisements fade into the background and all I see are pagodas, bell towers and ancient walls. This city was the capital of eleven different dynasties, and at its peak a thousand years ago, it was the largest city in the world.

I sit down by a window in a self-service restaurant and stare at my cup of black coffee. It is made with real Nescafé, but there are not enough granules, so it tastes like weak tea. The two peasants at the next table are sipping their coffee with a teaspoon. They look miserable.

'One yuan fifty for this tiny cup. We could have bought three pots of tea for that.'

'Stop whining. It was your idea to come here. Take some more sugar, it's included in the price.' I look at the small sausage rolls in their hands and know they could finish twenty and still leave hungry.

A few days ago I read up on the drug situation in China and discovered that drug abuse is more commonplace than I thought. The addicts come from ordinary backgrounds, and buy their supplies on the black market. Opium is still the most popular drug. Yang Qing is taking me to the detoxification centre this afternoon. I am visiting in the guise of a Shaanxi Press reporter.

When he steps out of the police car and taps on the restaurant window, I do not recognise him at first. He looks completely different in uniform. We make our way to the centre. I have never walked through the streets with a policeman before. At first I feel like a lowly criminal. Then I notice how people look at me and my confidence returns. As we advance, paths open in the crowd, children fall silent and snack vendors stop shouting their wares. I soon grow a taste for this vicarious power, and when we reach the gates I cannot help saying, 'The world looks very different from your vantage point.'

Yang Qing ignores my comment and says, 'The centre was converted from a guesthouse. It only takes female criminals.' He sounds very different from the man who spoke so passionately about Tagore last week. 'I must leave you after the introductions. I have a lot of work to do.' He combs his hair back and opens the centre's door.

About twenty young women are squatting in the corridor, none of them look up as we pass. The director leads us to an office on the first floor. She says she is happy for journalists to visit the centre. I ask if I can interview a patient and she takes me to a room at the end of the corridor. 'This is where we keep the new arrivals,' she says. Her face looks pale and tired.

'Why are they lying down?'

'We give them pills to make them sleep.'

There are about thirty women on the floor. Some of them stare at the ceiling. None of them see us walk in. They remind me of the buried warriors. The room smells of urine and the quilts are tattered and smeared with wet and dry vomit. 'This place is squalid,' I blurt out.

'Yes. The quilts were left over from the guesthouse. We couldn't afford new ones. You can mention that in your article.'

A girl at my feet sits up. She looks like any skinny girl you see walking down the street. I don't know where to start.

'Tell me about yourself,' I say, looking into her eyes. 'What made you turn to drugs?' The director goes to pour me a cup of tea.

'My name is Fang Li. I'm twenty-four years old. I have been here two months. I went to a labour reform camp last year. The police accused me of selling drugs. I told them I had bought drugs, but I never admitted to selling any.'

Her words sound forced. 'I can check the records later. Just tell me what turned you to drugs. I'm not a policeman, you can talk freely. Isn't that right, director?'

'Yes. Fang Li, tell the gentleman about the harm drugs did to you. Young people can learn from your mistakes. This is Comrade Ma, he is a guest reporter for Shaanxi Press.'

Fang Li tugs at the hem of her red jumper. I twirl my pen and say, 'Speak freely, Fang Li.'

'It's all my husband's fault. My parents are intellectuals. I graduated from Shaanxi Normal University, but I have always loved singing and dancing, even as a child. When the artists' salon opened in Xian, I went there to sing 'Count Your Empty Glasses' and 'When Tears Fall From My Eyes'. Men would always come up to the stage and shower me with flowers. He was one of them. He hired taxis for me around the clock, took me to the best restaurants, bought me expensive jewellery. I had just taken over my mother's job at the local nursery school, and was on a salary of fifty-three yuan a month. He gave me bunches of flowers that cost double that. How could I resist him?

'I spent my days hanging around his clothes shop, and met his low-life friends from outside town. It wasn't till he was arrested that I discovered he was the head of a criminal gang, and had already spent five years in prison. I had a terrible stomach ache the day the police caught him. His friends were lying in the shop, smoking opium. They told me to take a puff, said it would ease the pain. And it did. I took to smoking it every day, and told myself it was a luxury I could afford now. But before I knew it I had smoked through all my savings. When my husband was sentenced I sold the shop and smoked through that money too . . .

'I had tried giving up before they caught me last year. I was in a taxi at the time, on my way to do some business in Lingtong. I had just had a smoke and was half-asleep when the police stopped the car. They searched me and found some powder. I had forgotten I was carrying it. I said it was for my private use but they didn't believe me. They said, "Why carry such a big bag if it is just for you?" They didn't have handcuffs, so they pulled off my belt and tied my hands with that instead. When we arrived at the Public Security Bureau, I knew I was in trouble. There was a crackdown that night and the place was full. A policeman walked by and I asked him to untie my hands, but he kicked me to the floor, grabbed a rope from the counter and started thrashing me with it. I screamed, "He's killing me, he's killing me!" But no one came to my help.'

'Fang Li! Stop exaggerating. Now, tell Comrade Ma about the wonderful treatment you have received here.' The director looks angry.

'Of course, I deserved to be punished. The police were just doing their job. But first let me tell you . . .'

'Would you smoke again if you had the money?' Suddenly I

notice I have adopted the same tone as the policeman who interrogated me in Beijing.

'My family have nothing left now. We used to be quite well off, we had an imported cassette player, colour television, electric fridge. When I have given up the opium, I'll go to Shenzhen and try to make some money. Money means freedom.'

She glances at the director, my tape recorder, notebook, then wipes her dripping nose.

'Where did you buy the drugs?' I look into her vacant eyes.

'It's easy if you know the right people. I used to smoke three times a day when I had the money. Even when I was hard up I managed one fix a day. But I always ate fresh fruit afterwards – not like those layabouts. They wouldn't even stretch to a bottle of orange pop. I would like to give up but . . .'

There is a busy crossroads outside. Noises of car horns and voices merge into one sound. A bright beam of sunlight pierces through the open window.

I come out of the centre and stride through the streets relishing my freedom of movement. As the sun sinks below the clock tower, the sea of blue pedestrians drifts into the grey dusk. Perhaps an opium smoker is hidden in their midst, waiting to be caught by the police and thrown under the filthy quilts. I always associated drugs with the Opium War, imperial decadence and foreign exploitation. What place do they have in today's society? Perhaps when people have no ideals, money can only buy oblivion, not freedom.

Society's values have changed a lot in the short time since I left Beijing. Fang Li believes that eating fruit after smoking opium puts her a cut above the layabouts. I want to write a story about the people who live above ground and the souls who writhe below. I sit down at a Muslim restaurant and pull out the notes I copied from Fang Li's records. 'Son: 6. Mother: 52, senile. Father: 55, history professor at Northwest University . . .' I must talk to her again when she is released.

A beggar approaches, shaking an empty cap. I push the leftovers of my mutton soup towards him and leave the restaurant.

When the crowds and buses have disappeared, the weight of the night falls on the empty streets. The city walls look worn and defeated. The ground is so heavy I feel as though I am walking into my grave.

The next morning I am woken by the noise of footsteps thudding along the corridor outside. Yao Lu gets up and goes to fetch a thermos of hot water while I fold our camp beds and sweep the floor. When the canteen bell rings for breakfast, I go down and return to the office with half a jin of dumplings and a copy of the *Xian Daily*. Yao Lu hands me a cup of green tea and starts reading the newspaper. 'Says here a man put an advert in the Beijing papers announcing he was opening a modelling agency. He offered the girls a salary of forty yuan a month, and received 170 applications. He had permission from the Department of Culture. This is incredible. The first fashion models in the history of communist China!'

'Last year I was arrested for sketching a model in a life class. It is amazing what a free economy can do to society.' I arrange my pens and prepare to draw my twentieth illustration.

Yao Lu disappears for a few minutes and returns with a smile on his face. 'The leaders have approved your first ten illustrations. Looks like you have some more travelling money.'

'We must go for a drink tonight,' I smile. 'I read the book of legends you lent me. I like the one about tombstones. It has given me an idea for a story.'

'Don't start writing historical novels, please!'

'No. Or imitating Marquez!'

'Reality is just a loop in a greater chain.' He opens a drawer. 'Look at these manuscripts I get sent. The stories are shallow, they have no context . . . By the way, I gave your film to a friend who runs a photo lab. It should be ready in a couple of days.'

Just as we finish for the day, the telephone rings. It's Yang Qing. 'How were the addicts? Did they provide you with any literary inspiration?'

'I didn't realise there would be so many.'

'I have some news for you. The protracted battle against reactionary forces has finally reached completion.'

'What do you mean?'

'The Campaign Against Spiritual Pollution is over. You can go back to Beijing!'

'No, I don't think I will risk it. As soon as the Campaign Against Bourgeois Liberalisation finished this one followed hot on its heels.'

'It's up to you. Anyway, we've seen the figures.'

'How many arrests?'

'Over a million, and twenty-four thousand executions. Don't tell anyone though until you see it in the papers.'

I put the phone down and repeat what I have heard to Yao Lu. 'If I had stayed in Beijing I might be in my grave by now. We really must go drinking tonight, Yao Lu. It won't be long before they let you off the hook too.'

'I will take you to Old Sun the Daoist. He will read your fortune and give you an amulet to protect you on your travels.'

'Don't worry about me, Yao Lu. I never come to harm. I just hate to think of you spending the rest of your life marooned in this dead city.'

Lost in the Wastes

A cold wind sweeps through the village of Xinjie. I escape into a small restaurant and order a bowl of Mongolian milk tea and three steamed rolls. Three young men are huddled by the stove, smoking hemp rolled in newspaper. The smells of coal smoke and burnt ink sting my eyes.

I pull out a red pen, open my map and think back on the route I have taken over the last month. From Xian I walked west to Qianling. From a distance, the three mounds of Empress Wu Zetian's tomb resembled the curves of a reclining woman. At the peak of one mound I had a piss and the wind blew it straight back into my face.

At Baoji I stopped and saw an exhibition of ancient bronze vessels dug up in fields nearby. Outside the museum, a man stood handcuffed to a tree. A woman in an angora sweater struck a match and held it to the cigarette in his mouth.

On the train to Tianshui, the conductor discovered that twenty peasants in our carriage were travelling without tickets. When he went to lunch he asked me to guard the doors. I turned to the most genial-looking man and asked why he could not afford a ticket. He said, 'I sold five hundred jin of maize to the state this year and made three hundred yuan. But by the time I'd paid the agricultural tax, farmer's board tax, security tax and the telephone bills, I was seventy yuan in the red.'

'Why have a telephone if you're so hard up?'

'I've never touched a telephone in my life. But the village head wanted one in his home so we all had to cough up twenty yuan.'

I calculated his annual earnings would scarcely buy three puffs of opium so I opened the door and let him go.

From Tianshui I hitched a ride to the Maijishan Grottoes. The entrance ticket had a one-yuan supplementary charge for the road construction tax.

On 20 November I reached Lanzhou and stayed with Yao Lu's friend at the university. The next morning he gave me a thick jumper and I took a bus through the Liupan mountains to Guyuan in Ningxia Province. When Mao Zedong led the communists through those mountains in 1935, on the Long March to escape Guomindang persecution, he wrote: 'Heaven is high, the clouds are thin/ We watch the wild geese vanish to the south/ If we cannot reach the Great Wall we are not true men/ On my

fingers I count the twenty thousand li we have travelled so far. . .'
A nice poem, but what purpose did his crusade serve? This
region has suffered from famines every year since the 1960s.
Families own one pair of trousers between them, and the men
who share them nag their wives to get pregnant so they can sell
the babies for money.

It snowed all the way to the Xumishan Caves. A small copse of
pine trees rose from the bare summit. I bowed to the twenty-
metre-high seated buddha, ate some dumplings in the temple
restaurant, then hitched a ride north. The road was lined with
Hui traders, all wearing their distinctive white caps. Whether
they were busy weighing peanuts or arguing with their customers, they would always look up when a truck passed, so I saw a
continual stream of faces.

At Zhongwei town, cold winds swept sheets of newspaper
along the wide empty streets. The Yellow River nearby blocked
the southern advance of the Tengger Desert. Its waters seemed to
have aged on their journey from Qinghai.

In early December, I walked through the Helan range and saw
some Neolithic paintings in the caves above. The valley floors
were strewn with fallen rocks which local peasants used to build
houses and sheep pens. Trees sprouted from the stones. Peasants,
children and mountain goats watched me from rocky outcrops.
Usually all they saw was the empty road that cuts across the
waste. Tombs of the Western Xia Kingdom rose from the earth
like huge coal heaps. It is believed the kingdom built its capital
nearby in the lee of the mountains, and was destroyed in the
thirteenth century by the ferocious cavalry of Genghis Khan.

At Yinchuan I bought a face mask, some shoelaces and a pair of
gloves, and met up with two friends of Yao Lu. Their breaths
reeked of alcohol.

On 10 December I reached Baotou, the largest city of Inner
Mongolia. I had lunch with Chairman Xu of the local literary
society. He fed me noodles and dried meat and asked me if I had

a destination in mind. I said, 'My beginning and end are just points on the road. It is the journey itself that matters.' He said he had longed to travel as a young man, but whenever he ventured beyond a ten-kilometre radius the militia would always drag him back home. In the afternoon he walked me across Yellow River Bridge. I glanced back at the bald head he had forgotten to cover, and wished I had spoken with him longer. He will probably spend the rest of his life inside the walls of that small staff compound.

South of Baotou lay a vast, dry wilderness. Villages scattered the wastes like sheep dung.

I spent the night in Dongsheng with a friend of Chairman Xu, who gave me a pair of padded shoes and a woollen scarf. I hitched a ride the next morning, but a few hours into the journey discovered the truck was going the wrong way, so I jumped off and decided to cut across the Ordos Desert to my goal, Ejin Horo Qi. It looked no further than thirty kilometres on the map, the land seemed reassuringly flat – I could even see some shacks in the distance. So I checked my compass and walked into the wastes.

The grass and sheep dung disappeared and soon there were no more traces of man or beast.

At noon, I was walking through sand dunes. They were as soft as a woman's breast. Rosy halos hovered at each peak. I sat down to rest and sank my hands into the sand. The cold grains slipped through my fingers like water.

When dusk fell a biting wind blew up and my eyes filled with sand. I was glad that I had the padded shoes to keep my feet warm. I walked all through the night, but by the close of the next day I still had not reached the road. I began to panic. I had walked over fifty kilometres by now. It dawned on me that my compass must have broken. I started racing to every clump of grass, like a madman, screaming and shouting, telling myself I should never have travelled north. When the sun sank again, I ran towards it, yearning for it to take me away.

At night the desert was completely silent. I heard a plane pass overhead and imagined all the people sitting comfortably inside it.

By the third day I was afraid I was losing my mind. I forgot which side of the sun to walk towards. I had to think carefully before each step as I walked the trackless plain. The more freedom you have to chose your path, the harder the journey is. I talked to myself, decided on a course and committed it to paper. But three hours later, I still had no idea where I was. When I grew thirsty, I cupped a plastic bag over the sand and licked the condensation that collected inside. I threw away my water filter and books, then took a photograph of myself so that the person who discovered my bones would know who they had belonged to. My cold body was drying out. I knew it was futile to keep walking because when you are lost, there is nowhere to go. I was on the verge of collapse, but I talked myself forward and begged my legs to keep moving. Images turned through my head. I saw the moon above the desert, a bottle of beer on a friend's table, the lid to a fountain pen I lost twenty years ago. Sometimes I saw Xi Ping's chapped lips or a bowl of pork dumplings. But all the time my mind interrupted and said: keep walking, stop and you will die.

In the afternoon I woke by the side of a road. The man who had dragged me there had given me a swig of water before he left.

The restaurant's metal signpost rattles in the wind. I take a swig of milk tea, press my hand on the map and draw a large red cross through Ordos Desert.

I am tired of the dry plains. The land is so flat up here it can hold onto nothing, not even the wind. After a while you lose track of who you are and long to be squeezed inside the walls of a narrow valley.

Last week I reached Ejin Horo Qi at last and spent two days with the gatekeeper of Genghis Khan's tomb. The mausoleum was built in the 1950s to house what are believed to be the ashes of the dead Khan. A group of Mongolian pilgrims arrived and performed a ceremony in honour of their departed chief. The Chinese Mongolians wore blue army coats, their brothers from Outer Mongolia wore red robes and leather boots. The pilgrims roasted a sheep and shared the meat out. Everyone got some except me, so in the end the gatekeeper took pity on me and gave me some of his. Four white steeds were tethered outside the tomb in memory of the Khan's favourite horses. Old Sun's talisman must have protected me in the desert. When he placed it around my neck he said, 'Your fortune is good. Do not travel north. If you meet with trouble a gentleman will save you.' I wish I knew the name of the peasant who rescued me.

The gale outside has blown everything from the road except the houses and the two pool tables. I feel weak and tired, but the wind is north-easterly, so at least it will be behind me as I walk.

I fold up the map, fill my water bottle and pull up my face mask. Then I walk out and head east to the borders of Shaanxi Province.

Flies in Scrambled Eggs

When I step onto the high plateau of northern Shaanxi I feel I am walking towards my ancestors' heart. This land covered by fine dust blown from the Gobi Desert is the cradle of Chinese civilisation. The fertile banks of the Yellow River here have been cultivated for over eight thousand years. I have come in search of my roots. The frostbite on my feet burns with each step, so I shuffle rather than tread. My first destination is Hequ village, where I have heard the Yellow River is particularly wide.

I go straight to the banks when I arrive. This is how I imagined the Yellow River to be: a vast landscape of mud charging through a yellow ravine. The water near the bank is frozen solid. Torrents stand motionless and boulders of ice crash silently into each other, caught mid-flow. The huts on the far bank look like fine grains of sand.

I walk south through dry yellow hills. Fierce winds from the desert have scraped the slopes bare. Peasants live huddled in caves that honeycomb the soft cliffs. At a dirty street stall in Shenmu I eat a bowl of noodles and forget to chew a precautionary clove of garlic, and spend the next two days in bed with griping stomach pains. The frostbite on my ear has started to suppurate.

On the way to Yulin town, I see fragments of the Great Wall snake over the terraced hills on the right. The sky looks very blue against the yellow slopes. In the valley, I see stacks of dry hay and dead, seedless sunflowers bending on the marge of a frosty field. Only one side of the road is tarred, the other side is a rocky track. A truck approaches from behind. In the back stands a group of peasants with large red drums tied to their waists. The truck shakes so much as it passes that the faces are a blur.

When I reach Yulin, I walk into the hills to seek out Sun Xi's friend, Chen Jiang. He lives in a cave-dwelling on a cliff high above town. When I tell him I am a friend of Sun Xi, he shakes my hand and invites me to stay in his adjoining cave. The arched chamber holds a desk, a stone bed, some cabbages, and a fridge full of grain. I ask why he has a fridge when there is no electricity, and he tells me he bought it for when his little boy gets married.

At dusk, I sit on the terrace and watch smoke rise from the thousand chimneys of Yulin and hear children and dogs crying in the lanes. Chen Jiang's wife prepares cabbage soup and fried bread for supper. The men eat at the table and the women crouch on the ground.

I wake the next morning and see half the chamber fill with cool sunlight. It is nice to lie in a cave. I feel protected from the outside world. Next door, the entire family is sitting on the brick bed. The room smells of corn gruel. The children are doing their homework, the grandmother is twisting hemp and the wife is kneading a lump of dough on a wooden tray. Since the wife's hands are covered with dough, I help myself to a cup of hot water, then sit down and chat until noon.

In the evening, Chen Jiang takes me to a folk singer. I listen to his songs and jot down some interesting lyrics. In Shaanxi, folk songs are called 'sad tunes'.

The next day, I stroll through the narrow lanes of Yulin, and am amazed to see Liu Yu, the patriotic walker, marching towards me, hair down to his shoulders and dressed in nothing heavier than a sky-blue shirt. He shouts my name and laughs with joy and astonishment. I am the first friend he has met since he set off from Jiayuguan. We find a small restaurant, order two beers and talk until dusk. I tell him about my journey then he tells me about his. In the evening we order some noodles. He says loneliness is the greatest hardship, everything else he can get used to. I tell him the biggest problem is finding shelter for the night. He says he usually sleeps outside. He practises qigong and has learned to sleep sitting up so that the slightest noise will wake him. He has twice been attacked by wolves. When the restaurant closes I take him back to my cave and we talk until dawn. He says when he has finished walking the Great Wall, he plans to trek across the Taklamakan Desert. I tell him I never want see another desert as long as I live.

In the morning, I walk him back to the Great Wall, and we promise to meet up next year in Beijing. Then I climb the ramparts of Zhenbeitai Fort and gaze into the northern wastes. For thousands of years, nomadic tribes from the northern steppes charged through these plains to wage attacks on Chinese farm-land. The Great Wall was able to keep them at bay, until Genghis Khan united the tribes and led his cavalry south. For a hundred years the Khan's descendants ruled the Chinese empire, but their dynasty was doomed from the start. The Mongols are wanderers of the wide steppes, and are not suited to sedentary life. The Great Wall here resembles China's compound wall, and the yellow earth that sweeps to the south is China's garden.

In the afternoon I leave Yulin and reach a fork in the road. I wait for half an hour, but no one passes to tell me the way, so I flip a coin and head west. Twenty kilometres on I come to a village and see a tractor parked by the side of the road. I walk over, hoping to wangle a lift. Four peasants are squatting on the mound behind having a smoke. I ask them for a ride but they say they are not going anywhere soon. Then I ask if there are any sites to see in the area and they tell me there is 'White City', a ruined town that is protected by the provincial government. As they speak, a jeep drives by and gets stuck in a ditch in the road. The driver struggles for a while, then gives up and shouts, 'Twenty yuan!' The peasants reply, 'Eighty, nothing less!' At last they settle for fifty, and haul the jeep out with their tractor. When the jeep disappears, the peasants rush over to deepen the ditch, then return to wait for their next victim. I ask them how much they make from this and they say more than they used to make on the fields.

The next village stands at the edge of a large gravel plain. I see a man sitting by a stream and ask him the way to White City.

The ruined city was built by the Western Xia Kingdom. Its walls lie half-buried in the gravel. They are constructed of ground stone and rice glue, which explains the white colour. Locals use them as sheep pens.

Another twenty kilometres south I cross a frozen river and reach the village of Qingbian. A child carrying a basket of firewood sits down and watches me pass.

Further south the road winds back into the yellow hills. I see a beacon tower on the Great Wall to the right and walk towards it. There are peasants crouched below the ramparts. A man in a nylon jacket drives up to them on a motorbike, balancing a large wooden cross over the handlebars. It looks like the central cross of a window frame. One of its four nails is missing. When he dismounts and takes the cross in his arms the peasants fall to their knees.

I walk up to him and ask what is going on.

'Jesus Christ was born today,' he says. 'I am here to lead the prayers.' I think how strange it is that Jesus should share a birthday with Mao Zedong.

'I couldn't make it yesterday,' he continues. 'Too many villages to visit. There are three hundred Christians in the area now.' He is the priest of the local Christian society which has recently been restored after two decades of religious persecution. I ask him if I can borrow his bible, but he tells me it is on loan from the library, and is the only copy in the county.

I reach Jiaxian the next day and go straight to Baiyunguan, a large Daoist temple on the banks of the Yellow River. The muddy beach below is strewn with black boulders and blocks of ice. I seek out the sage Yao Lu told me Chairman Mao used to consult, but am told he has travelled to Xian for a meeting with the religious affairs committee. So I shake the divination box myself and pull out a stick.

> When roaming the land keep your face hidden.
> Conceal yourself in the cities;
> Nurture your spirit in the wilds.

I register the advice, drop a coin into the collection box and step outside. A song celebrating the ninety-first anniversary of Mao Zedong's birth blares through the village speakers. 'The Red Army climbs a thousand mountains and crosses ten thousand rivers, yearning for a moment of rest . . .'

In the hostel courtyard a troupe of peasants practises their red drums for the New Year parade. The noise is deafening.

The next morning, I continue down the main road south. As the cold wind blasts the sweat from my face an old folk song comes to my mind: 'I live on the Yellow Plateau, where the wind scrapes down from the hills. Whether it blows from the north-east or blows from the north-west, the wind is always my song.' A bundle of straw sits on the roadside, waiting to be squashed by a passing truck.

I hear a sudden burst of firecrackers and notice two cars parked outside a house. I poke my head over the gate. It's a wedding. Before I know it, a middle-aged man in a Mao suit drags me into the courtyard. The villagers sitting down eating sunflower seeds clear a path for us. Every door and window is pasted with the words DOUBLE HAPPINESS cut in red paper. The bedroom is crammed with silk quilts and metal thermos flasks – gifts which the family will later wrap up again and pass on to the next couple in the village to get married. I am introduced to the bride and groom and given a seat and a pair of chopsticks. I wolf down some fried cakes and drain a bowl of soup. When I lean over the table to take some fish I discover it is rock hard. The person next to me explains that it is made of wood. I am reminded of how my mother used to boil stones in a pan of water so the neighbours would think we had food in the house. When my stomach is full I take a group photograph as thanks for their hospitality, and instantly my pockets are filled with sweets and sunflower seeds.

In the next valley I see a school in the caves on the opposite bank. Classes have finished for the day and children are sweeping yellow dust from one side of the yard to the other. I am curious to know what these children want to do when they grow up. I decide to cross the river and pay them a visit.

A dirt track leads me down to a village of mud huts but there is no sign of a bridge. Four or five women are leaning against a wall, soaking up the winter rays. I ask them the way to the school. They laugh. I assume they find my accent difficult so I repeat the question slowly.

A women in a green scarf says, 'It's a long walk.'

'But I saw it just now from the path.'

'If it's across the river it's a long way. The nearest bridge is seven kilometres down that track.'

Patches of snow lie on the mud fields next to heaps of dry manure. There probably is a bridge down there but I suspect it is further than she says. When you ask peasants for directions, the distances are never reliable. You can walk for hours and still be told your destination is seven kilometres away.

I watch a woman feed her baby with a piece of bread from her mouth, and ask her how many children she has.

'None,' she says, looking at the track behind me.

'Isn't that yours then?' I say, pointing to the baby in her arms.

'Doesn't count, it's a girl.' The baby's mouth is smeared with wet dough.

'Women are equal to men now, haven't you heard?' I say. I watch an insect land on the baby's chapped cheek then fly away again. The mother tuts and rolls her eyes to the sky. I ask if there is a hostel in the village. They tell me the nearest one is in Mizhi, fourteen kilometres away.

I ask them if the Mizhi women are as beautiful as people say and they collapse into giggles. One woman pulls off her white scarf and walks away. I give the baby a sweet from my pocket and walk back up the way I came. From my map I see that Mizhi is twenty kilometres away. With no stops I should be there in three hours.

As I walk into Mizhi, I remember Fan Cheng saying he wished he could marry a northern woman. He said southern girls are weak and flighty, but northern girls are strong and chaste. That comment has always stuck in my mind.

It is market day. The path is muddy from melted snow. Pigs, sheep, dogs and bicycles jostle for space. The man selling rat poison shows a pile of dead rodents to prove the efficacy of his potion. The tooth puller displays a heap of teeth to prove his skills in dentistry. His gaze is unnerving. I suspect there are dog teeth and pig teeth mixed in his pile. A girl walks by with a steaming roll. I am too embarrassed to ask where she bought it so I walk behind her, breathing the sweet smell.

When the crowd becomes overbearing, I sit down at a food stall, order a bowl of noodles and watch the villagers walk by. There are men in blue overalls and young girls with red scarves tied at their necks and big rosy cheeks. On my left, a freckle-faced women sells plaster casts of the goddess Venus and slices of yellow cake. The fruit stall on the right must have caught fire earlier. Its burnt frame lies toppled on the ground. Charred apples and oranges steam in a puddle of water. An old woman in an army coat swears at a child. Six beautiful pheasants hang limply from the side of a bicycle rack.

I mop up the remains of my soup with a piece of dry bread from my pocket, then go to look for a place to sleep.

In the morning I search the streets for beautiful women, but see none, so I wander into a video room and watch a Hong Kong action film instead. Halfway through I realise it is *Beyond Forbearance*, the film I saw in Golmud. The worse something is, the easier it is to forget. Suddenly I hear the thud of drums. I step outside to see what is going on.

A crowd has lined the street. Through a cloud of dust, a yellow dragon advances, swaying above the heads of ten burly men. Behind it march peasants in yellow tunics beating the red drums fixed to their waists. Next come acrobats hobbling on high stilts dressed as Guanyin, Black Face, White Beard, and Pigsy and Monkey from *Journey to the West*; then singers with rouged cheeks and red cummerbunds and dancers with babies in their arms. I remember being paraded like that in the National Day processions. My headdress was so heavy it nearly broke my neck. The huts along the street are old and ramshackle, but the red flags and exploding firecrackers liven them up. The po-faced crowds, however, look completely out of place. They are still clutching live chickens and bags of flour, and their battered shoes are covered with dust.

For me, New Year's Day is no different from any other. The fleas that plague my body will not leave me for the holiday. I walk back to the hostel, slip a towel into my bag and take to the road.

Beyond Mizhi the bare terraced hills follow in endless succession. No grass, no trees, no rocks. When the wind blows the air turns yellow and I cannot see a thing. But I will walk the road however hard it is, because only on the road can you see that yesterday lies behind you and tomorrow waits on the path ahead. The road measures life in distance. The further you travel the longer you live.

The yellow plateau resembles a wind-dried skeleton, and its insides are as pitted as an ants' nest. After days of tramping the empty road I long to see a sweep of houses.

Sometimes I see shepherds and sheep searching for grass, but at dusk they all scurry back to their holes. When night falls I switch on my torch and keep walking.

Finally I reach Suide and go to find Sun Xi's friend, the poet and doctor, Yan Hu. He lets me stay in his room in the hospital dormitory block, and in the evening invites his literary friends over to meet me. We finish four bottles of rice wine and litter the floor with cigarette stubs and owl bones. We stole the bird this afternoon from a glass jar in the hospital dissection lab. It reeked of formalin, but after braising it in ginger and soya sauce the taste was quite bearable. We embrace for jovial group photographs, then everyone starts accusing me of being a fake and a scrounger. 'Swanning down here from the big city looking for your bloody roots. What a joke!' Then Yan Hu mumbles from the floor, 'I'm the only real poet in this room.' His ambition is to secure a transfer to a Xian hospital.

Before my departure, Yan Hu agrees to show me the maternity ward. I have always wanted to visit one, but would never get a chance in a city hospital. The ward is so crowded the women have to sleep two to a bed. Four women lie in the delivery room with their legs wide open. A piece of string tied to a jar of water dangles from one woman's vagina. Drops of blood fall into a washbowl below. Yan Hu tells me the other end is hooked to a five-month-old foetus. 'She's an unmarried mother. Doctors don't have time to give women like her a proper abortion, so they just attach the string and let gravity do the rest.' I watch her pale, damp face stare at the ceiling and wish someone would put an end to her agony.

The woman on the next bed screams as a doctor drops a slimy infant into the nurse's hands. Another child born to gather firewood by the roadside and watch the traveller pass.

When I come out of the hospital my bag is packed with frostbite ointment and a roll of bandages. Yan Hu has some fresh placenta that he will use to stuff dumplings tonight.

I leave Suide in the dawn mist. The wind is north-easterly in the morning and south-westerly in the afternoon. The road south to Yanan follows tributaries of the Yellow River through a maze of dry ravines. Everything that grows on the yellow soil is yellow too. In the north, the Chinese eat yellow gruel, drink yellow wine and when they die they go to the Yellow Springs. I never used the colour in my paintings, it set my nerves on edge, but now I have grown numb to its effects. Life is so precarious here that people learn to change with the wind. Sons of men killed by the Party work for the Public Security Bureau. Families destroyed by Mao Zedong hang posters of him on their walls. Because they all know Chinese history changes as frequently as the Yellow River floods its banks.

I reach Yanan at last, and decide to stay a few days. Mao Zedong's ten-thousand-kilometre Long March came to its end here. He chose to build his communist stronghold in this town, because he knew that once he controlled China's heartland the empire would be his.

My doss-house is in a cave in the hills above the town. The tap in the yard leaks and the frozen puddle below is dotted with tea leaves and melon seeds. When the ice melts at midday I have to throw down a path of cabbage leaves before I can walk over to wash my face. At night the yard is pitch black. When I finish cleaning my teeth on the second night, a cold wind blows me back to the room. The light in the cave is dim but I can see each face clearly.

The middle-aged man stirring the pot of noodles on the stove is still wearing his nylon jacket, his shirt collar is black with grime. He sells cats for a living. There are three cages of them stacked by the door. I ask how much they cost and he says he buys them for two yuan each, and sells them for ten.

'Why do people need cats?' I ask. Behind the chicken wire, the cats' eyes sparkle like glass balls.

'Rat poison can kill farm animals so it's safer to use a cat.' He asks me what I do for a living and I tell him to take a guess.

He glances up from the pan of noodles and says, 'You sell nylon rope.'

I remember the rope seller I saw in the market today, and can think of nothing that was particular about him.

The cat seller says you can buy rope wholesale from government depots at two mao a metre, and make a fortune selling it in the markets.

The peasant on the brick bed removes his padded jacket and starts squeezing his fleas.

'Aren't you cold like that?' I ask him, scratching my legs.

'It's boiling in here. This is the hottest room I've been in.'

Next to the fire under the brick bed are bags of rice and pork scratchings, and a horse's bridle that stinks of urine. There is a mound of quilts on the bed, but I prefer to sleep in my coat. The bed is only big enough for four, but there are five sharing it so we have to sleep diagonally. I will do what I did last night and wait for the others to nod off then stretch out on top of them.

The room warms up once the door is closed, but the smell of

charcoal smoke and dirty feet is so strong I have to soak my nostrils in tiger lotion. The man in the purple jumper sells peacock feathers for a living. He says business is bad.

I advise him to hawk them outside universities, or the hotels where foreigners stay. He says he tried selling them on Mount Hua, but was arrested by the police and fined twenty yuan. He says he has a hundred feathers left and when they are sold he will start selling women instead.

The boy warming his hands over the stove is still chain-smoking. I ask him to show me his calendars and he passes me one with a photograph of a blonde woman standing on a beach in a swimming costume.

The peasant has never seen a foreign woman before. He examines the picture, and mumbles, 'She won't get a husband now – flashing her arse like that.'

'You can have one for two yuan. It has Western and Chinese dates.' The boy fails to mention it is last year's calendar. I want to say something, but keep my mouth shut.

'I have nowhere to hang it,' the peasant says. 'Besides, if the police saw it they would put me in handcuffs.' His fingernails are filled with the blood of squashed fleas.

The calendar seller is not ugly exactly, but there is something not quite right about him. He looks as though he was moulded by a moron. It is hard to pinpoint the problem. Perhaps his chin is too large for his shoulders. The uncertainty makes one long all the more to squash him into a ball and start again.

The peacock-feather trader cleans his teeth with some scouring powder he has stolen from the kitchen.

'That's for scrubbing saucepans!' I tell him.

'Never mind,' he says. And suddenly I think of a way to make money.

The peasant snuggles under the quilts and laughs. 'City folk only wash their teeth because they eat too much good food!'

'Brushing keeps teeth clean and white,' I say. 'Haven't you noticed what white teeth the city people have?'

The conversation soon dries up. My roommates have little to talk about, as their only concern is to make money and stay out of trouble. An hour later, I stretch over the snoring bodies and let my mind drift to Hangzhou. I picture myself sipping brandy in Wang Ping's room. I am sitting on her chair, wearing her slippers. I wake up to find someone's dirty sock stuffed up my nose.

In the morning I buy two mao's worth of scouring powder and a sheet of red paper. I fold the paper into a hundred small envelopes and fill each one with a pinch of powder. Then I amble through the street and quietly tout my wares. Three university students in sun hats who are travelling in search of their roots buy two envelopes from me. I tell them it is particularly effective against tobacco staining. I only sell ten that day, but I find the street inspector, give him a pack of cigarettes and he says I can set up business on the pavement tomorrow.

The following day I come equipped with toothbrushes and a cardboard box which has pictures of smiling faces cut from a magazine stuck on the sides and the words MIRACLE TEETH WHITENER painted on the front. As I sit behind it and shout my wares, I understand why the Mizhi tooth puller had such an unnerving gaze, because I too just stare at people's teeth now when I speak to them. A middle-aged man with a scraggly neck sidles up and demands a demonstration. His teeth are black with nicotine. I brush the two front ones for free. By the end of the day my entire stock is sold. I count my earnings and decide to move to the People's Hotel.

My room has four beds, a desk, a coat stand and a broken mirror with a sticker that says NO GAMBLING OR WHORING.

After a hot shower I lie in bed with a cigarette. A guest walks in and sits down on the next bed. It is the man whose two front teeth I brushed this morning.

'That powder you sold me was lethal. My teeth may be clean, but my mouth is all swollen.'

'It is a French product. Perhaps the formula is little strong for Chinese gums.'

I ask him what he does for a living and he says anything that keeps him away from his village. He says he has been to Beijing and seen Mao's Mausoleum, and I tell him he is the first person I have met this month who has travelled to the capital.

We chat for a while, then in the evening we go out for a meal. His name is Liu Jingui.

I notice him staring at the waitress and ask if he is looking for a girlfriend.

He gives a loud cackle that sounds like a branch breaking from a tree. Then he whispers, 'I run a little business, brother. It's top secret. If the police find out I'm finished.'

Hoping to find out more, I chat about women and ask if he has had any luck recently.

He sniggers. 'Can't play around, brother, I have a wife at home.'

'You sell women, don't you? Never mind, you don't have to tell me. I just thought we were friends, that's all. I was obviously mistaken.'

He presses my hand. 'You are an educated man, brother. It is an honour for me to call you my friend.' He moves closer. 'I don't have many skills, I'm just trying to get by. If I can go home with a thousand yuan in my pocket at least I won't have disgraced my ancestors. All right, might as well tell you, I am a – how shall I phrase it – coil remover. I give discounts to the poor.'

'What type of coils do you remove?'

'The ones placed inside women after their first child. I help take them out again.'

'Have you had medical training?'

'No, but no one has died yet. Some women bleed a little but they are fine after a couple of days. First I removed my wife's coil, then she told her friends and soon everyone in the village wanted theirs out. I made a lot of money, but then someone reported me to the family planning officer and I had to run away.'

The scrambled eggs I ordered are riddled with flies. They crawl from my mouth as I chew. I ask the waitress when the eggs were cooked. She says yesterday, so I tell her to bloody well heat them up again.

From Yanan I travel a hundred kilometres east to the Hukou Falls and see the vast Yellow River charge through a narrow channel and gush down a precipitous cliff in wild yellow waves.

It is almost dark when I reach Yichuan. I spot a mud hut with a light on and knock on the door. The old man who opens it tosses some straw into his storeroom and says I can sleep there. We talk for a while by candlelight. I ask him what is the furthest place he has travelled to in his life.

'The top of the hill by the Yellow River,' he says.

'How far is that?'

'About eight kilometres.'

'Have you never wanted to go a little further?'

'They say there is nothing but fields beyond that.' His face is like the furrowed earth.

'Not all the land is tilled.' For a moment I forget what towns are for.

'What do the town folk eat then? People die after three days without food.' He picks a burning twig from the stove and lights his cigarette.

Later the old man remembers he did go further than eight kilometres once. He injured his eye on the fields one day and was taken to the county hospital, but his eyes were shut all the way there and all the way back so he never saw a thing. He says he lost his wife in 1961. She was sowing melon seeds by the banks of the Yellow River and was washed away by a sudden flood.

As I approach the town of Hancheng, the road becomes black with soot. When trucks from the nearby mines rattle past, people as black as the road slide from their shacks to collect the coal that has toppled to the ground. The ditches they have dug into the road are so deep that even the best drivers cannot help losing some of their load.

From the hills above Fenglingdu, I see the Yellow River run

through its wide valley like a thin trickle of urine. I am exhausted. China is too old, its roots lie too deep, I feel dirty from the delving. I have seen enough. A month walking these winding roads has twisted my mind. I need to find a patch of flat land and rest for a while.

6.

Wandering down the Coast

Immerse yourself in nature.
When you can't be out doors,
feel deep within you
the cleansing breeze,
the lake's calm,
the bud's promise.

让自己沉浸于大自然,
纵使无法出门,
也可以用心感受那微风的清新,
湖泊的静谧,
以及花蕾初绽的悸动

House of Memories

A week later, I take a train to Qingdao to spend Spring Festival with my family. As I walk out of the train station, I hear the wide ocean and smell its damp, salty breath. The noise of the crashing waves holds memories of my childhood, my first love, my early passions for art and life. I glance over the tiled roofs to the highest hill, and see the Catholic church whose steeple was removed in the Cultural Revolution. The Germans took control of Qingdao at the end of the nineteenth century, and during the seventeen years of their rule, transformed it into a replica of a Middle European town. The elegant architecture had no effect on the chaos of my childhood.

It is nine years since I last visited my parents' house. The yard seems to have shrunk. The red characters LONG LIVE MAO ZEDONG THOUGHT I painted on the wall at thirteen have almost flaked away. The sky looks a familiar blue above the red-tiled roof. I open the wooden door. The brass handle is still missing its inner ring and decades of turning have scraped a large hole into the wood. I removed that ring myself at the age of eight when my parents were out and donated it to the school furnace so that my teacher would praise me for my selfless contribution to the communist revolution.

The inside is as shabby as ever. The leaky lead kettle still hangs from the same nail on the kitchen wall. My school maths book lies in the dust on top of the bookshelves, my Young Pioneer's badge pressed between its pages. It takes me back to the Cultural Revolution, when my high-school friends and I would jump into the classroom through the window. The teachers had lost control. I remember when my English teacher tried to teach us to say: 'Long live Chairman Mao. Long, long live Chairman Mao!' my classmates threw paper darts at her desk and shouted, 'Stop

205

spouting the language of our capitalist enemies! Shut up and go and clean out the toilets!'

My brother has a child called Ma Yong and my sister is pregnant. My old classmate Wang Jun got his feet stuck on a railway line last year on his way back from work and a train drove right over him. My other classmates are all married now, but they still seem to be stuck in the 1970s. Their only new topic of conversation is which factories give the highest bonuses. I do not tell them that I am a rootless vagabond now, who has travelled down from the Yellow Plateau for some rest and some good food.

My mother does not reproach me when I confess that I have resigned from my job, but she is very upset when I tell her about my divorce. So for her sake, I pretend to the neighbours that I am still married. My father urges me to stay in Qingdao and find proper employment. He has some contacts in the printing trade and suggests I start a small publishing company. I tell him I am planning to find a job at Shenzhen University, then settle down and get married – so there is no need for him to worry.

When I sit on the sofa I can hear the clock turning back twenty years and start ticking again. But my childhood memories no longer tug at my heart. They lie quietly on the bookshelves or under the bed. That piece of wood wedged under the leg of my parents' bed is the lid to my old pencil box. I remember holding it over my penis one day in the classroom when Rongrong was sitting next to me, and whispering to her, 'Go on, have a look. Boys can piss standing up, you know.' She leaned her head on the desk and I slowly pulled the lid away. The rusty metal leg pins that memory to the ground.

Although I grew up in this house and this town, I feel they have both moved away from me. I can no longer find my place here. The more I retreat into my past, the more dislocated I feel. The person I was and the person I am are two quite separate people.

Three days later, I catch a train to Hangzhou, desperate to see Wang Ping. I pick up a note from her at her office and join her at her parents' house in Zhenhai. The house sits on the edge of a cliff with views onto the open sea. Fishing boats chug over the waves below leaving trails of smoke in the air. Two tall parasol trees shield the sunlight from the yard. The mother puts up a camp bed for me in the damp kitchen, next to a vat of pickled vegetables.

Wang Ping and I spend every day together, walking along the beach and talking, and my feelings for her grow like the beans her mother has left to sprout in the pot by the kitchen stove. I like to see her face change when she laughs. Her expression is usually blank, but she has a sweet little nose that makes her look amusing and intelligent, and detracts from her vacant eyes. Only once, when she discusses her plans to study abroad, do I see her eyes flutter with life briefly, like a bird trying to land. She is very quick and capable. When two policemen come to the house one night to check my identity papers, she sees them off with a few polite words and they never bother me again.

I finish writing a story about a scene I witnessed as a child, and I give it to her to read. In the 1960s, Qingdao fishermen were ordered to abandon their petty capitalist trade and devote their lives to studying Mao Zedong thought. They soon could not afford to feed themselves. One day they were so hungry they swam to a seaweed farm run by the local commune and stole handfuls of kelp that had drifted through the nets in a storm. Militiamen spotted them as they were swimming back, caught up with them in rowing boats and beat them with wooden oars. Some of the men were pulled aboard and tied up with ropes, but most were beaten so badly their stiff bodies were just left to float on the water. The men were stark naked. The wives who were waiting with their clothes on the beach looked on in horror and screamed.

Wang Ping puts the manuscript down and says, 'Your writing

is too coarse. Whenever I look at the ocean again, I will see a mass of white corpses. *Disgusting!*' She often drops a few words of English into her speech, knowing perfectly well I don't understand them.

When I mention that Lingling has asked me to help with an exhibition on the minority ethnic groups of Yunnan Province, she says, 'Who wants to go to an exhibition like that? Yunnan is such a dirty, backward place. Do you know that most American families own two cars these days?'

I look at her clean, white ears and say, 'Yunnan has the most diverse population in China. Each minority has its own unique language and culture, and the lives they lead are much more interesting than the American lives you dream about. There is more to China than communism and the Han Chinese. If you don't understand your own country, you will feel lost when you go abroad.'

She tells me about an exhibition on American domestic appliances that she reviewed last month in the *Hangzhou Daily*. She rhapsodises about the miraculous technical advances, but her descriptions of electric kettles and formica worktops leave me cold.

One afternoon, when the people next door are quarrelling, and babies' screams mingle with smells of powdered milk, Wang Ping's mother leaves us alone and goes to buy some meat at the market. The sea breeze in the yard tastes salty and sour. When I step into the room my eyes meet Wang Ping's gaze. She has washed her hair and has a towel wrapped around her head. Time condenses. I move towards her and take her in my arms. And suddenly, for some reason, my mind flashes back to when I was fourteen and was touched by a man with big, rough hands. I had gone to visit my brother in the countryside, but he was away the day I arrived, so I stayed with his neighbour, and that night the bastard slipped under my quilt and rubbed me until I went soft.

When Wang Ping walks me to the Zhenhai train station, a soft rain starts to fall. It reminds me of the time I walked Xi Ping to the station before she left for the shoot in Guangxi. Sometimes memories can make life seem very sad.

'Promise to send me a letter when you reach a city.' Wang Ping's hair and shoulders are damp. Her white ears look empty.

Time is Money

'Guangzhou in June is as hot as a burning wok. The people who live inside it either fry to a pulp or jump for their lives. No one looks at you in the streets. No one even looks at the sky. All eyes are fixed straight ahead. Everyone rushes about, shouting Hurry, hurry! as if it were the last day of their lives.'

Lingling frowns when I finish speaking. 'You northerners are too slow. If everyone in China was as lazy as you the country would be finished. China's success springs from Guangzhou's hard work. This city is the dragon head of reform, China's gateway to Hong Kong.'

'The only thing this city has produced is a mountain of consumer goods. Where are the thinkers? The artists? Guangzhou people know only how to make money, spend it and die. What is the glory in that? I saw a big banner on the streets today that said TIME IS MONEY, EFFICIENCY IS LIFE.'

'Shut up, you northern twit.' Lingling is angry. We are sitting in the shade of a hut that doubles as my bedroom and the exhibition headquarters. During the last month we have built a small Yunnan village in a corner of Guangzhou's main park. The site has a food alley, two exhibition rooms, four straw huts, and is surrounded by a tall bamboo fence. Now that the electricity and water is finally installed, we are practically self-sufficient.

In the evening, I sit on my camp bed and deal with my post.

Yao Lu's letter upsets me. He says the friend who was developing my films has been arrested and his shop ransacked. The pictures I took in the north-west are lost for ever.

I whisk the mosquitoes from my face and open a letter from Fan Cheng. He has just returned to Beijing after nine months in Xinjiang. He says he is fed up with his job at the tax office and has sent an application to the Shenzhen government for the post of resident writer. I write back, urging him to make it up with Chen Hong.

> She is a fine woman, and still loves you very much . . . I seem to be entangled myself, with a girl from Hangzhou. I would like to stay close to her, but in my restless state it is impossible to form a stable relationship . . . After Hangzhou, I spent a month in Shaolin Temple, climbed Mount Huang, then followed the coast down here to Guangzhou . . . Now that you have finished exploring the deserts of Xinjiang, come and visit the cultural desert here. The south is another country. You will like it. Hong Kong seems just a stone's throw away.

Da Xian has been with us for a week. I invited him down from Beijing to paint our ornamental gateposts. His girlfriend Chun Mei studies English three hours away at Shenzhen University, so they see quite a lot of each other.

Li Tao's letter is a week old.

> I know just how you felt when you found out about Xi Ping. I popped round to Da Xian's house yesterday and saw Mimi's bike outside his door. I had no idea she was in Beijing. I knocked but no one answered. Then I smashed the window and Mimi came running out . . . This is too much. I can't take it. I knew Mimi was unhappy, but I would never

have guessed she could betray me like this. I want to kill someone. Make sure Da Xian has left Guangzhou by the time I arrive. You better tell Chun Mei about this too, she has a right to know. Fan Cheng says we have opened our door too widely, and should rid our gang of scum like him. Mimi weeps outside my door every day, begging me to take her back. She looks like a drowning woman grabbing for branches. But my heart is numb ... I will arrive in Guangzhou next week. Shenzhen University has offered me a teaching post in the economics department.

Da Xian is coiling a piece of wire in the sun. I remember Qiuzi and Xi Ping and I want to strangle him. He turns round, sees my face and realises his secret is out.

'And what's it to you, then?' he snorts. His nose is always blocked.

'When Chun Mei comes tonight I will tell her the truth and she can make up her own mind. It was Li Tao who suggested I invite you here, and all the while you were sleeping with his girlfriend. You dog.'

'It's not as simple as that, Ma Jian.'

'I don't want any explanations. You must leave in three days. If your work isn't finished by then, you won't get paid.'

Chun Mei arrives at dusk. She always smiles before she speaks. Her red lips and white teeth show she is in the prime of youth. She hands me a cassette and says, 'I recorded this for you, Ma Jian. I hope you like it.' She gives Da Xian an affectionate smile. I remember her lying in his arms last week. She was wearing white shorts. Her curved knees reminded me of Xi Ping's.

'Sit down, Chun Mei.' I glance at her bare legs. She sits on the camp bed and strokes Da Xian's hand. 'I have something to tell you. Da Xian has been sleeping with Mimi in Beijing. I got a letter from Li Tao today. He wanted you to know. Well, I've told you now. I'll let you sort out the rest yourselves.' As I walk to the door I see a tear drop from Chun Mei's smiling eyes.

Outside the park gates, I turn right and head for the banks of the Pearl River. Both ends of the distant Huaizhu Bridge sparkle with lights. Small ferry boats chug back and forth. Lingling's husband Wang Shu said that visitors from the north always assume the opposite bank is Hong Kong. At the dead of night they swim to the other side, crawl up the beach, and have just enough time to shout 'I'm free at last!' before the police pounce and put them in handcuffs.

At this time of night the lights in Beijing have already sunk behind the courtyard walls, and anyone walking the streets is liable to be arrested. In the north, even the air is hard. But in the south people live in the open and the air is soft and warm. No wonder everyone wants to live here.

A banner across the road on the left reads A SON WHO JOINS THE ARMY BRINGS PRIDE TO THE FAMILY. A SON WHO ESCAPES TO HONG KONG BRINGS SHAME TO EVERYONE.

When a son joins the army in the north, it is an occasion for celebration, but no one wants their son to be a soldier here. In the south, if a young man has not escaped to Hong Kong and made his fortune, his mother will curse the day he was born.

The entrance to the restaurant is lined with cages of snakes, cats and tortoises. A man takes a skinned dog off his bicycle rack and delivers it to the kitchen. The fish and prawns jumping in enamel basins splash water onto the stone floor and remind one the sea is not far away.

There really is nothing Guangzhou people do not eat. Tonight I have tasted snake, cat, turtle and raw fish. Lingling has invited the manager of a printing factory and a photographer from Guangzhou Press who owns a Hasselblad. They have agreed to take our publicity photographs and print our posters and tickets for free because they are friends of Wang Shu. Lingling promises to pay them when the exhibition starts making money. As they chat away in Cantonese, I sample the dog dumplings and deep fried dove. Lingling asks if I have decided on a model yet, and suddenly I wonder what to do if Chun Mei decides to back out. I had planned to dress her up as a Yunnanese girl and plaster her photograph across the city.

Day and Night

The next morning, Da Xian, Chun Mei and I scour the shops along Zhongshan Road for film, candles, coloured paper, paints and pens. Chun Mei's unsmiling mouth looks like a man's.

Cantonese pop booms from every radio, and each television is tuned to the same Hong Kong soap opera. The noise on the street is so loud we have to retreat into shops before we can hear ourselves talk. The portable electric fans that stand on the counters churn smells of roast duck through the air. The advertising hoardings on the streets and the blonde mannequins in the shop windows give the city an air of opulence and sophistication that is worlds away from the north. Streaming past me are businessmen with leather briefcases and baggy trousers, women with dainty handbags and heavy make-up, and workers in vests and shorts. Housewives carrying plastic bags weave through the bicycles and motorbikes. Southerners move with fluid steps, their bodies are light and supple. Posters of Hong Kong pop stars cover the walls of every grocery store, and make the Marx, Lenin and Mao posters in the Xinhua Bookshop look like museum pieces in comparison. I browse through the magazine section, then buy some pens and paper, as well as Updike's *Rabbit, Run* and Joyce's *Dubliners* which I will read and then send to Wang Ping.

We turn into a narrow lane of small brick houses. Smells of fish and incense pour from open windows, the rooms inside are black. Pink and yellow underwear hang from bamboo poles above. I go to a public phone, give Lingling a call then wait for her to call me back. The heat is unbearable. A table on the pavement is set with cups of tea. We each buy one, but Da Xian and I have to spit ours out. Chun Mei tells us this is called 'bitter tea'. Two old men on plastic stools stare at us then gaze at the line of shops behind. A furniture store sells goldfish in its doorway. A man who cuts keys, prints name cards and mends watches has set up business in the entrance of a shop that sells hats, cosmetics and Hong Kong cigarette lighters. Outside the radio repair shop, a tethered cat claws at a plastic bag as it tries to break free.

Life is easy here. Women stroll to the public toilets in their nighties and stop to buy rice on their way back. Children wash their feet and sandals while they clean vegetables under the street tap. A man on a motorbike pulls up beside a fruit stall and leans over to select his tangerines.

In the afternoon, Chun Mei appears to take a turn for the worse. She is wearing brown make-up and a grass skirt for the photo shoot. When I look at her through the lens, her ears seem very white. The photographer forbids me to touch his Hasselblad, so when I need to take a picture, I tap his hand and he presses the button for me.

Having seen Chun Mei on to the train back to Shenzhen, Lingling and I return to the exhibition ground. I lie down on my camp bed and tell her how much I appreciate her finding this job for me.

When the gates close for the night we have the whole park to ourselves. We take a boat out and row into the middle of the lake. The water smells of jasmine. She tells me she likes me.

'No you don't. As soon as I got up from your sofa the other day you wiped it down with a wet flannel. You treat me worse than a dog.'

'That's not true. When Wang Shu and I have a flat of our own, we will make a room up for you and you can stay with us whenever you like. As long as you have a shower before you arrive.'

Lingling is terrified of dirt. She always carries a packet of tissues with her to wipe her hands and face, her restaurant chopsticks, or her seat on the bus.

'We have been married six months and are still living with Wang Shu's mother,' she says. 'There is no privacy. We still haven't made love yet.'

I catch her eyes and hold them until at last she looks down. The night sky behind her has turned a deep red. This city never sleeps. I drag the oars through the water and hear the splash stretch to the bottom of the lake.

Women offer me peace and security, but I am afraid to get too close. When I took the Buddhist vows I pledged that I would fend for myself and depend on no one. My feelings for Wang Ping are confused. I try not to think about her too much. But part of me hopes that once my mind has calmed down a little, I will be able to build a life with her.

To fill the silence, I talk about Da Xian's decision to split with Chun Mei and return to Beijing. The boat glides under the bridge, scattering its reflection across the lake.

'The quickest way to commit suicide is to marry an artist,' she laughs.

'Well, you can come and marry me then when things get too much!' I smile. Then I pause and say, 'I will always be a good friend to you, Lingling.'

She tosses her tissue into the air and it floats through the night like a patch of day.

Building a Park within a Park

Three days before the exhibition is due to open, the photographer Shen Chao arrives on a bus with twenty people from remote villages of Yunnan. After twelve days on the road everyone is covered with mud and dust. Most of them have never been on a bus before. As they step off, some of them start to vomit. Wang Shu leads them to the exhibition rooms where he has laid out mattresses and sheets he has borrowed from the local hospital.

Now that everyone is here, the place comes alive. We hold a lunch meeting in the park teahouse. The park's Party secretary gives a welcoming speech. Shen Chao stands up and announces this is the first exhibition of its kind in Guangzhou, a very important event. Wang Shu lists the prestigious guests who will be attending the opening ceremony. Then Shen Chao's girlfriend Pan Jie briefs us on our sponsors and I talk through the rehearsal schedule for the bonfire dance. Suddenly everything seems to be falling into place.

The next morning I run to the station to fetch Li Tao and Fan Cheng from their train. Northern peasants spill from the exit carrying their quilts, padded coats and dreams. In this hot, bustling city, they appear slow and clumsy. They wipe the sweat from their brows, stand at the crossing and stare blankly at the passing traffic. I climb over some cardboard boxes, squeeze to the front of a long queue, flash my journalist card to an aggressive policeman and buy a platform ticket.

Fan Cheng steps off the train. He has a beard now, more wrinkles and less hair. Li Tao still looks pale but he is smiling. Perhaps he has pushed the Mimi episode to the back of his mind.

In the afternoon, Hu Sha comes from Beijing, and Yang Ming from Chengdu. They arrive on the same train, so I presume they met up at a town along the way. Yang Ming is wearing leather boots. We exchange a smile. She thanks me for inviting her and asks whether the post she sent on for me arrived.

Chen Hong turns up the following day, but Fan Cheng ignores her. Yesterday, he told me, 'I have no intention of going back to her. Horses never eat the grass behind them.' I wrote to Chen Hong a while ago, suggesting she forget about him and start a new life for herself, but she wrote back and said: 'That's easy to say, Ma Jian. If you lose a finger it takes your body two years to readjust. And what I have lost is a hundred times more vital.'

I invited Wang Ping too, but she wrote back last week to say she couldn't make it. 'The leaders refused to give me leave. *Hangzhou Daily* published "Escarpment" last month, so I've enclosed a postal order for 70 yuan. I hope you like the T-shirt. Thank you for the Hong Kong birthday card. It's beautiful. I passed it round the office and everyone was very jealous.' Those birthday cards are sold in every shop in Guangzhou. I sent one to my sister as well, along with a leather satchel with shoulder straps which I asked her to give to Nannan.

Everyone from Beijing uses my hut as a meeting point. It takes me back to my life in Nanxiao Lane. Chen Hong and Hu Sha decide to visit Shenzhen, and ask me to help them apply for the permits.

The opening ceremony is a great success. Everyone from the local media and arts turns up, even the mayor makes an appearance. The black-bean soup, rice gruel and pork dumplings our Beijing cook made are finished in a flash. Pan Jie is dressed to the nines, she looks like Imelda Marcos. Shen Chao is wearing a suit and tie and is walking through the crowd shaking hands like a proud father at his daughter's wedding. He has reason to be pleased. He spent two years in Yunnan taking the photographs for this exhibition. The men and women in Dai, Tibetan and Jingpo dress are the friends he made there. This is his dream come true, and I am happy for him.

The Qingke wine he has brought from Yunnan is very strong. Six Lishu women invite the male guests to drink from their cups. They have got quite a few of them drunk already. When dusk falls, we light the bonfire, and our friends from Yunnan perform their dance. After the official guests leave, we laugh and hug and take jovial group photographs. The Jingpo men fill our bamboo cups and teach us the pony dance. Then the Lishu women stand up and sing 'We came into this world weeping, but we will leave it with a smile . . .' At midnight we retire to my hut. I lay the leftover snacks on my table and sneak in another bucket of Qingke wine.

Hu Sha has drunk too much. He has been sick twice and is now sprawled on my camp bed cursing the city. 'All these bloody crooks think about is money, money, money . . .'

'Stop flinging your arms about. If this net tears, the mosquitoes will bite us to death!'

Hu Sha bought a tape recorder in the market yesterday but when he came back and opened the box there was nothing inside. I put a Jean-Michel Jarre tape into my cassette player and turn the volume up.

Fan Cheng examines the exhibition poster on the wall. 'I like this photograph, Ma Jian. You've made the site look like the paradise garden in *A Dream of Red Mansions*.'

Yang Ming wipes the sweat from her brow. 'Transplanting a primitive village into a modern city – it would be a good subject for an avant-garde poem. Are you tempted to visit Yunnan after this, Ma Jian?'

'Yes, I would like to explore the whole of the south-west, and then perhaps move on to Tibet. I try not to make any fixed plans though. I prefer to follow my instincts. So, Fan Cheng – what do you think of the south?'

'The north is a yellow wasteland, the south is a green wasteland.'

Li Tao is sitting in the corner, having a serious conversation with Chun Mei. Last night he drank so much, he sweated like a pig and stripped to his underwear. 'My job at the bank was a nightmare,' he says. 'I had to have lunch every day with our Party secretary. He didn't have a clue about finance. This province shows us the way forward. Social progress depends on a strong economy . . .'

'Stop lecturing the poor girl,' Fan Cheng says, snatching a Marlboro from Li Tao's pocket.

Chen Hong is standing in the doorway. She is still wearing her sunglasses. Her hair is a mess. 'Our Beijing circle is falling apart,' she tells me. 'Everyone is just out for themselves now. They all want to move to Shenzhen. Hu Sha is the only one with any ideals left. By the way, did you see my poem in this month's *New Era*?'

Lingling has started an argument with Hu Sha.

'In Beijing, people just sit back and complain,' she says. 'But in Guangzhou, we get on with the job. Now that the economy is booming, you politicos have become irrelevant.'

'Bullshit! We need politics more than ever, now. These reforms have given us freedom of thought. You southerners don't know how to take advantage of that.'

'It's not what you think that matters, it's what you do. The future is forged through action.'

'All right then. Let's build that cattle ranch in Hebei. Ma Jian! Show them your photographs!'

'I left them in Beijing. I can draw a picture though.'

Fan Cheng rises to his feet. 'Ma Jian and I have been planning this for a year now. Each member invests a thousand yuan. It's a beautiful spot. We can live surrounded by nature and concentrate on our writing.'

'I thought you wanted to move to Shenzhen and write stories for the government. You won't find much nature there.'

'We could buy some horses and run riding holidays. I could set up a travel agency here.'

'No. We should turn the place into a country club. We could restrict membership to people in the creative arts.'

I draw a sketch of the site on the wall. 'There's a lake on the right and a forest on the left. We can put the ranch in the middle and the house here. It'll be a wooden house with a large veranda where we can store our gumboots and farming equipment. It will have fourteen single bedrooms and a large sitting room where we can sit around a kerosene heater and talk about art.'

'Can women join?'

'Of course. We can't leave the kitchen empty!'

The Lishu women, Cangcang and Caidan, walk in and ask me to drink from their goblet. We have spoken a lot over the last days. They have told me many interesting folk tales. Caidan complained that Shen Chao never said she would have to perform. She hates wearing her national costume in this heat. Cangcang presses her lips next to mine and we drain the goblet dry. The wine burns down my throat. Shen Chao flushes a deep red and raises his glass. 'I'm so happy that you are all here today. Any friend of Ma Jian's is a friend of mine. Stand up, everyone! To your health!'

Before I go to sleep I take a photograph of Chen Hong for her Shenzhen permit. When she removes her sunglasses, I notice her eyes are red with tears.

The Opening Ceremony becomes the Closing Ceremony

The next day we sell just twenty-seven tickets, and no one stays for the bonfire dance.

The opening ceremony could have doubled as the closing ceremony. We call an emergency meeting and decide to split forces. Lingling goes to stick posters up at the universities. Pan Jie returns to Beijing to pressure the national media to cover the event. Shen Chao talks to Guangdong Television about filming a documentary and I offer to repaint the sponsors' advertisements that have washed away in the rain.

But our problems begin to multiply. The clay figurines Shen Chao commissioned his friend to produce for our gift shop were so ugly we had to send them back, but now the factory insists we cover their costs. Our guests from Yunnan go shopping and fall prey to southern ruthlessness. Li Xueyong from the Jingpo tribe buys a watch, but when he opens the box he finds a nut and bolt inside. The Wa man comes back with a new cassette player, but when he opens the box he discovers a red brick. Tsering the Tibetan buys a Hong Kong T-shirt, but on his way back to the park the design washes away in the rain and leaves red blotches of ink on his chest. The exhibition room is in chaos. The women are in tears, the men are shouting and cursing. Their families have toiled for years to make the money they have lost in just three days. There will be terrible trouble when they get home. The Beijing cook is complaining about the lack of customers and is threatening to pack up and leave.

While I sit on our gatepost repainting another hoarding, I catch sight of the Great China Hotel across the park, and it occurs to me that if we managed to stick some posters in there we might get some foreigners to come. So I jump down, roll up a couple of posters and go to try my luck. A crowd of northern peasants stands at the hotel gates, staring at the brightly clad foreigners who stream from the minibuses. A doorman in a red uniform and round cap bars my entry and chuckles as I walk away.

Ten minutes later I return in long trousers and leather shoes, and sneak in through the duty-free shop on the right. I have visited the shop twice before to admire a beautiful assistant Li Tao has discovered. She stands behind an array of frighteningly expensive perfume bottles, making it impossible to find an excuse to approach. On both occasions I paid a visit to the gentlemen's lavatory to steal a roll of toilet paper. It is the most elegant room I have ever seen. It has gold taps, potted plants, air-conditioning, piped music. When I sit on the toilet seat I can almost imagine I have escaped to Hong Kong.

The man at the reception listens to my request and calls the public relations officer. The pleasant Hong Kong woman with gold earrings takes my posters and agrees to visit the exhibition. I rush back to the park and tell Shen Chao to fetch her and give her a guided tour.

A few days later I find my way to Guangxiao Temple, one of the oldest Buddhist sites in Guangzhou. The twin iron pagodas that stand in the courtyard look rough and wild. I step into the Hall of the Sixth Patriarch and see a large brass statue of Huineng, the founder of the southern school of Zen Buddhism. As a young man Huineng travelled north to seek religious teaching. When the Fifth Patriarch balked at taking on a southern disciple, Huineng swayed him by arguing that while men are divided into northerners and southerners there is no division in buddha-nature. Upon his return to Guangzhou, Huineng entered Guangxiao Temple and heard two monks arguing over a banner fluttering in the wind. One monk said it was the banner that was moving, the other said it was the wind. Huineng said, 'Neither the banner nor the wind moves. It is your mind that moves.' He understood that man's greatest enemy is himself. A side-chapel holds the ashes of a thousand dead sages. A black-and-white photograph is pasted to each box. If the sages have managed to transcend the fetters of samsara, why do they feel the need to leave these mementoes behind?

I come out of the temple gate, go to a cake shop and order a glass of papaya juice. A little girl is leaning over a plastic table doing her homework. A sour smell of sweat wafts from the soles of her feet. My daughter's feet used to smell like that. She could never keep them still. By the time her homework was finished, the floorboards beneath her chair were always hot and shiny.

I ask her how old she is and what she wants to do when she grows up.

She swings her legs about and says she wants to make money.

'Why do you want to make money?' She is only seven years old.

'If you have money, even the devil will scrub your floors,' she says, paraphrasing an old proverb.

'Where is your father?' I ask.

'Gone to fetch cash.'

I ask her mother what she means. 'He's gone to work. In Cantonese fetching cash means going to work.'

I check my watch. The bonfire dance is about to start. Unfortunately, this is a city where no one has time to be a spectator.

On the way back I walk past the Sacred Heart Church. From close up it looks old and dilapidated. It is hemmed in on all sides by tall concrete buildings, its two steeples struggle towards the sky. A hundred years ago French missionaries came here to build a heaven on earth, but now their heaven is suffering the tortures of hell.

Although I too feel squashed as I chase through the city streets, I can always sense the sea is just around the corner.

Walking to the End of the World

After the exertions of the exhibition, I take a rest for a while and move in with Li Tao at Shenzhen University. For a month I work on a story, but find the money I earned in Guangzhou and the comfort of being among friends has dulled my creative spirit. I feel the need to start travelling again, and decide to take a boat to Hainan Island, the most southern province of China.

An hour before my boat is due to leave, I make my way to the bus stop. Workmen are hammering cement blocks into the pavement. The newly tarred road in front is covered with sand that has spilled from a nearby building site. Two trucks drive past leaving a cloud of yellow dust, so I retreat into the doorway of a hairdresser's salon. The girls inside stare at a television screen as they shake their hairdryers about. Suddenly I see Fang Li, the Xian drug addict, walking towards the door. Her dark shiny hair does not match her yellow skin. She smiles and says, 'Mr Ma, isn't it?'

'Fang Li! What are you doing here?'

'I was discharged from the centre in March and flew straight here. What brings you to Shenzhen?'

'I'm just off to Haikou. My boat leaves in an hour.' At last my bus arrives.

'Let me see you off then.' Her miniskirt is very tight, so I help her onto the bus. Her arm feels cool and dry. At the traffic lights the conductor sees a policeman and tells the standing passengers to crouch down. When we have crossed the intersection, we stand up again, and she starts telling me about her life.

'This is the year of the ox. I was born in the year of the monkey. They say monkeys leap over the ox's back, so it should be a good year for me. I met a guy on the plane here. He fell in love with me at first sight and asked me to move in with him. It was two months before he realised I was using drugs.'

Shenzhen is a vast construction site. There are no corners. Parallel roads lead straight into open fields. People from every province wander the streets in their best clothes, searching for a new life.

'He is a model worker,' she continues. 'If his unit knew about his relationship with me he would get into terrible trouble. I told him I would keep quiet for ten thousand yuan. His wife and daughter are transferring here soon . . .'

The air outside the window smells of manure and tilled earth. The high-rises sprouting from the ground make the fields look smaller. Local peasants in new shirts drift aimlessly between the buildings. The young men pouring from the office blocks with polystyrene lunch boxes have light blue shirts and shiny shoes.

When we get off the bus she says, 'You must write a story about me. I lied when I told you I never sold drugs. I lost ten thousand yuan the last time. I have a girlfriend now, you know. We met at the Palace Ballroom. I fell in love with her when I heard her sing. When my husband gets out of jail next year I will file for divorce. A lesbian? Me? I don't think so. Go back to Xian? Never. I met a Canadian man last week. He works for a Hong Kong company and sends me flowers every day. I can't speak English so we have to talk through the dictionary. Love him? I don't know yet. I'll wait for him to take me abroad then see how things go. The other guy? He's terrified to touch me now. I'll move out as soon as he pays up . . .'

I watch her figure disappear into the crowd. She looks like any other pretty girl on the street. You would never guess she has a child in nursery, a husband in prison, a married boyfriend, a girlfriend, a Canadian lover and an opium addiction.

As the boat casts off, I think of Li Tao and Chun Mei. They are in love now. Mimi has agreed to a divorce. Yesterday, Chun Mei came with me to the post office when I sent my letter to Wang Ping. On the way back she stopped and said, 'Ma Jian, by the time you have finished your travels, Li Tao and I will have an apartment. You must come and stay with us. Shenzhen is a new city, an empty shell. It is waiting for us northerners to come and fill it with our dreams.'

When the Haikou writers' association see my introduction letter from Guangzhou Press they give me a free room in their guesthouse and pass my story to *Horizon* magazine. Three days later I follow a line of coconut trees to Wenchang town. Lingling's cousin Chen Xiong runs a photographer's studio here. His front window displays a huge photograph of two palm trees bending towards the sea. He tells me he took the picture in Dongjiao, a village twenty kilometres away. It is a photograph that hangs in almost every restaurant in the country. I stay for three days helping him paint a mural of Beijing's Beihai Park for a portrait background, then take to the road again.

The next day I reach the coconut plantations of Dongjiao. The blue sea and green palms are as close as two lips, separated by a long white beach. Time settles like the flat sand. I sit beneath a tree, inhale the sea breeze and try to let my thoughts grow as large as the ocean . . . The letter I received from Ai Xin in Wushan was just seven characters long: 'I am off to see the ocean.' I wish that smiling girl was sitting beside me now. Wang Ping said I was rigid and judgemental, and difficult to be with. What is it that draws me to her? On my last night in Shenzhen, Li Tao asked me why I always fall for women called Ping. It is strange. Guoping, Xi Ping, Lu Ping, Wang Ping . . . 'Ping' means small green leaf that grows on still water, and the women I love are true to their name. They drift through my life like rootless weeds floating across the surface of a pond. Xi Ping taught me never to trust a woman again. Lu Ping's pirouettes have long since faded from my mind . . . Women are like the sea though, they are not just there to be looked at. I throw off my shorts and plunge into the water.

In the evening I come to a village lit by lamps that burn on coconut oil. The fragrant huts stand under dense palm trees. The only break in the canopy is the hole above the village well. A hunched old woman walks home barefoot, beating her way through the leaves. I knock on a door and ask if I can share a bed for the night.

A week later I stop below Five Finger Mountain at a village inhabited by the indigenous Li tribe. Director Huang of the hygiene office puts me up in his house. He advises me not to climb the mountain. 'There are poachers' traps everywhere. If you tread on one you will either fall into a ditch or be catapulted into the air. They only check the traps once a week, by which time you will be drinking tea with the immortals.' I tell him that sounds fine to me.

I set off at dawn and reach the top at noon. A few dead pines rise from the two-thousand-metre summit. The limestone crags have blackened in the wind. My feet start to squelch inside my shoes, and I find it difficult to walk. I sit down, remove my socks and discover about thirty fat leeches stuck to my toes. I beat them with the soles of my shoes then rip them off one by one.

I follow a river to the Li village of Shuiman. There is a folk song that goes 'Shuiman girls, Shuiman tea . . .' I take out my camera hoping a pretty girl might pass, but it frightens the children so much they run away in tears. Some of the grass huts have side sheds for grown-up daughters. Girls who do not become pregnant bring shame to their families. No Li woman can marry unless she has a bulging stomach. I go to a hut with a smoking chimney and ask for a bowl of tea. The old woman pulls a branch of tea leaves from a cloth bag and drops it into a pan of water. When it comes to the boil she empties the brew into a bowl. The taste is slightly bitter. She says she is seventy years old, and her grandsons are all married. I tell her I organised an exhibition on minority nationalities in Guangzhou, and have come here to photograph the Li. She eyes me coldly. 'The Han came here when I was a girl and took twenty-four of us to Guangzhou. We were exhibited in iron cages in Yanghan Park for three whole months. They told the visitors the Li are born from monkeys and raised by snakes.' Her lips quiver with anger. I let the matter drop. Despite our noble motives, the exhibition was a failure, a fantasy within a tropical garden. The old woman's face is covered with tattoos. I ask to take her photograph but she still doubts my credentials so I show her the red stamp on my introduction letter. The sad lines inked onto her face as a girl have faded over the years. I promise to send her the photograph. She tells me Li girls tattooed their faces to repel the Han invaders.

The mountains beyond the village are green, but there are no more oil palms or coconut trees. I walk downhill through bamboo groves and double-spring trees in full blossom, and spend the night with a Li family in their roadside hut.

The next morning, I crest a hill and see a large forest fire. The area is cultivated by slash and burn, but this fire is out of control. There is no one about. If the wind changes, the flames will swallow the bamboo hut nearby. I run over and bash through the door. Inside, there are rugs, clothes, pots and pans. I toss everything into the stream outside and weigh them down with stones. The last time I enter, waves of heat roll towards me. I try pulling the jar of rice wine across the room but the bamboo ladder is in the way, so I dip my hands inside and scoop some wine into my mouth. As I stagger out of the door, ribbons of smoke curl up the ladder.

Two days later I stop at Tongzha, then continue my journey south. I skirt the foot of a cool mountain, descend to fields of sugarcane and spend the night with some labourers from Guangdong. They have contracted to farm a mu of land for fifteen yuan a year, and will share the profits between them. They puff at long water pipes. Their hair has turned dry and yellow in the sun.

The road scorches during the day, but at least the passing trucks leave a pleasant breeze. The people who live by its sides wander up and down all day then retire to their homes at dusk. At night the boys come out and flash their torches into the dark. I rarely use my torch for fear of attracting mosquitoes. Two weeks later I arrive at Sanya, the most southern tip of China.

The sea washes straight into the streets. The small wooden boats moored at the shore smell as sour as my damp plimsolls.

I have come to the end. Ahead of me lies the blue-black sea. My footprints stop where the sea begins. I can go no further. I long to, though. The oceans haunt my dreams. But I belong to the earth and can only walk across land.

Two women clutching handfuls of sunglasses run up and ask if I want a digital watch. I walk to a seaside restaurant and buy a packet of biscuits. The boss puts a new tape in the cassette player: 'Fate has sent me far and wide to wander the distant wastes . . .' It is the theme song of an Indian film I saw as a child. With my canvas bag and walking stick I look just like the wanderer in the film – only I am wearing sunglasses.

A child gives me a prickly pear then steps back to stare at me. A girl on a bicycle stops to wave. As I get to my feet, the boss wipes the sweat from his face and says, 'Why not have something to eat before you turn back.' He too knows this is the end of the world.

7.

The Abandoned Valleys

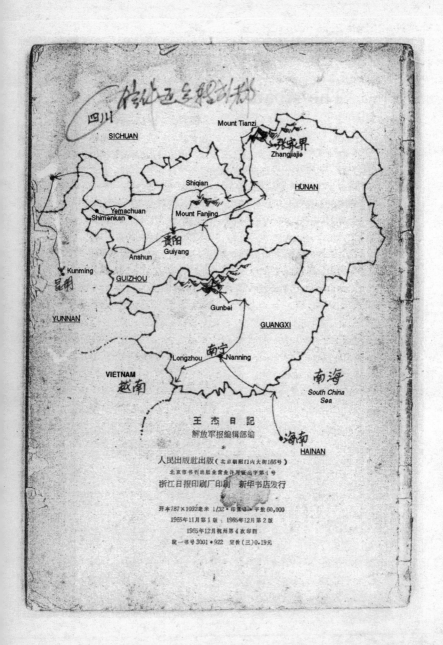

The Silent Beat of the Drum

Dear Wang Ping. I wish I could lie in your arms for hours on end, but my mind is too restless. Sometimes I sense I am walking to a final destination, but I don't know where it is yet. In fact I am just drifting in circles, swirling like a loose leaf on a stream.

Today is Saturday, 10 October. I have just arrived in Gunbei, a remote village in the mountains of north Guangxi. Tomorrow I will cross the Motianling range and proceed into Guizhou.

I spent most of the last month in Longzhou village near the Vietnamese border. Limestone pinnacles rose from wide paddy fields, and the sun moved through the sky, illuminating the landscape like a huge stage light. The scenery was beautiful, but the local Zhuang nationality live in dark dank hovels. The peasant I stayed with lent me a musty blanket he brought back from the Korean war. Thirty years of body odours clung to me like a wet skin, it was impossible to sleep. I thought of the students in the neighbouring village who butchered their teacher in the Cultural Revolution. To prove their devotion to the Party, they cooked his chopped corpse in a washbowl and ate him for dinner. They developed a lust for fresh offal, so before they killed their next victim, they cut a hole in his chest, kicked him in the back and the live liver flopped into their hands. Local villages were able to consume an average of three hundred class enemies during those years. The Zhuang wore long black tunics and sipped beer from each other's spoons.

I walked to the border near Pingxiang, and was arrested on suspicion of espionage. Fortunately, I had a letter of introduction from the Guangxi writers' association. The police phoned them the next morning, then let me go.

I visited the provincial museum in Nanning and saw an exhibition on the natural history of sex. It was very interesting. It made me realise how much our lives are governed by ovaries and semen. In the next room I saw huge bronze drums that were excavated in fields nearby. Some were over two thousand years old. The sides were carved with images of rain clouds and shamans in feathered headdresses dancing themselves into a trance to the beat of ritual drums. They could not hear the noise of the modern world. I could not hear it either . . . I have drawn a map for you of my journey down the coast. I will write to you again from Guizhou.

There is no postbox in Gunbei, so I put the letter back into my bag, and go to a shop to buy firecrackers for this afternoon's party. The village head has told everyone to take the day off and prepare a dance for Comrade Ma who is here to write an article on minority culture.

Gunbei is enclosed by mountains, only one or two trucks pass each day. The villagers belong to the Miao tribe. They live in round wooden huts with roofs made of bark. The girls usually dress in clothes from the local town's discount stores, but for the dance today they are wearing traditional costume: hand-dyed purple tunics, embroidered cummerbunds and intricate silver crowns. They step into a gentle dance as the bamboo pipes begin to play. The instruments range from small flutes to pipes five metres long. The girls hold their backs straight, sway their hips and stamp the rhythm with their feet. There is a controlled restlessness to their movements. The whole village gathers round and children join in the dance. At dusk the firecrackers are let off. Everyone laughs and cheers, the pipes play a new tune, and for a moment I almost forget I am a stranger.

Later the village head invites us home for a bowl of butter tea. His wife is a school teacher. She has removed her traditional

234

costume but her neck is still purple from the dye. She serves us sticky rice and pickled fish. I ask the white-bearded man next to me where the fish was caught.

'They grow in the paddy fields,' he says. 'When the rice is cut, we drain the water from the fields and grab the fish with our hands. We rub them with salt, chilli powder and herbs then keep them in a earthenware jar for two years. It is our custom to give the head to the guest.'

I scoop a handful of sticky rice, squeeze it into a ball and bite. 'That is a fine beard you have, grandfather,' I say.

'I have to let it grow. If I cut it I fall ill!' Everyone laughs politely. A bowl of wine is passed around the table.

After the meal, the young villagers take me to the house of an old widow who sings me some Miao love songs. I cannot understand the lyrics so I just look at the woman's expressions. As the wine drifts to my head I fall into a doze and dream of my first love. She is standing on a Qingdao beach, wearing a long black skirt. The sea breeze streams through her hair. She says, 'My parents don't want me to see you any more. Go away now. Go!'

At Motianling Pass I light a cigarette, glance back at the path I have taken through Guangxi then at the wilderness of Guizhou that lies ahead. On the map this region is called the Land of Ninety Thousand Mountains. Only the wind can cross this sea of green heights, I will never make it. At first, the mountains seem to laugh at me. Then, as I climb one after another, I discover each one has an individual weight and form, each is as unique as a human face. The mountains I painted in Beijing were just lifeless protrusions of earth.

I take off my 'journalist shoes' and change into my plimsolls. The further I walk the less I know why. I have become a marching machine. As long as I have a bag on my back I will walk, until I drop. The path takes control, I follow it blindly. I have lost all sense of direction. Why did I choose to live this way? I am not a dog, after all.

The money I made in Guangzhou is almost spent. The capital of Guizhou is not far ahead now. Perhaps I can pick up some work there. I follow the wind north, and two weeks later tramp into the dirty streets of Guiyang, 'City of Petty Tyrants'.

Entering a Strange Circle

I find the house of the dissident poet Li Zhi at the end of a long narrow lane. There is a two-metre-high brick kiln outside his door. It looks as if he has made it himself. I hear rhythmless chords crash on a piano inside. It is the kind of piece parents force their children to play. When I step inside, Li Zhi clasps my hand. His wife goes to pour me some tea and his two little boys clamber up to the gallery and jump around like monkeys.

'I got your letter last month, but I never thought you would make it! Sit down and I'll show you my new work.' He hands me two clay masks. The features are hideously deformed and painted in garish colours.

'When masks are this ugly they're not frightening any more,' I half-joke and take a sip of tea. 'What happened to you last year at Hu Sha's house? I heard the police broke up your poetry reading.'

'Yes. The cops arrested me and dragged me back here. Said I could never visit Beijing again. I haven't written any poetry since then.'

I cut to the chase, and tell him my money is running out and I need to find some work.

'Well, you have come to the right person. I know everyone in Guiyang! A friend of mine has just opened a sofa business. I'll see if he needs any help.' When I spoke with Li Zhi in Beijing he used standard Chinese, but now he has slipped back into

Guizhou dialect. Fortunately it sounds similar to Sichuanese so I am able to get his drift.

His brick house is tiny. There is a double bed downstairs and a mattress in the gallery for the children. A piano and two lamps occupy the remaining space. A dim light bulb shines on the cucumber, exercise book and half-eaten meat pie on the piano lid. The meat pie looks delicious.

'Is there anything you would like to see while you are here?' Li Zhi waves his hands as he speaks. His fingernails are filled with clay. He looks as fragile as the broken pieces of terracotta I saw by the kiln outside.

'Something different. I have become very interested in minority cultures since I worked on that exhibition in Guangzhou.'

His wife starts to wash the dishes. She has thick glasses and soft, pale skin. She looks like an accountant. One of the boys swings from the edge of the gallery, kicks into his mother, crashes onto the piano, screams, falls to the ground and scuttles under the stool.

'Do you know Old Xu?' I continue. 'He's a friend of Yang Ming's. Works for Guizhou Press. No? Never mind. So, tell me about Guiyang.'

Li Zhi shoots a furious glance at his children. I can tell they are in for a beating when I am gone.

'Of the artists, Tang De is quite good, and Dong Kejun is listed in the *World's Who's Who*. Everyone else is crap. Tian Bing is the only poet now that Huang Zhang is in prison. The writers are shit. I am the only famous person in Guiyang, really.'

The boys start throwing paper darts at my head.

'Have you somewhere to stay tonight? No? I'll take you to Tang De then. He'll put you up. As for you rascals, just wait until I get home!' The little monkeys slip through his hands, leap up to the gallery and giggle, their faces as scrunched as their father's masks.

On Saturday afternoon, Tian Bing takes me to a quiet, forested park in the outskirts of the city. As the rain clouds clear, we head for the park's highest hill. The smell of dust fades slowly as we climb. I have been staying with Tian Bing and her husband Tang De for a few days now, and have found a job making sofas. Tang De is a woodcarver. The whorled patterns he creates echo the lines of his face. Tian Bing is a poet and a reporter for Guiyang Television. She boiled all my clothes this morning, and gave me a new pair of jeans. She tells me Yang Ming is coming to visit her next month. They were at university together in Chengdu.

Halfway up she stops and shouts, 'Slow down, will you!' Her skin looks transparent in the sun, the downy hairs on her face sparkle with sweat. Sometimes she reminds me of a sick chicken. We sit under a tree. She is as damp as the bark. 'Gorgeous view, isn't it?' Her Sichuan dialect reminds me of Ai Xin. I keep seeing visions of that beautiful poetess waving at me from the wharf.

'Everything looks nice from a distance. See that yard over there? That's where I make the sofas.' Then, turning to her, I say, 'Why did you move here, Tian Bing?'

'One grave is as good as another,' she sneers. Last night she showed me her poetry. I pencilled some corrections and her face went red with fury. 'Who do you think you are?' she said. 'You Beijing writers are all the same. The arrogance!' She has been sharp with me ever since.

'You don't seem at home here. You are too sophisticated. This place is so cut off, everyone is slightly strange. I haven't been able to think straight since I arrived.'

'Stop thinking then! You're so self-important, wanting to meet every little intellectual in town. So much for detaching yourself from the mundane world!' This fragile-looking woman has a spirit of steel. 'I didn't like this place at first,' she concedes, 'but I am a woman after all, and where my man goes, I go.' She tears a handful of grass and scatters it over my trousers. I think of the line from her poem: 'The lover's zip has rusted.'

'I like that line: "A woman as strong as rock." ' Then I pause and say, 'Tang De is a good man.'

'I like the way he sits around all day smoking and drinking. I can't bear those polite men who help with the cooking and washing up. If it weren't for Tang De I would have left years ago.'

'But what brought you here in the first place?' The saying goes that in Guiyang, you never see three days of clear sky, three li of flat land, or three coins in your pocket.

'My first boyfriend moved back here after university. I joined him later, six months pregnant, only to discover he was living with another woman. Son of a bitch.' Her eyes begin to redden.

'Bastard.' I imagine he is one those cringing young men who become transformed into petty tyrants on home ground.

'You mysterious wanderer, dropping into our lives like a gift from the sky. Tell me, is there any cure for jealousy?' When she fixes her eyes on me, she looks like a little girl whose neck still smells of milk.

'Control your desires. If something does not belong to you wipe it from your thoughts.' My voice is trembling.

Suddenly she puts her arms around me and kisses my lips. I hold her for a second, then she breaks free and walks away. The blades of grass in the sun still sparkle with raindrops.

Two tourists with backpacks walk past a goldfish-shaped dustbin.

She leads me back to the town centre along the banks of the Nanming River. Her jeans are identical to mine.

'This river is disgusting,' I say. 'There must be half a century of rubbish buried in there.'

The men digging muck from the riverbed are covered in mud. The stench is vile. Old women scavenge on the banks for wire and umbrella frames, and pile their loot on the pavement. It is already four o'clock, but people are still sloping out in their slippers to brush their teeth by the riverside.

'Each work unit has been assigned a section to clean. We have contracted some peasants to do our share of the work. It means no bonuses for two months though.'

The town centre is so crowded we can hardly move. An ear cleaner waves his twig and shouts, 'One mao an ear!' A blind masseur in dark glasses rubs his hands, waiting for his next customer. A spit-patrol officer grabs a middle-aged man and charges him a one-yuan fine. A beggar plays a three-stringed lute on the street corner and sings with his eyes shut: 'Chairman Mao's kindness is deeper than the sea. He comes like thunder in spring to rescue the Communist Party . . .'

'What did Old Mao do for him, for God's sake!' I shout over the clatter of bicycles. By the time I have bought my socks and gloves the sky is already dark.

We sit at a street stall and share a plate of dofu. 'It's stuffed with chilli sauce and big enough for two, so they call it lovers' dofu,' she says with a smile.

A bicycle mender crouched below us is removing drawing pins from a rubber tyre. I lean down and whisper, 'Bet you sprinkled those pins on the road yourself, little devil.' He pulls his cap round and shoots me a sideways glance.

Tian Bing kicks my foot. 'Don't pick a fight in Guiyang,' she says. 'Everyone carries knives. Someone got stabbed yesterday in the train station, and all they wanted was his watch.' Splinters of light flash from an electric welder across the road.

'This chilli's hot. So who else writes poetry in Guiyang?' I ask distractedly. The crowds of the city appear to be closing in on us.

'Look at these wastrels! What kind of shit do you expect them to write? When you give your lecture at the university, whatever you do, don't talk to them about poetry.' Her voice sounds as angry as it did last night. It seems that, like me, she is not at home with herself either.

A few days later I move in with Zhou Long, a friend of my workmate, Fu Yi. He is a member of the provincial acrobatic troupe and has a large bald patch from years of balancing urns on his head. He puts his mattress on the floor for me and says he will sleep on the wooden boards of his bed. His girlfriend is a tightrope walker, and lives in the room across the corridor. In the evening Fu Yi, Zhou Long and I go out for a beer. We order a plate of 'cloth dolls' – small pancakes which we fill with one of thirty stuffings laid on a table before us. They swig the beer and start a drinking game, waving their fingers in the air and shouting, 'One: bed! Two: lovers! Three: mouths! Four: feet! Five: legs! Ha ha!' A cold wind blows up. After my lecture this morning at Guizhou Normal University the students took a collection for me, much to my embarrassment. I will buy them a dictionary with the money. I stand up and suggest we take the beers back to Zhou Long's room.

When I am out making sofas every day, my hair and nostrils fill with fluff and sawdust. I cut timber into planks, fix springs, and help Fu Yi attach fake leather covers. For this I earn eight yuan a day. Our yard is heaped with timber, metal rods and wadding, and the ground is strewn with sawdust and string. When my hands get tired I join Fu Yi for a smoke and a cup of tea and we while away the time watching the girls walk by. In their shiny black leggings, they look like little black ponies from behind.

Fu Yi always carries a magazine, so he knows about everything from butterflies to Freud's theory of sexuality. He knows that the new president of the Soviet Union is called Gorbachev, that the Chinese women's netball team won the world cup again and that the American rocket Challenger exploded live on world television. He knows a lot but does very little. He attaches the springs with two nails instead of six and says, 'Don't worry, it will look fine once the vinyl is on. Everyone has to live, you know!' He repeats that last phrase at least twenty times a day.

If a bird flies overhead or his saw hits a nail he shouts, 'Typical!' and sits down to admire his biceps.

'Look, her arse has dropped,' he says, lighting a cigarette and gobbing onto the floor. 'Must have got laid last night.' The girl who passes at this time every afternoon is wearing ankle socks with her stilettos today. The road is muddy in the rain and dusty in the sun, but the girls who walk past always look good enough to eat.

'It was still tight yesterday. One more virgin lost for ever . . .' Fu Yi stretches his legs over the half-upholstered sofa.

I walk to the corner for a piss. The pack of Marlboro Lingling sent me from Guangzhou is nearly finished. In her letter she said Shen Chao is having an affair with the Hong Kong hotel manager and Pan Jie has returned to Beijing in a huff. The printers are still nagging Wang Shu for their costs.

She said she typed up my story 'Yin Yang' and sent it to *Flower City* magazine, but the editor wouldn't touch it. I will post it to Old Xu this afternoon and see if he wants it. It is the story of a girl who gases herself after being raped by a gravedigger. Her family take her for dead and bury her the next day. The girl wakes inside the coffin, struggles to escape but dies slowly of suffocation. Later that night, the gravedigger opens her grave, hoping to rape the corpse, but when he sees her tormented expression and the scratches on her face he understands she was buried alive, and is overcome with pity and remorse. He climbs into her coffin, lies down beside her and slits his wrists.

I return to the sofa.

'O virgin, thy trembling lips . . .' Fu Yi waves his head and flashes his yellow teeth.

'Save me your poetry, please. You are lucky to have a nice girlfriend like Xiao Yu. Why are you so obsessed with virgins?' Last night, his girlfriend walked into the communal bathroom with a washbowl and toothbrush. I could not see her face, but when the moonlight from the open window fell onto her shoulders I wanted to take her in my arms.

'Take it from me, Old Ma, virgins are something special.' He rolls up his sleeves and flexes his muscles.

I am tempted to tell him Wang Ping was a virgin, but decide to keep it to myself. She seems very far away now. I have felt restless these last days. I went stiff just now when I pissed in the corner. 'I could do with a woman tonight,' I say, sucking on my cigarette.

'You can borrow my mistress if you like. She's got much bigger tits than Xiao Yu.'

'All right. Tell her it's just the once though. No strings attached.'

'Fine. Yanzi likes artists, she'll be happy to help you out. Hey! I read they spike Marlboro with dope to get you hooked. What? I know they taste good. Just think though, I have to work a whole day for just one pack. What a life! In foreign countries the restaurants let you eat bread for free. It's true, I read it in a magazine.'

'You have to order a meal too, though. You can't just sit down and eat bread all night.'

'Tell me, Old Ma, why do you write stories? What? To feed yourself? Hey, do you believe in wild yetis?' Then he tosses a cigarette stub on the ground and says, 'You're not happy, are you?'

'Pick that stub up, you bloody idiot!' I remember hearing that if anyone drops a stub in the meadows, the herders will beat them to death.

'Calm down, brother. Everyone has to live, you know.'

When we finish for the day he rinses his hair under the tap and carefully buckles his watch. He is taking me to the library tonight.

The boss finally agrees to my idea of selling paintings together with the sofas. He hands me a photograph of an evening seascape and promises to pay me fifteen yuan a copy. I go out to buy canvas and paints and finish two pictures before dusk. Once I get the hang of it I manage to churn out six paintings a day.

On Tuesday afternoon I visit the offices of Guizhou Press to see Old Xu. He hands me a pile of letters that have accumulated for me over the last month. There is a lot of news about the stories I have submitted to magazines. Wang Ping tells me *Northern Fiction* has accepted 'The Last Rain' and *Beijing Literature* will publish 'White Fruit'. Li Tao says 'Black Earth' will appear in next month's *Modern Writing* and that *Special Economic Zone Literature* is interested in 'Virgin'. *Horizon* magazine writes to says 'Waves' was published in their autumn issue and my fee has been sent to Wang Ping. I decide to give up the sofa job and wait for my cheques to roll in.

Old Xu says he liked 'Escarpment' and 'Yin Yang' but his boss said they were too dark and decadent and refused to publish them. I say, 'Never mind, there are two thousand literary magazines in China, one of them is bound to take them.' Old Xu has arranged for me to talk to the Guiyang Teachers' Book Club tonight. I will receive a fee of twenty yuan. We make our way to a classroom in the Telecommunications College, and with the aid of some notes I have scribbled in the library, I ramble on about the influence of Daoism on modern Chinese verse, then discuss my approach to creative writing.

When I am finished, fourteen teachers seated behind a horse-shoe of school desks start firing questions at me.

'My name is Zheng Guang. Please tell me, do you think traditional culture will influence the future development of society?' Zheng Guang is the chairman of the book club. He wears a suit and tie and has a big smile on his face, and looks very out of place in this cold, dark classroom.

'Well, it can't influence the past, can it? Tradition is an inevitable part of life. Of course it will influence our future. But modern societies are driven primarily by the concept of individualism.'

'Mister Ma, the reforms have so far been limited to the economic sphere, but I feel that what our country needs most is political liberalisation. What is your opinion on this?' I glance at the questioner opposite me: bald, smiling, middle-aged, doesn't look like an informer. He cracks his knuckles as I reply.

'I was asked similar questions at Anhui Normal College and Shenzhen University. The authorities talk about reform but they have no intention of loosening political control. Political freedom gives one a sense of self. Economic freedom encourages greed. If one has the latter without the former then society becomes warped and this can be very dangerous.'

'I read in a magazine that robots have reached the intelligence of a three-year-old child. Does this mean that in fifty years' time they will achieve the intelligence of an adult?' The questioner at the back clenches his hands into tight fists.

'Forgive me, all I can tell you is that foreign countries use calculators to control their production lines. I know nothing about computers.'

'Why are you a Buddhist? Do you believe in heaven?' The man in the front row has no legs. All I can see is a head perched on the table.

'Buddhism eases one's spiritual pain. I will not let a political party tell me how to live, when to die or what to believe in. Our souls are linked to the universe, but we can never see heaven, because our flesh ties us to the earth and the people around us. But when the people around you have lost their will to be free, then earth becomes a hell.'

'Do you think dogs can predict earthquakes? Have you ever seen a ghost?' Before my talk, this man told me he was a professor of biology at Guizhou University. Either his hair is very greasy or he was caught in a shower on the way here.

'As man's brain has evolved he has lost some of the subtler sensitivities. Animals are more attuned to nature. The dogs in the street outside know we are sitting in this classroom, but we have no idea where they are. Sometimes when I practise qigong I feel my soul leave my body. I have never seen a ghost, but I hope the Buddha will appear to me one day.'

'What is your opinion of Bao Yu's love for Lin Daiyu in *A Dream of Red Mansions*?' This woman is sitting right in front of me. She has a small mouth and thick white glasses.

'I read the book when I was sixteen. It's a wonderful novel. We all want to live a dream life in a beautiful secret garden. But when the dream shatters, we wake up and see through the red dust of illusion. I too write about love and death, or, to be precise, about how love can only exist in death, because only death is eternal. What? No, I have not seen through the red dust yet.'

The questions come to an end. During the applause Zheng Guang presents me with a brand new nylon shirt, and everyone begs me to show them some qigong.

A few days later, Tian Bing and I go to Zheng Guang's home for a drink. He and his wife are divorced but they still share their one room. His wife is a Beijing Opera singer and gave me twenty yuan for my copy of Van Gogh's cornfields. Tonight she has fried some wild onions and spicy fish. Everyone from the book club is here. They say they paid me too little for the lecture and slip a hundred-yuan note into my pocket. I sit on the floor and give them another qigong demonstration. Everyone gasps as my palms turn red and the sweat pours from my head. When I open my eyes I see Tian Bing weeping on Old Xu's shoulder. As I open another beer, she walks over and slaps me hard on the face.

I decide to take a trip into the countryside. Yang Ming is due to arrive soon, but I cannot bear to stay in this city any longer. The next day, I walk to the train station and buy a ticket for Zhangjiajie Nature Reserve in northern Hunan Province.

Abyss of Desire

I wake in the morning to a white universe. It snowed last night. The toilet hut looks like a fairy-tale cabin. I walk past it and crunch through the snow to the edge of the 'One Step Crevasse' I jumped across yesterday. The snow has narrowed the gap, but the drop is still as deep. The opposite side is slightly lower, so the leap across is easy, but the return jump is perilous. Last summer a Beijing tourist jumped back with so much force he ricocheted off the wall and fell into the abyss. I remember the fear that seized me yesterday, a sudden clenching between my thighs. They should build a footbridge across the damn thing and put an end to it.

I walk back to the timber frame of the condemned house that stands at the foot of Mount Tianzi. When this spot was turned into a tourist site, the village committee decided the house spoiled the scenery and ordered it to be knocked down. I stayed with the owner's uncle last night in his warm and comfortable flat. He showed no concern for the fate of his nephew's family when the snow started to fall. 'Let them freeze to death!' he said. 'Serves them right for not listening to the village head.'

I see smoke rising through the roofless frame. Since there is no door, I walk straight in. The wife is feeding logs into the stove, and the five-year-old daughter is clutching a hand warmer. I touch it. It is stone-cold. Her frozen fingers look like little red carrots. She says her daddy has gone to the village. Hanging from the central beam is a mirror, a string of chillies and a calendar torn to today's date: 1 January 1986. 'Snow on the first day of the year. That must be a good omen.' I try to give them some words of comfort, then take my leave and set off for Zhangjiajie town.

In the white mists of Tianzi I felt cut off from the world, but Zhangjiajie pulls me back to earth. Tourists fill the streets and restaurants. Late at night, the police break into my hostel and drag a naked couple into the corridor, threatening to inform their work unit unless they pay a three-hundred-yuan fine. The man's feet turn white and the woman's thighs tremble with cold. They fetch 170 yuan and say it is all they have. The police grab the money and let them go.

Back in the dormitory, everyone lights a cigarette and discusses the naked woman.

'So that's what women look like with no clothes on.'

'Such shiny skin, lovely white bottom.'

'Serves them right, sleeping around like foreigners.'

'They were up to no good. He looked old enough to be her father.'

Director Liu of Shaoyang Food Supplies describes how counter-revolutionaries were dealt with during the Cultural Revolution. 'They were shot, then stripped naked and tossed into the river so everyone downstream would know. Once I saw a whole family floating by, threaded together with a piece of wire.'

'What about the women?' asks the man who had never seen a naked woman before tonight.

'No chance of a cheap thrill, my friend. They hacked the tits off before they threw the women in.'

I read the hotel regulations pinned to the wall. The last one says: 'Men and women can only share a room if their age gaps exceed seventy years.' I guess that rules out grandmothers sharing a room with their grandsons. I crawl into bed, but cannot sleep. The room is still murmuring with gossip.

I hate people gloating over the misery of others. When the police drive criminals to the execution ground, the streets fill with gawping crowds. Women are always treated the worst. In a Beijing suburb I saw a woman being dragged through the streets by a wire hooked between her vagina and anus, while the male prisoners were just hooked at the shoulder blades. When a woman steps before the firing squad, people point and whisper, 'Look, it's a woman.'

In the 1940s Chinese men could take fourteen wives, but a decade later they had to limit themselves to one. But the thwarted desires for domination and voyeurism still seethe inside men's hearts and explode at every opportunity. On an execution notice today, I read of a Sichuan man who, having raped a young girl, stretched his hand up her vagina and ripped out her womb. When a country is ruled by a band of thugs, men behave like savages. Another naked couple stand shivering on the street outside. The police must have found some more victims. Inside our room, six stinking mouths chew over the details of the scene. Before day breaks I pack my bag and leave.

I return to Guizhou Province the next day and climb the sacred Mount Fanjing. There are stone steps all the way up. When the black rain clouds lift, the mountain is bathed in light. The Buddhist temple at the top is under restoration, the shrine is empty. I stand and watch the clouds race through the sky below. There is no one in sight. It feels good to be away from the crowds and breathe the clean mountain air.

Two days later I descend the mountain and trek to Shiqian village to bathe in the Ming Dynasty spa.

When the Shiqian Library manager reads my letter from Guizhou Press he smiles and hands me the keys to the building. There are four thousand dusty books to browse at will. I decide to stay a few days.

The next morning I buy a ticket for the hot springs. There are three connected pools: officials' at the top, men's in the middle, and women's at the bottom. The middle room is thick with steam. About ten men are wallowing in the bubbling water. They mop their faces with flannels then use washing powder to scrub their dirty clothes, plimsolls, slippers and sheets. The water is filthy, but at least the heat soothes my chapped skin. The stream that arrives from the officials' pool is far from clean, I imagine it is black by the time it leaves the women's pool.

The old man beside me stands up and tries to piss over the ledge, but his aim is poor and the urine dribbles back into the pool.

'Sorry, my friend,' he says, wiping the ledge with his flannel. 'I'm getting old. I will be eighty-one this year.'

'Congratulations, that's a fine age.' I look at his little penis and edge away. I am not in the mood for conversation.

Soon the stench of chlorine and filth brings tears to my eyes. I stand up and stick my head out of the window. A few women too poor to buy tickets are washing in the black stream running from the lower pool. As the water continues down the narrow valley the steam slowly disappears.

In the evening I lock up the library and walk back to the hostel. There is a light still on in the village. An old man has passed away and a crowd has gathered at his house hoping that the sight of an aged corpse will bring them long life.

I squeeze through the door. The couplet hung on the back wall reads THE SOUL RETURNS TO HEAVEN, CLEANSED OF WORLDLY DUST. On the funeral altar, a photograph of the deceased is lit by two flickering candles. I recognise the face. It is the old man who pissed in the pool this morning. His relatives pull me inside and give me a seat at the front, right next to the corpse. There is no escape.

The woman on my right hands me some melon seeds. I stare at the dead man's sunken chin and the yellow teeth behind his dry lips. In this room full of living people he is the only one who has walked to the end of life and stopped. His death draws the living around him, while the living try to suck life from his death. Today, this man is their role model, the guide to their future.

'He lived to a fine age. Had a tumour removed last year, big as an apple.'

'Never lost his appetite. He ate a bowl of gruel yesterday and peeled two hard-boiled eggs by himself.'

At last the Catholic priest walks in with a red cloth over his shoulders and a prayer book in his hand. I saw him this morning at breakfast in the hostel canteen. I take advantage of the confusion and squeeze outside. It is less crowded on the street. A hush falls, then the people inside start chanting with the priest: 'Almighty God, when the earth shakes and the mountains crumble, you will come on your horse to pass final judgement. We wait in fear. Have mercy on our sins, absolve us from punishment, lead us to heaven and grant us life eternal. Amen.'

After breakfast the next day, I buy the prayer book off the priest for two yuan, and set off back to Guiyang.

Rain over the Leprosy Camp

With a letter of authentication from Old Xu, I go to the post office to cash my cheques and come out with nearly three hundred yuan. Fu Yi takes me to find the sofa boss who still owes me money for my paintings. Fu Yi works for someone else now, making picture frames for double his old wage. He says, 'Yanzi thought you were quite nice. She keeps asking where you've gone.'

'Don't tell her I'm back,' I say, remembering the cold, hard soles of her feet.

The sofa boss lives in an old courtyard compound. The tree in the middle is dead. Each coal shed is filled to the brim. There is a coffin outside the boss's door. Fu Yi tells me it was given to the boss's father as a retirement present. The boss is not at home, but later we find him playing drinking games in a nearby restaurant. He gives me 150 yuan. I painted thirty-five pictures so I was owed more than seven hundred.

When I leave for Huanguoshu Falls the next day, Old Xu walks me to the bus station. He says, 'Tian Bing wanted to run away with you, but when you showed us your qigong she decided you were a cheap prankster and now she never wants to see you again.'

'I am sorry she feels that way. She never really cared about me though. I just fuelled her dreams of escape.'

Is it love that keeps her in this city, or hate? Would she really have run away with me? I don't think she knows the answers herself.

The winter has been so dry that the Huanguoshu Falls are reduced to a trickle. A dam will be opened tomorrow for a foreign tour group, but I decide not to wait. Spring Festival is two days away. I want to head into the mountains and see it celebrated in the Miao villages.

On the sixth day of the Chinese Lunar Year, I continue west and meet a companion on the road. We spend all day together, walking through deep, green valleys. In the evening we reach his uncle's house, and he invites me to share a meal and stay the night. The uncle tells me there is a bus to Anshun tomorrow, so I change my route and decide to loop north before I head into Yunnan.

A month later I pass through Yemachuan village on the Guizhou–Yunnan plateau, and take a red path that runs along a ridge like a fresh wound. Green weeds lining the path stretch towards the sky. Suddenly, a black cloud appears from nowhere, and in the downpour that follows, the path turns to mud and I slip twice to the ground. Through the sheets of rain I see a white house ahead, and wade through the wet grass to its gates. The sign on the door says SALAXI SANATORIUM FOR INFECTIOUS DISEASES.

I walk inside. The place is empty. A cold wind blows through my wet clothes. 'Anyone there?' I shout, but all I hear are my creaking footsteps. As I climb the wooden staircase I wonder whether the residents have been wiped out by a fatal plague. It is dark upstairs, the only light is from a window above the stairwell. I grope along the corridor and see a splinter of light shining from a crack in a door. The plaque says DIRECTOR'S OFFICE. I walk in. The room is small and tidy. There is a newspaper and inkwell on the desk, and an acupuncture chart on the wall. I take a tea cup and open the thermos flask but there is no water inside.

The rain outside the window is so heavy I cannot see beyond

the vegetable plot below. I take off my wet jacket and sit in the armchair. If no one turns up I might as well spend the night. I didn't pass any hostels on the way.

Soon the building begins to creak. Footsteps climb the stairs and tread down the corridor. I stare at the door. It opens and a girl walks in. She speaks to me in a Guizhou dialect. I tell her I am a journalist and produce my letter of introduction. She puts down her umbrella and smiles. 'You are the first journalist to visit our leprosy camp. Wait here, I'll call the director at once.'

My eyes dart around the room. Now I know why there were no guards at the gate, the fear of leprosy is a sufficient barrier. I take out my camera and notebook and pass a comb through my hair.

The director is a young man of about thirty. He pours me a cup of tea and tells me the history of the sanatorium.

'It was built by Italian Jesuits in 1933, specifically for the treatment of leprosy. How many patients now? About thirty. Their conditions are stable. Most could go home if they wanted, but no one will take them back. Symptoms? Skin thickening, ulceration, partial necrosis, hair loss . . .'

'Would you allow me to meet some of the patients?' I ask, closing my notebook. 'We can continue this talk later.'

'You are very brave. Most people are terrified of infection. In the past, the staff had to wear gumboots and surgical masks before they entered the camp.'

The camp is situated just behind the building. In the drizzling rain it looks like a pretty mountain village. The path is lined with sick rooms, most of them empty.

The director knocks on a door and we walk inside. The windows are grimy. Through the darkness I can see white bowls and farm tools on the floor. Two camp beds are pushed against opposite walls. There is a large leek on the stove in the middle. The air is stale and musty.

'Get up, Jiefang. A journalist has come to speak to you. You can say what you like.' The director is a small man, his gumboots look huge on him.

'S-sit down, please. I'll light the stove. Is it still r-raining outside?' Jiefang throws off his bedcover and picks up a box of matches.

'I'm not cold. Please sit down. You seem to be in fine health.' He looks perfectly normal to me.

'I'm much b-b-better. Came here in September and the m-medicine worked at once. Went home, but my w-wife didn't w-want me, wouldn't even let me see the ch-children. Went back to my f-factory, but they wouldn't take me. They gave me some money and told me to go away. No hostel would have m-me, so I had to come b-back here in the end.'

'We wrote to his work unit to say he was not contagious, but they wouldn't listen. The fear runs too deep.'

'How do you spend your time?' Jiefang looks about thirty.

'My hands still work, so I am needed on the fields. My boys? One's n-nine, the other's five. No, they have n-never v-visited me.' His lips continue to quiver long after he finishes speaking.

A woman hobbles in on crutches. Her clothes are filthy. She is wearing an army cap. Her twisted mouth is half-open. A blind man with a haggard face follows behind her. They are joined by ten or more patients. Some have lost a hand, an ear, a nose, but most of them can walk and their skins seem quite healthy. The room is too crowded now, so I suggest we move on.

I open the next door and see an old woman crouched by the stove. Tufts of hair rise from her bald head like clumps of weed. Her eyes follow me as I enter the room, then return to the chillies behind the door. Another woman is asleep in the bed. All I can see is a patch of skin – a face or shoulder – peeping out between the blanket and the pillow. Her breathing is loud and chesty. An old flannel and a card printed with the words DOUBLE HAPPINESS hangs from the hook of a grey mosquito net. The smoke-stained wall behind the stove is pasted with pill-bottle labels. It looks like fungus sprouting on rotten wood.

'The lady in bed is fifty-one. She suffers from gastric bleeding and can't speak any more.'

The next room is a little brighter, the walls are lined with newspaper. An old man with white hair sits on the edge of his bed watching flies dart about. His face is gaunt and twisted. Streams of saliva dribble from the corners of his mouth and run down his padded jacket like rail tracks. He clutches the bedside table with his two remaining fingers. There is a newspaper on the table, an apple and a muddy pair of gloves.

'Where are you from?' he splutters with great effort.

'Comrade Ma is a journalist from Guiyang, Old Wu. He has come to investigate our situation and will report back to the higher authorities. Old Wu has been with us for thirty years. He studied at Kunming Normal College and worked for the local government. Everyone here comes to him when they need to write letters.' The director obviously gets on well with his patients.

'We only receive twelve yuan a month, but prices keep going up, we can hardly afford to feed ourselves.' Old Wu dribbles, tapping his knuckles on the newspaper. 'We have written to the public health department three times asking for help but they still haven't replied.'

The other patients start chipping in.

'The reform policies have improved people's lives, but we still live on maize gruel here. In Hezhang Hospital they have televisions in every room.'

'The county sent us some hats this year, but we need soap and new farm tools.'

'And a television.'

'We can never go shopping.'

'Me? I was nine when I arrived. I've only been home once.'

'This is our little orphan. His family lives in Sichuan. He went home in 1968 but the villagers beat him up. He hid in the bushes by day and walked back to us under the cover of darkness.'

'We have four hens, two of them lay eggs.'

'Comrade Journalist, please send our message to the government. I am a Party member, I led a production brigade ...'

I ask to take a picture of them outside and suddenly they freeze.

The director pulls me aside and whispers, 'They never take photographs of each other. Haven't you noticed there are no mirrors in the camp?'

'Comrade Journalist has shown us respect. We should allow him to take our photograph.' Old Wu waves his hand and everyone returns to their rooms to change into their best clothes. Old Wu has no feet but he sticks his leg stumps into a pair of old leather shoes, leans on the table and pushes himself up.

It is still drizzling outside. A wet hen scuttles out of the chicken coop. Everyone helps carry the old woman out of her room and comb her hair in place. Thirty disfigured faces stare into my lens, their eyes crying out for help. The women brush their hair back. The director holds an umbrella over me, my hands are shaking. I don't know what I can do for these people.

Back in his office, the director tells me that without the vegetable plots and three apple trees the patients would starve. 'No one could survive on what the government gives.'

'But they are crippled. How can they work on the land?'

'Two of them still have use of their hands and the staff help out with basic necessities.'

'The old woman they carried out is not well, is she?'

'She's been ill for ten years. She has never had leprosy though. Her boyfriend caught the disease in the 1960s. They came here together, and had their wedding in the camp. He died four years later and she has been here ever since.'

'How many patients were here at the height?'

'Over a hundred, I think. They used to have dances on National Day. But conditions are terrible now. We never have enough medicine. The doctor's salary is just a hundred yuan a year, no bonuses. The local peasants assume the staff are contagious and refuse to come near us.'

'Can't you get a transfer?'

'Probably, but I have grown attached to the patients, I can't just abandon them. Last year they caught a wild bird, made a bamboo cage and gave it to me for Spring Festival. They know it is dangerous to make gifts of food, so they keep all the apples for themselves.'

In the morning I return to the red path. The sky is clear now, but the air around the wall-less camp looks cold and stiff. I glance back at the white building rising from the neat vegetable plots. It looks like an empty shell hovering above the ground. If it hadn't rained yesterday, I would have walked straight past.

Mountains behind Mountains

It is the middle of April but the rivers are still ice cold. Whenever I wade across one, my legs go numb for hours. I climb two mountains a day and at last reach Shimenkan village, drained and exhausted. The village head gives me a friendly welcome and offers me a bed in the committee house.

'This house was built by English missionaries. It used to be a church.' He was sent here by the local government to work on poverty relief.

In the evening I open my map. I am at the north-western tip of Guizhou Province, near the borders of Yunnan and Sichuan. I close my eyes and picture the mountains I have crossed during the last month, and wonder how Mr Bagley and his wife managed to make it here all those years ago. They came in 1902 to build a school and a church for the villagers, and stayed until Mr Bagley's death from typhoid thirteen years later. I visited the school this afternoon. The children sleep on wooden planks now. When they are hungry they take a potato from a cloth sack and cook it on a fire of dried leaves.

The next morning I visit the cemetery and see the open graves of Bagley and a fellow missionary who was murdered by local tribes. The smashed tombstones lie scattered on the grass. You can still see the English letters and Chinese characters of the inscriptions. After the men were buried, the villagers continually unearthed their graves looking for treasure. In the end they took everything, even the bones.

Bagley's only real legacy is the group of thirty children he sent to England for a secondary education. When they returned they became the cultural elite of the province, and occupied the most important posts at Guiyang schools and colleges. Not one of them returned to Shimenkan though.

The poverty in these mountains puts me to shame. Most people have never worn shoes. The family I stayed with a few days ago cooked their food on a piece of broken terracotta. They served me a bowl of maize gruel and a cup of salt water, and I gave them my last packet of biscuits. They told me they grew enough grain to eat for two hundred days, and the rest of the year have to make do with husks and potatoes.

That afternoon cadres from nearby villages gather at the committee house to read the central authorities' 1986 agricultural plan. There are ten Party members, but only five know who Deng Xiaoping is and none have ever heard of Secretary Hu Yaobang. At the close of the meeting, the Party secretary announces that tonight's mission is to arrest a man who has fathered four children and owes the state thousands of yuan in family-planning fines.

'We ransacked his house last month, but he still won't give himself up. He was seen creeping back to his house two nights this week, and leaving before dawn, but his wife will not admit to it and refuses to tell us where he is hiding. Tonight we must surround his house and catch him red-handed. Liu Wang, you place six men in ambush outside his uncle's home, and don't forget the torches. The rest of you must guard the village gates.'

In the middle of the night, twenty militiamen arrive at the

committee house and wait for their orders. When I see their guns I suspect the peasant will not survive the night.

Surprisingly, though, he surrenders without a fight. The men bring him to the committee house, tie him to a table, open his abdomen and snip his sperm ducts. In the afternoon he squats in the office refusing to leave, but no one takes any notice.

'Why not go home? Your wife will be getting worried.' If he stays here all night I will not get any sleep. He rolls his eyes, one hand still clutching his bandaged stomach.

'I am not going until they give me back my bull.' Ever since they cut through his skin, he has looked like a deflated football.

'You haven't done so badly. You still have four children at home.' He looks away and ignores me from then on.

The village committee confiscates his door, window panes, roof tiles and farming tools, but these are still not sufficient to cover his fine. At dusk they drag him outside. After a meal of mutton noodles with the village cadres, I open the front door to see if he is still there, but he has vanished into the black night.

Between Daxing village and the Jinsha River, the temperature suddenly rises, and banana and prickly-pear trees appear by the side of the road. I cross the river at dawn and start my ascent of Mount Daliang. At noon it is so hot I climb stark naked, but when I reach the two-thousand-metre peak I shiver in my down jacket.

That evening I reach a village called Mayizu and stop for the night. A Hong Kong–Shenzhen production is shooting a movie here and has transformed the village into a film set.

In the morning, the Yi villagers dress in their national costume and parade through the mucky lanes, laughing and kicking dogs out of the way. No one goes to work on the fields. When the crew start shooting, the Yi follow them from location to location, brandishing wooden chests, hip knives, earrings and bracelets, hoping the director will need to hire them for the next scene. When the director picks someone for a role, they moan at the injustice. They cannot understand why the dirtiest layabouts and ugliest women are always given the best parts. After the director shouts, 'Action!' the villagers start laughing and crying as if they were watching a film at the cinema. The puny director's constant pleas for quiet are translated into Yi by the security guard sent down from the county town.

The film is based on the true story of an American pilot who parachuted here in the 1940s after his plane was shot down by the communists. The Yi found him and made him their slave, and it was nine years before they let him leave their mountain enclave and return to America. They would never have imagined that the 'foreign monkey' they released would one day bring them such fortune. The Hong Kong director is at his wits' end. 'This is a nightmare,' he says. 'The Yi charge us for everything, and their prices go up every day.'

Money has changed these people's lives and their way of thinking. What would I do if I came into some money now? Would I still be wandering through these mountains? My poverty allows me to move as freely as a leaf in the wind, but sometimes I wish a stone would fall on me and pin me to the ground.

The American pilot was able to stay here all those years because he had a goal in life: he wanted to go home. I have no such goal, so I must keep walking.

I check my compass, head south and a week later arrive at Yunnan's capital, Kunming.

8.

Life at the Border

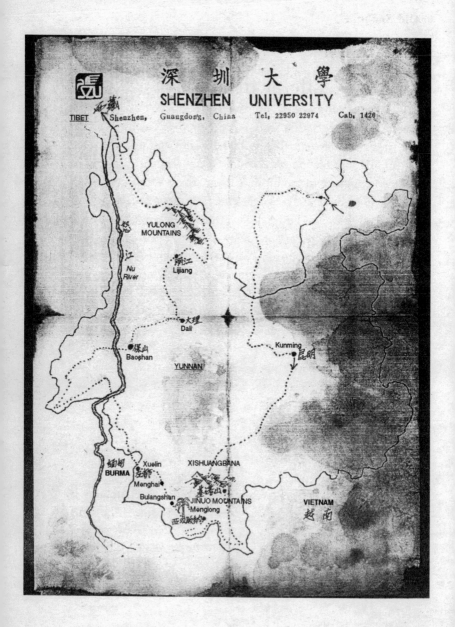

深 圳 大 學
SHENZHEN UNIVERSITY
Shenzhen, Guangdong, China   Tel: 22950 22974   Cab: 1426

TIBET 西藏

YULONG
MOUNTAINS

怒
江
Nu
River

麗江
Lijiang

大理
Dali

保山
Baoshan

YUNNAN

Kunming 昆明

緬甸
BURMA 雪林
Xuelin
Menghai
Bulangshan

XISHUANGBANNA

基諾山
JINUO MOUNTAINS
Menglong

西双版纳

VIETNAM
越南

Old Shabulu

On 2 June, two hours after leaving Baoshan, the long-distance bus stops at a small hamlet, halfway up a steep mountain valley. The driver jumps off and says he needs to find some water for the engine. The passengers start lighting cigarettes. The baby next to me wakes and screams. His mother lifts her vest and stuffs her left nipple into his mouth. The bus is hot and stuffy.

This is my second month in Yunnan. Six weeks ago, I gave a lecture on modern poetry at Kunming University which attracted a small audience. The next day the students told me their university's propaganda department had issued a warrant for my arrest. The alleged crime was 'disseminating liberal propaganda to impressionable youths'. I ran away to the border region of Xishuangbana, but on my second day in the capital, Jinhong, the poet who was hosting me said the local writers' association had received notice that an officer had been sent to Beijing to investigate my case, and that pending the results, they should have nothing to do with me. He gave me a nervous glance and said, 'Please, if they catch you, tell them we've never met.' I left town and headed into the mountains, and have been racing through the borderlands since then like a hunted animal.

The baby has fallen asleep again. I open the window, take out my notebook and read through the last few entries.

28 April. Still wandering through the Jinuo mountains in the Xishuangbana region of southern Yunnan. The landscape is green and tropical. I have seen oil palms, papaya trees, pineapple trees, tropical orchids, climbing wisteria, fire flowers blazing on rotten wood, leafless bachelor trees and chameleon trees with leaves that change from yellow to

263

green to red. The slopes cleared twenty years ago by city youths to make way for rubber-tree plantations are now dry and barren. By the banks of the Pani River, I saw the graves of fourteen youths who died in the fires. Two of the tombstones bore the inscription: POSTHUMOUSLY AWARDED MEMBERSHIP OF THE CHINESE COMMUNIST PARTY.

The Jinuo village I am staying in has a long bamboo house that is shared by 29 families who belong to the same clan. The families live in separate rooms, but cook their meals on a communal fire in the long central corridor. The house is cluttered with farm equipment, baskets and stools. There is little attempt at decoration.

Jinuo custom allows members of the same clan to fall in love, but not to marry. When the time comes for a clan couple to separate, they exchange gifts with each other as pledges of undying love. The girl gives a leather belt and the boy gives a felt bag. These gifts are then taken to their new marital homes and displayed on the wall. When the clan lovers die, they carry their gifts to the mythical Nine Crossroads, meet up and travel together to the underworld where they can marry each other at last. For the Jinuo, husbands and wives in this world are mere companions of the road, true love must wait for the afterlife. I have seen these belts and bags hanging on the walls of several village huts. When a girl gets married, her clan lover splashes her with water from a dirty washing-up bowl as a show of jealousy. It is considered a great humiliation for a bride not to be drenched at her wedding. Jinuo women wear white, peaked hats and long black skirts.

. . . Last night I visited the folk singer's hut. He was out, but his son sang for me instead. Two of the songs were about lovers who yearn for the day they will meet again at the Nine Crossroads.

Our driver has been away for an hour. He has obviously had a drink with a friend. He clambers back on to the bus and flings a bag of live chickens under his seat, takes a quick swig of tea, mumbles 'What a life!' and switches on the ignition. As the engine heats up, the chickens kick frantically inside the darkness of the cloth bag.

I remember seeing the little girl called Meina crouched in a doorway of that Jinuo village. She had stepped on a rusty nail the week before and her foot was swollen with pus and blood. She could hardly walk. I washed the wound, smeared it with antiseptic cream and covered it with a clean bandage, and she didn't flinch once. When I finished, she hobbled inside and fetched me a banana. Her mother was sitting by a loom, ears pricked. An older woman was smoking in the dark corner behind. All I could see were her silver earrings. That evening, Secretary Li told the children to take me into the hills to see Shabulu, the old shaman who had spent eighteen years in prison for cursing an innocent man. In the 1950s, he was the richest man in the village and owned more rice than he could eat.

Shabalu wore an old army cap that night. When he looked up there was sadness in his bloodshot eyes.

'I am a journalist, but a Buddhist too,' I said, 'so you can speak freely.'

'Mmm, is that so? Some government officers visited me last month. Asked me lots of questions for a religious survey. I let them record my answers.'

'I am writing a story about the Jinuo and would like to know more about your religious customs. Can you tell me about the sacrifices? How often do you perform them?'

'We hold sacrifices all year round. Before we sow the seeds, cut the corn, hunt, build a house.' He bowed his head when he spoke.

'And funerals?'

'When someone dies we kill a pig and hang the head and trotters on a tree above the grave.'

'I saw a grave hut on the fields today. There were bones inside. I suppose the dogs must have dug them up.'

'No, it wasn't the dogs. Most families can only afford one grave so they must dig up the old bones before they can bury the new.'

'What if two people die in the same week?'

'Mmm, that hasn't happened yet. A year after the funeral, families stop putting food in the grave hut and perform a ceremony to send off the soul. After that they can remove the bones.'

'What do you chant in that ceremony?' The oil lamp was too dark for me to see my notebook, so I switched on my torch.

'Mmm, I have forgotten most of it.' He began to chant in Jinuo, translating some words for me as he went along. 'Valley path . . . twin boulders . . . Hill of the Parting Stream . . . horsegrass, brushwood . . . White Ghosts' Lair . . . Cave of the Spirit Lovers . . . It describes the route the soul must take on its journey home. At the end of the ceremony I say: "Go! It is time for you to leave and return to the land of our ancestors. We have killed a chicken to see you off. Go! You will not miss us." Then I repeat the details of the route.'

The glass shade above the oil lamp was encrusted with burnt mosquitoes. We sipped the rice wine I had bought in the village store, and chewed on some raw spring onions. Shabulu looked down and stroked his enamel cup. His tall shadow on the grass wall behind made him look very small.

'The villagers say they come here when they are sick and you drive the demons from their bodies.'

'Most illnesses can be cured by eating some food from one's uncle's mouth. If the sickness is serious, relatives bring me rice, salt, eggs and ginger, and I recite from the scriptures. For very severe cases I kill a pig, but I need some help with that.'

While taking photographs that morning, I had seen two small

boats made of plantain leaves set on a mountain path. The Jinuo believe these 'spirit boats' carry diseases away from their villages. There were spells written along the sides and incense sticks burning on the prows.

'Sometimes it is necessary to take medicine though,' I said. 'Little Meina's foot is gangrenous. She will lose it if it isn't treated. Whatever her family smeared on the wound didn't seem to be working. I hope it wasn't food from her uncle's mouth.'

'Mmm, surely not. No one comes to me for cuts and bruises. I too believe in pills and injections.' He glanced up nervously.

'I've heard you can speak to the spirits. What do they look like? What do they say to you?'

'I never went to school. My father taught me everything. He could see the ghosts, I think. The teachings have been passed through my family for generations. I don't really understand them. I've forgotten a lot.'

Finally I asked him why he placed a curse on the village teacher. Apparently, when Shabalu drew lots and announced the teacher was possessed by demons, the villagers beat the poor man to death and chased his wife into the jungle. She was found a few months later hanging from a tree.

'Mmm, I still don't know why I said that. I have done my time in prison for it though. I won't make that mistake again.'

He was released from prison a while ago, but the trauma of his years behind bars was still etched on his face. He missed the upheavals of the Cultural Revolution and the hordes of city youths who flooded the village to eradicate feudalism and superstition. By the time he got out, the village had four Party members, nine league members and the head of the Jinuo Autonomous Region was a graduate from Beijing Nationalities Institute.

The white enamel cup and grey mosquito net were the only bright objects in the hut. Everything else was buried in darkness.

When the unexpected happens, people seek answers in rocks, trees and stars. The fear of things we can see diverts us from the fear of things we cannot. When I was lost in the mountains at night and a bright light appeared before me, my first thought was that my grandfather had come to rescue me.

Into the Jungle

All afternoon the long-distance bus trundles into the mountains up a narrow, twisting road. I am lucky to have a seat. Although the plastic seat-cover sticks to my sweaty thighs and my headrest is torn and filthy, at least I am not squashed among the passengers in the aisle. I close my eyes and remember how green the air was during my trek through the jungle to Bulangshan. When I entered the rainforest at Menglong, the air smelt of green sap, and huge pineapple trees towered above me. I crawled like a mouse between fallen trunks and through chinks in the walls of leaves. My feet seldom touched the ground. The long, musty lianas hanging from the canopy made the jungle look like a deserted cathedral. Insects stuck to my hands and face and bit ferociously.

That area of primeval forest is still inhabited by the Bulang, Lahu and Ake tribes. An hour into my trek the path petered out. I pushed through the leaves and found a track of broken branches and followed it for three hours until I came to a clearing on a mountain top. Someone had died in Menglong, and their family had come here to fell a mahogany tree for the coffin. The track I had just followed was the path the trunk had made. The cut branches lying on the ground were over ten metres long and the tree stump was big enough to sleep on. Sunlight poured through the hole in the canopy. A circle of mushrooms rotted among the leaves on the ground. Looking through the trees I could see more mountains in the distance and a river in the east.

I climbed down and discovered the river emptied into a huge swamp, enclosed on three sides by tall mountains. Branches and weeds floated on the surface and a buffalo carcass protruded from the reeds. I had no choice but to retrace my steps and loop round through the jungle. The forest was dark now. Thorns and brambles ripped my clothes and dug into my skin. I thought of Zhao Lan who spent five years in these forests during the Cultural Revolution. Her watercolours are always huge and green.

My two compasses were giving different readings, so I split the difference and headed towards what I hoped was north-west. As dusk fell, birds swooped back to their nests and small animals croaked in the undergrowth. Insects suddenly filled the air and swarmed into my mouth when I coughed. I chose a tall tree and climbed to a branch halfway up. I stuck my knife into my belt, tied myself to the branch with a length of rope and doused myself with tiger lotion. After draining the last drops of beer from my water bottle, I tied a chiffon scarf around my face and looked up. In the fading light, I saw a patch of white flowers above, but when I touched them they transformed into a swarm of white ants. I pulled my hand away and shook them off. Some hours later I heard a loud cracking of branches. It sounded like a family of bears. The moon was out but I could not see beyond my hands. It was long time before the noises stopped. I sat on my perch, terrified and exhausted, counting the hours till dawn.

The following day I reached a small village of grass huts, asked directions, downed a bowl of bitter tea and continued on my way. Before dusk I came to a Lahu settlement in a remote fold of the mountains. A naked child sunning himself on the balcony of a bamboo hut saw me and screamed. His mother came out and leaned over, her breasts tilting up like the eaves of her roof. When she realised a stranger had arrived, she shrieked and ran indoors, leaving her son to cry on his own. Soon, heads peeped out from every balcony. Two men smoking in a doorway watched me pass.

A half-naked woman with a shaved head sat with one breast in her baby's mouth, the other drooping towards her thigh like a courgette. A skinny chicken stared at me then jumped onto the village fence. A dog barked at the stick in my hand. A girl stood in the high grass chewing a stick of bamboo. Her cotton tunic was missing a sleeve, and her bare arm hung down like a peeled twig. A man crouching on a balcony stared at me blankly. He was wearing an old army suit and had a blue bag over his shoulder.

The Lahu believe all paths are evil. When the Han tried to build roads through the jungle in the 1950s, the Lahu waged a bloody attack. The few members of the tribe that survived the battles retreated deeper into the hills and refused to have any contact with their 'liberators'. The woman with the shaved head must have just married. Before their wedding day, Lahu women shave their heads and throw away all their jewellery. As I left the village I decided to hide in the mountains and loop back to spend the night in the valley behind. I suspected the Lahu might pursue me. They never kill on home ground. When I passed through the village again the next day, they took me for a ghost and ran away in terror.

A Han woman with long hair stood by a path, wearing a shirt, trousers and shoes. I ran up to her and said I was travelling to Bulangshan to interview the village head, but was afraid I would not make it before dark. She told me she taught in a school nearby and invited me to spend the night in her bamboo outhouse. Her husband examined my introduction letter under the oil lamp. He was having difficulty reading the handwriting so I told him he could take it back to his room and read it at his leisure. I asked them about their lives and they went blank for a second. The man said he worked on the fields and grew cabbages on their private plot. The woman said she had eleven students, and taught them writing, arithmetic and domestic chores. 'Is it safe for the Han to live here?' I asked. 'Yes, but the villages are a little backward. Some parents refuse to send their children to a

Han school. They say, if you want to teach them to speak your Han language, it is you who should be paying us! Only five or six children stay to the end of the year.'

I put some clean plasters on my cuts and blew out the lamp to save them the oil. I felt as weak as a punctured tyre. My spirit can return to nature, but not my flesh.

A bird sang out as it flew over the roof. I opened my eyes and saw the morning light filter through the bamboo walls and the cracks in the wooden door. I stepped outside. Clouds of white mist still shrouded the forest. The clearing was no larger than half a basketball court. The thatched hut opposite served as a cattle shed by night and a school by day. A few cows had pushed through the door and were strolling in the yard. I stepped inside the shed and found it filled with flies and dung. There were wooden stumps on the floor for the children to sit on. A blackboard hung on the bamboo wall at the back. I could still see some chalked characters from yesterday's lesson.

'Mao Zedong said: "China is poor, we must learn to be frugal ..." Read the text and explain how we know that Chairman Mao lived a simple life ... His socks are darned ... New words: frugal, remind, sofa, bodyguard, interview ...' The other characters had been wiped off by the swish of a cow's tail. I used that same textbook as a child in the 1960s. It had a story about Mao Zedong tucking his feet under the sofa when foreigners visited so they would not see his darned socks. To this day, whenever I see pictures of Chairman Mao, my eyes always go straight to his feet. A portrait of Mao Zedong hung from a metal wire above the blackboard, out of tails' reach.

The mist slowly lifted. I was very grateful for the good night's sleep, and to thank my hosts I offered to take their family photograph. The man said, 'Bet you'll never send it to us,' while the woman rushed indoors to comb her hair and dress the children. When I took out my camera, the man decided to join the group after all. The two boys sat on wicker baskets, rigid with fear. When the four startled faces stared into my lens the distance that separated our worlds seemed magnified. The sun rose above the school roof behind. I put on my pack, scribbled their address on a cigarette packet and promised to send them a copy. But the ink was washed away when I fell into the Nu River, and the photograph is still at the bottom of my bag.

In the morning I passed through a small Ake settlement, a remnant of a much larger village that was razed by the Han. I entered the largest hut and asked for a bowl of tea. The owner's possessions consisted of an iron pot, a woman, the string of shells around her waist and the key that hung from her necklace. The key was puzzling, because he clearly had no need for a lock. I gave them a snake I had killed on the way and took my leave. As I continued up through the mountains, I saw peasants prodding terraced fields with bamboo sticks and dropping seeds into the holes. The dung heaps that littered the path were covered with large tiger butterflies.

On the third day I finally reached Bulangshan, the mountain stronghold of the Bulang tribe. Women in blue tunics and black turbans twisted cotton and kicked their buffaloes along as they returned from the paddy fields. The little baskets swinging from their waists were full of insects they had collected for the evening meal. I stayed with the village head, Secretary Lu. His grandmother was over eighty. When I asked to photograph her, she smiled and flashed her black-stained teeth. The secretary's two daughters had beautiful eyes. They had not yet reached the teeth-staining age, but knew how to be shy in front of strangers. I gave them two lead pencils. I noticed a pair of plimsolls in the corner of the room and asked the secretary about them. He said he wore them to meetings at the town committee house.

In the next village I was told a frontier regiment nearby offered beds to visitors, so I marched there at full speed. When Instructor Chen heard how far I had walked he assigned me a bed and told me to rest. 'It is a miracle you didn't lose your way,' he said. 'You can relax now though. There's a road just north of here that goes straight to Menghai.'

My skin was lacerated with sunburn and insect bites, but I gritted my teeth and washed with soap and water. I had to sleep on my side that night. Instructor Chen came to me the next evening and said, 'How's your back?' I had taken a horse out that morning and when it cantered into the hills, I got caught in the branches and fell to the ground. I said, 'Better, thanks,' so he invited me for a stroll. Two kilometres beyond the camp, he took a gun from his pocket. 'You wanted to try your hand at shooting, didn't you? Here, have a go.' He pulled out a sheet of writing paper and stuck it to a branch twenty metres away. My first shot missed, but the next two went straight through the middle. The bangs echoed through the forest.

On the way back he told me he wanted to leave the army and return to his wife in Chongqing. He said she had visited him one Spring Festival, but had gone home after three days, vowing never to return to the mountains for as long as she lived. He was worried that after eight years in the army it would be difficult to find a job in the city, as employers demanded skills and qualifications now. We spent a lot of time together over the next two days, drinking tea and smoking. I told him about my friends in Chongqing, and the ballroom where I hugged a girl and danced the chachacha. He told me that in the Cultural Revolution he was political instructor to a group of city youths from Kunming. His wife was one of his students at the time. She was the prettiest girl in the group.

My cuts and bruises were beginning to heal. At noon on the fifth day, I said goodbye to Instructor Chen, folded up the map I had copied from his, and set off for the main road.

From Traveller to Fugitive

Just before dusk the long-distance bus stops again in the shade of a high mountain. There is a traffic jam ahead, apparently. We all stream off to take a look. A boulder as large as an oil barrel has fallen from a cliff and landed in the middle of the road. I push and it moves a little. I call the men crouched under the tree to come and help, but they just smirk, so I give up and walk away. Trucks loaded with produce are parked on either side. The evening sun sinks towards a distant mountain, then birds swirl in the sky and disappear. I wish I too had a nest to go to.

I remember that it was this time of day, two weeks ago, that I reached the Nu River and gazed upon its flooded expanse. The roadworkers I had passed the day before had said there was a ferry here, but it obviously did not operate during the rainy season. There was not a soul about. The nearest bridge was a fortnight's trek upstream. My heart sank as the rain poured down my face. The misty cliff on the opposite bank blotted out half the darkening sky. After the Nu leaves its source high in the Tibetan plateau it thunders south through steep, inaccessible ravines, and is of no use to man whatsoever. When it reaches the Burmese border though it slows down and becomes the mighty Salween – Burma's Yangzi. I waded down to the muddy bank and discovered the ferry boat tethered to a tree. It was a long flat raft consisting of eight bamboo rods, bound together with rope.

I examined the river. The water was grey with sediment. From the branches floating on the surface I could tell it was moving quite fast, but reckoned that with the aid of a pole I should be able to make it to the other side. I hacked off a stick of bamboo, tied my pack to the raft, pushed off from the tree and punted into the river. The water was calm at first, but halfway across it deepened suddenly and a fierce current swept us up. The raft

274

started hurtling downstream, straight towards a line of boulders. I rushed to the front and just as we were about to collide managed to jam my pole against the rocks. The raft turned in a circle and careered downstream backwards. I fell over, dropped the pole and grabbed onto the raft's rope.

The Burmese border was just thirty kilometres away. I knew that if the river swept me across the frontier I would be a rifle target for both the Chinese and Burmese armies.

A few minutes later we entered a whirlpool behind another line of rocks. Branches jutting from the boulders thrashed me as we swirled. I tore off my jacket, jumped into the river and tried to push the raft free. If I hadn't been holding the rope the whirlpool would have pulled me to the bottom. I held my breath and kicked to the surface. My eyes were filled with water, I couldn't see a thing. Another twirl and the raft swept free at last and continued downstream.

I saw a bend in the river ahead and knew it might be my last chance to make it to the other bank. I kicked my legs desperately trying to steer the boat to the right. As the raft slowed I grabbed hold of a branch and locked my legs around a boulder. At last my feet touched the riverbed. I pushed the raft onto the rocks, staggered to the beach, fell to the ground and retched. I lay on my back, limbs splayed, too weak even to move my face from the vomit.

It was still light when I woke. The rain had eased and the raft was still perched on the rocks. I felt as helpless as the fallen leaves drifting down the river. On both sides I was enclosed by high boulders, and behind me a sheer cliff towered to the clouds. Small clumps of weed jutted from its damp cracks. I was trapped, but I knew that somehow I would have to climb out of here before dark. I splashed my face in the river, took a swig of water and wrung out my jacket and plimsolls. Then I tied the bag to my back, stuck my knife in my belt and started up the cliff, carving footholds as I went. My legs tensed with fear. Occasionally, when

I grabbed hold of a firm clump of weed, I could pause for a moment and take a deep breath.

What was going through my mind? I knew if one stone slipped underfoot, if one clump of weed came loose in my hand I would drop to a certain death. I heard the torrents crash below and felt a damp wind wipe across my face. I wondered what to shout if I was to fall. I wanted to shout an obscenity, but could not think of one strong enough. I wanted to shout the name of a women I had loved, but no name came to mind. So instead, I focused my thoughts on the cliff and talked myself up. Don't touch that stone, it's loose. Put your foot here. Careful, that branch might pull your bag off. Those roots are firm. Grab them – that's right. Now, pull your right leg up. That hole should be deeper. Dig your nails in. The knife snapped suddenly and sand flew into my face. Don't touch your eyes, your fingers are covered in mud. I cursed, and with one eye closed, stared into the face of death. Two hours of climbing and I was still only halfway up. My bones were numb with fear. At one point I was so tired I almost gave up, but something inside drove me on.

The sky was nearly black when I reached the top. I lay down and stroked the firm, flat ground. After the hours of terror and torment, a strange calm swept over me. I knew now that I wanted to live. I wanted to walk into a warm house and speak to people. I wanted to go back to my home in Beijing and make a cup of tea. I found a path and, without thinking, followed it downhill. Before long it brought me to a small village.

As I walked through the gates two militiamen shone torches on my face. They pulled me inside a bamboo house, woke the policeman and announced they had caught a Burmese spy. The policeman sat on the edge of his bed and lit a candle. He then emptied my bag onto the table and told me to step back. A few children wandered in to stare. He shooed them all away apart from a girl with a runny nose who was probably the village head's daughter. When he realised he was still in his Y-fronts he took a uniform from under his pillow and hurriedly got dressed. My camera, cigarette pack, penknife, compass, rope and water bottle were arranged neatly on the table. I told him to check my documents first but he paid no attention. The elation I had felt at escaping death vanished at a stroke. My wet clothes stuck to me like a second skin. I was too numb to speak.

Man's greatest enemy is his fellow man, because only men take pleasure in inflicting pain. It is easier to battle against the forces of nature than to live among people. 'When did you cross the border? How many were there of you? What is your assignment?' The policeman launched into an interrogation. I asked to sit down. 'You have seen my documents. The introduction letter got wet in the rain, it's not my fault you can't read it. Give me some food and water, or I will not say another word.' The militiamen were still examining the photographs and tickets that had fallen from the pages of my notebook. The policeman ordered them to fetch 'Old Beijing', the village teacher.

After the teacher had deciphered the blurred characters of the introduction letter and exchanged a few words with me, he could tell I was not a spy. 'I saw a lot of his type when I was at the county school,' he told the policeman. 'Long-haired artists. The larger the town, the longer the hair. This gentleman has had lunch with a Party secretary and the camera you found in his bag is worth three tractors.' The militiamen looked startled at this news. The teacher told them to fry me some potatoes, while the policeman continued to thumb through my papers, trying to hide his embarrassment. I gobbled a bowl of rice and chatted with 'Old Beijing'. He told me he had visited the capital once during the Cultural Revolution and had shaken the hand of a Red Guard soldier who had shaken hands with Chairman Mao. He said the militia head attended a meeting in the county town recently and came back with the policeman's uniform, and that I should feel flattered, because he only wears it on special occasions.

The policeman tried to plot my route from the pile of wet bus tickets but found too many gaps. 'My director warned us that spies carry used bus tickets to trick people into thinking they live here,' he told the teacher. 'None of the tickets add up. Look, there is a ticket to Menglong, but no ticket out.'

'I trekked through the jungle to Menghai.'

'Trekked? A real Beijing journalist would get a chauffeur-driven car from the county government.' The policeman showed the teacher a plastic bag printed with the characters MADE IN HONG KONG. 'Look, where do you suppose he got this from?'

The teacher was stumped. I told them it was a bag that had wrapped a pair of socks I had bought in Guangzhou, but they did not believe me. In the end, the policeman decided I should be taken to the county town's Pubic Security Bureau.

They gave me a bed upstairs and told me not to leave the room. They said if I needed to piss I could do so out of the window.

The floors of the bamboo house creaked loudly. The only way to escape undetected was to jump out of the window. From the splash of my urine I could tell it was about a four-metre drop. I walked around the room trying to remember which floorboards creaked the most, then put my pack on, sat on the bed and closed my eyes.

I knew if they took me to the county town my life would be over. The police there would have been informed about my lecture in Kunming and my criminal record in Beijing. I would have been sent straight back to the capital and locked up for vagrancy and sedition.

I was woken by buzzing mosquitoes. It was past midnight. I could hear snoring next door. I shook my bed a little, the snores didn't stop, so I carefully crept to the open window and eased myself down. I left the village and climbed the hill, not daring to turn my torch on. Soon I could hear the river again. When my hand touched a concrete bridge I switched on my torch and ran.

Half an hour later the batteries ran out and I was plunged into darkness again. Cold shivers ran down my spine. I was on a narrow path on a high mountain ridge. One false step and I would roll to my death. I could hear the wind rustle through treetops in the valley far below. I wished I had the eyes of a mouse and could see in the dark. I crouched down and began to crawl like a pig. If my hands touched mud I shuffled forwards, if they touched grass I shifted to the left. I groped like this for hours until I could go no further. At last I collapsed and sank my face into the ground. Even if the militiamen had run at me with their guns, I would still not have had the energy to move. I was no longer a traveller, I was a fugitive on the run.

At that very moment a light appeared in the darkness. It was neither a torch nor a candle, nor a glow-worm shaking in the breeze. It seemed to come from another realm. It rose from a stream and floated through the trees then stopped by some branches ten metres away and slowly dropped to my eye level. I shut my eyes and tried to compose myself. Suddenly I remembered a story my father told me as a child. One night, when my grandfather had lost his way in a field of sorghum, a ball of fire appeared before him and guided him back home.

I opened my eyes and stood up. He is here. My grandfather who died in a communist jail before I was born has come to my rescue. I walked forward and the ball of fire followed me through the branches, guiding my way for twenty kilometres until the sky turned white.

Selling Chiffon Scarves in a Traffic Jam

The driver grumbles, 'Looks like we're stuck here for the night,' then swings his legs onto the dashboard and falls into a doze. We should have reached Dali two hours ago. The passengers start fighting for sleeping space. I cannot sleep while it is still light, so

I wander outside and count the stationary vehicles. Seventy trucks, three tractors. If that boulder isn't moved, there will be even more tomorrow. Thank goodness I have a seat. I climb back onto the bus, sit down, tug the raincoat from my bag and drape it over my head.

I am woken in the morning by rowdy peasants banging on the bus trying to sell us their boiled eggs. At noon they are joined by people selling home-made ice lollies, biscuits and sugared prunes. One man turns up with a wok and starts selling pancakes and fried rice. The road inspector arrives in the afternoon. He has a gammy leg. He clambers onto our bus and says, 'I'll call the roadworkers out, but it'll take them a day to get here,' then he takes a cigarette from the driver and hobbles away again. Suddenly it occurs to me that even if the boulder were shifted no one would be able to move because the trucks are double-parked. I feel tempted to take my bag and walk, but decide it would be a waste of a four-yuan ticket. So I stroll outside instead, buy a bag of boiled eggs and sit under a tree with my notebook.

Last week, when I arrived in Baoshan after my narrow escape from the police, I sought refuge with Li Chengyuan, the editor of *Peacock* magazine. I was afraid to venture outside in case the local police had been notified about me. So I stayed indoors most of the time, writing letters. I sent Wang Ping a poem and a large butterfly. I wanted to ask her to write back to me, but was still not sure where I would be next month. I sent Lingling my notes on the Wa tribe, and an embroidered bag I bought last month in Xuelin market.

Xuelin was a small Wa village in the Awa mountains, close to the Burmese border. On market day, Wa peasants came down from the mountains to sell their meagre wares. Their skin was dark and coarse, and brought to mind their mythical ancestors – the mud creatures. According to legend, two sexless creatures walked through a garden and heard a snake tell them to pick fruit from a tree. The first creature ate two and the fruit became breasts, the second ate one and the fruit became an Adam's apple.

Although the Wa women had torn clothes and callused hands they found ways to express their femininity. Some had woven black skirts and embroidered the hems with yellow and red flowers. One old woman wore a bicycle chain as a necklace. Girls who could not afford bracelets wore rubber bands instead, and rouged their cheeks with spit and a rub of cheap red paper. Women who owned no scarves wrapped shirts around their heads and decorated them with sprigs of wild flowers. Traditionally, Wa women spent their time making life beautiful while the men were busy severing heads. A nearby village once stole a bull from Xuelin, and in the fight that ensued four hundred people were decapitated.

An old woman selling a garlic bulb bought a bunch of herbs and stuffed it through the large hole in her earlobe. A little girl sat on the pavement trying to sell a scrawny hen. I gave her five mao, told her to feed it up and sell it when it was bigger. Naked children scoured the streets like hungry chickens, searching for grains of rice. Occasionally a Wa trader from Burma strode through the dirty crowds in clean clothes and shiny shoes.

I will never forget the Xuelin villagers who lived in those conical straw huts. They each carried a bamboo pipe that was specific to their gender and age. Boys played loud courtship tunes on four-holed *dangli*, girls blew love songs on small, flute-like *lixi*, and old women whistled simple melodies on their two-holed *enqiu*. After a day on the fields, they would return to their huts, pour themselves a bowl of home-made rice wine and listen to an old man play love songs on a one-stringed lute. In the morning they would run to fetch mountain water from the village pipe, tie their babies to their backs and set off for the fields. I stayed with the village head. On my last night, his wife cooked a chicken stew. After dinner we huddled around the pot of simmering pig slops, and I asked them what they wanted most, because I could not believe that life could be so simple. Almost everything they wanted I could buy in a flash, but I still did not know what I wanted. My notebook says:

Bilisong, village head, 47: I want a brick house that keeps the rain out, like the ones in the county town.

Kanggeng, Bilisong's wife, 43: I want a gold tooth. (She smiles. Her teeth are perfect and white.)

Sangamu, Bilisong's daughter, 25: A watch, and an alarm clock.

Abengyi, Sangamu's husband, 30: When I'm rich, I will buy a bicycle.

Junmei, Sangamu's daughter, 5: I want an ice lolly.

Biniou, Sangamu's son, 10: A dog like the frontier police have. One will do.

Eiwo, Bilisong's daughter, 18: I don't want anything.

Eiwo is weaving cloth for a skirt. She always curls her toes when she speaks. I gave her a chiffon scarf the other day and she has worn it ever since. She always sits furthest from the fire. The pigs in the sty below stick their tongues through the floorboards by her feet, licking around for scraps. I've lost two pencils to them already. Eiwo's lips are so thick they stick out beyond her nose. When she sings her nostrils tremble. Last night she sang a Wa folk song called 'Let Me Run Away With You'. The translation goes: 'Let me come with you. If our water runs out, we can drink our saliva. If our saliva dries up, we can learn from the wind-monkeys and drink the wind.'

The Wa believe a new hut has no soul until the house spirit has been summoned. They entice the spirit into the hut with chants and a potion made from wine, oxtail and dried rat. Whenever an object is bought, money-ghost ceremonies are performed to ensure the ghost does not stay with its past owner. If a stranger approaches the hut during the ceremony, they rush out to shake his hand, as they believe he carries the money ghost.

The next page says:

May 21. Beautiful weather. I hired a guide in Xuelin to smuggle me across the Burmese border. We looped round the official border post and sneaked into Burma at Zuodu. The exhilaration of leaving China was overwhelming. I felt like an escaped prisoner. I tore off some leaves for mementoes. We crossed ancient woodland and fields of high grass and saw a mountain village with the same conical huts as Xuelin and Zuodu. We climbed over its wooden fence. There were lots of pigs but very few people. It looked like a model primitive village. My guide was afraid of crossing Decapitation Gully alone, so he found a local to take us through. The gully was indeed quite frightening. Looking up, all I could see was a thin line of sky. In the past, neighbouring villages met here to fight their battles. The victors would march home with severed heads and stick them on the village gates. I remember Chairman Mao politely suggested to a Wa delegate in Beijing, 'Now that we have entered the modern age, surely you could rethink the custom of placating grain gods with human heads. Perhaps you could use monkey heads instead.' Following that remark, the skulls were removed from the Wa gates and the decapitation custom slowly died out.

Suddenly my two guides stopped and started whispering to one another. I was afraid they were discussing my head. The knives dangling from their waists were longer than mine. I sneaked a knife from my bag and stuck it in my belt, then asked them what the matter was. They muttered in Wa and pointed to the sky. At last I guessed from their gestures that a bird had flown across our path and it was dangerous to proceed. I said we could rest for a while and wait for a bird to cry out ahead. According to Wa custom, if a bird sings on the path behind, you should turn back immediately.

I put my notebook down, lean back against the tree and close my eyes. All I took from that foreign land were memories of old women with caved stomachs, girls with bloodshot eyes selling loose tobacco, a desperate mother crouched by a pothole, dropping potatoes to her son who had fallen down four days before while out picking berries, and a man dragging a banana tree to market hoping to earn some drinking money. People who live isolated from the modern world maintain their traditions, but also their poverty. In just thirty years the population of Xuelin has grown from three hundred to two thousand. The mountains' resources are stretched to the limit, and the people have no choice now but to build a road. I rushed across that land, knowing I would never return. Those villages belonged to the past. My destination still lies ahead, somewhere on a different path.

The next day the roadworkers have still not arrived and the line of trucks is nearly four kilometres long. Business is roaring. To pass the time, I take out the chiffon scarves I bought in Kunming and planned to use as presents, and start selling them for two yuan a piece. Our bald driver is still standing inside the bus trying to sell off his consignment of ducks before they die of starvation. He charges one yuan for a live duck and five mao for a dead one. Peasants who bought the birds yesterday have roasted them at home and are now selling them for twenty yuan. The makeshift stalls are selling their chillied beans, spicy peanuts, tobacco, tinned beef and beer at double yesterday's prices. A couple of newlyweds take turns to guard the presents stacked in the back of their truck. The bride's dress is filthy. She is asleep in the driver's cabin now, mouth wide open. The pink silk roses in her hair are crushed flat. The groom is in the back, whisking the flies away as he rubs his dead pig with salt. Someone tried to steal some cement from another truck last night and the driver beat him so badly he had to be rushed to the county hospital. The policeman who has come to investigate told me the driver is the son-in-law of a local Party secretary, and will probably be let off scot-free.

I sell ten scarves in an hour. As I sit beneath the tree on my folded jacket, my mind returns to Li Chengyuan's comfortable sofa that I slept on a few days ago. His study was neat and tidy. There was a potted jasmine in the corner and all his books were bound in leather. His wife belongs to the Dai nationality and is a nurse in Baoshan Hospital.

Li Chengyuan is a very cautious man. He does not smoke or drink alcohol. He insisted I visit the local clinic for an inoculation against Japanese encephalitis. He is one of the few city youths who decided to remain in the countryside after the Cultural Revolution. He said there were subsidies for living in the frontier regions, and that the salaries were higher. The stalls outside his house sold large-grain Zhefang rice, the smell was delicious. The streets were full of foreign goods that had been smuggled across the border at Wanding. But drugs were rife too, and the town already had two detoxification centres.

He told me many of his friends escaped to Burma in the 1970s to join the communist guerrillas. I asked him how the city youths managed to clear so much of the rainforest. He took a swig of tea and said, 'We burnt the trees then detonated the roots. Our political instructor made us dig one metre into the soil. He checked it with a ruler. Said it was our political duty to "expose the roots". Chairman Mao wanted us to "Change Heaven and Earth". We worked like slaves.' He told me a girl from his group went for a piss in the jungle and was attacked by a swarm of hornets. The boys stood and watched her writhing in the sea of yellow insects, but not one of them dared go to her rescue.

His group spent a week in the Jinuo mountains, felling a sacred banyan tree to make way for terraced paddy fields. The tree had one hundred trunks. The locals called it Niunaixiu. All that remains of it now is a patch of dry land.

'How did you get through those eight years? I wouldn't be able to last more than a month in those mountains,' I said, rubbing cream onto my insect bites.

'There was a road seven kilometres away, with a petrol station and a farm shop that sold ice lollies and mangoes. We went there every Sunday to buy tins of canned meat. We sat under trees with a lolly and cigarette, and watched long-distance buses pull up at the petrol station and passengers get off to stretch their legs. Those people were our only contact with the outside world. They told us about the arrest of the Gang of Four, bell-bottom jeans, ballrooms opening in Shanghai. We knew about tight trousers two whole weeks before the central authorities banned them.'

'But you could write to family and friends, surely they kept you in touch.' When my brother was sent to Inner Mongolia, he visited us every two years and always left with large supplies of lard and soya sauce.

Li Chengyuan stared at the tea cup lid twirling between his fingers and said, 'I have not told anyone this before, you must promise to keep it a secret. My real name is not Li Chengyuan, it's Li Aidang. My parents were murdered in the Cultural Revolution because of the names they gave to my brothers and me. Being the youngest child I could have stayed in the city, but I knew it would be safer to leave.'

'Aidang – love the Party. What's wrong with that?'

'My brothers were called Aiguo and Aimin. Get it? Love the Guomindang!' He smiled bitterly. 'My parents had no idea, you see, never occurred to them. Guo-min-dang. Who would have guessed? In 1979, there were still seventy thousand city youths stuck in Yunnan. Forty thousand went on strike, demanding to be let home. I didn't join them though, I had just got married and wanted to stay out of trouble. Then the government announced that everyone could go home except for married couples. The next day a few shame-faced couples filed for divorce. By the second day, there were five hundred of them queuing outside the registrar's office. The government then stipulated that divorces would have to be registered within the next seven days to have any effect. You can imagine the chaos. Suddenly there were seven thousand couples queuing for divorce. It was a sobering sight. Half an hour before the deadline, hundreds of frustrated couples stormed the office. The walls collapsed and several people died in the crush. In the following weeks the streets were filled with abandoned children. Some parents tied their babies to bicycles and stuck notes on the handlebars that said: "Whoever takes my child can have this bicycle." '

When people have no sense of self, relationships are just temporary distractions from the inner emptiness and fall apart at the first obstacle. My brother's friends used every means possible to secure return permits to Qingdao. Some slept in tight bandages for six months and were sent home with crippled limbs. Some chopped their fingers off. Our neighbour Zhang Li took pills on the sly and was discharged with liver disease. They were proud of their injuries. But proudest of all were the girls who gained their return permits by sleeping with village heads and political instructors. Li Chengyuan never wanted to leave though. He was afraid of the cities. He was afraid of himself. He said life was safe in Yunnan because if the government decided to launch another campaign he could escape across the border.

My last scarf is sold. I have made twenty yuan, but feel uncomfortable seeing all the women walk by with my pink chiffon scarves on their heads. A man walks up to me and asks whether I want to buy one of the water bottles dangling from his neck. I tell him I have an army bottle. He says plastic bottles are much lighter, and he'll sell me one for just two yuan. I tell him to bugger off.

My patience has run out. I fetch my bag from the bus and start walking. I reach a hostel before dark. Dali is just a day's trek away now. Next week, I will continue to Lijiang and explore the matriarchal Naxi villages around Lake Lugu, then I will cross the Yulong mountains and head into Tibet. I hope that there at last I will find a place where man can live close to his gods.

9.

A Land with No Home

Buddha and the City

He strides ahead, waving me on occasionally with his army cap.
We are nearly four thousand metres above sea level and climbing
a hill, there is no way I can keep up with this local boy. On my
first day in Lhasa I played basketball with Mo Yuan and Liu Ren
and collapsed after just ten minutes. The boy has followed me all
day, watching me take photographs. He loves to look through my
camera at the crowds on the street.

We sit down for a rest. At our feet lie broken prayer stones and
yak horns carved with the six sacred syllables. The view is
perfect. Not a road or telegraph pole in sight. Just the red and
white Potala Palace rising from the cliff, swallowing the sun's
rays and the hearts of the pilgrims. I have been here a month, but
have still not visited the palace. Every day a man crouches below
its walls carving mantras, boddhisattvas and auspicious symbols
into the rock. He strikes his chisel with complete concentration
as the dust flies into his face. When he pauses to rest or meditate
his body seems to merge into the cliff. The images of Avalokiteshvara, Boddhisattva of Compassion, daubed with rainbow
aureoles stare at him with piercing eyes. He has carved the cliff
for five years, apparently. The pilgrims who pass on their way to
the prayer wheels drop coins or food by his feet. Once I spent a
whole day seated behind him, trying to discover the source of his
faith.

I look in wonder. The boy seems pleased with my expression.
He is a good guide. He led me here through a maze of side alleys
and backyards. I would never have found it by myself. I position
my camera on a heap of stones, adjust the focus and aperture,
place the boy's finger on the button and ask him to take my
picture. But before I get to my feet, he presses the button with the
force of a shepherd restraining a wild sheep. I sweep the broken

291

stones away, reposition the camera and take a picture with the self-timer instead.

The boy gestures it is time to leave. I follow him through more narrow streets to a small hillside temple. He walks in and wriggles up a tunnel at the back. I climb up behind him to a cave filled with the acrid smoke of yak butter lamps. I move forward and see a lama seated beneath a gold buddha. The lama lifts a black stone in the air and slams it onto the back of a woman crouched at his feet. The woman looks up, bows appreciatively and disappears down a hole behind. The stone then crashes on the boy's back, and he wobbles and creeps to the side. Without thinking, I crawl up and close my eyes and wait for the stone to strike. But the lama sees me and shouts in Chinese, 'Han man! Han man!'

I glance at the stone hovering above and say, 'No, no, I'm from Hong Kong!' This is not the first time in Lhasa I have used this lie to get me out of trouble.

After a moment's hesitation, the lama bangs the stone on my spine then shouts, 'Hong Kong man, go!' and I crawl out behind the boy's bottom.

As we wander along the Barkhor – the pilgrim path that circles the Jokhang Temple – the boy sticks his hand into cracks in the wall and pulls out clay tablets delicately moulded with images of Manjushri, Boddhisattva of Wisdom and Vajrapani, Eliminator of Obstacles. From a gap in a large incense burner he takes a warm tablet of eleven-faced Avalokiteshvara and gives it to me as a present. After that I become his obedient pupil. He teaches me the correct way to rub a buddha's feet and spin the prayer wheels. When he sees a hole in a rock he tells me to insert my hands. I cannot understand his explanation, so I content myself with feeling the cool. He makes me copy his every move. At the banks of a stream, he leans down to drink then waits for me to do the same. I put my mouth to the water but only pretend to swallow because a few metres upstream a pack of crows is devouring a dead dog. He performs a full prostration, then I too fall on my stomach and scrape my forehead on the ground. At last he looks satisfied. I sit down to catch my breath, my back still aching from the lama's stone. Then a voice calls from a window and the boy runs away. I never even got to buy him an ice cream.

In the evening I return to Mo Yuan's room in the grounds of the Tibet Autonomous Region Radio Station. Mo Yuan is a friend of Lingling's. He left for Guangzhou last week to attend a writers' conference and see his girlfriend Dali who has just graduated from Shenzhen University. He said I could stay in his room while he was away, as long as I look after Beimu, his Alsation puppy. He is very attached to her. He bred her himself. When I walk into the yard, Beimu jumps towards me and wags her tail. I feed her half a steamed roll and some leftover noodles, then go next door to have supper with Liu Ren.

A beef stew is simmering in his pressure cooker. We have had supper together most nights, taking turns to cook. Last week I made a hundred yuan from painting two large advertisements on the hoardings outside the radio station, and then the local government contracted me to design an exhibition on the geology of Tibet. To celebrate my good fortune, I bought two bottles of rice wine and some tinned meat yesterday and invited some friends round. It is impossible to cook at this altitude without a pressure cooker, though. My stir-fries were raw and tasteless.

Liu Ren hands me another book on Tibetan Buddhism while I tell him which temples I visited today. 'I seem to have lost some of the excitement I felt when I first arrived. Especially after talking to the lamas. Many of them are probably just peasants who were too lazy to work on the land. When the Dalai Lama fled to India, he must have taken the best lamas with him. The communists did not just drive the spiritual leader from Tibet, they removed the soul from its religion. The temples feel like museum pieces. When my designs are finished, I might travel into the countryside. Get a change of air.'

'You're in luck, then. A group from my office is going to Yangbachen next week. I'll ask them to give you a lift.' He pulls on a woollen tank top. The nights are cold here even in the middle of summer. Liu Ren's face is identical to mine. Same beard, same ponderous eyes, same involuntary scowl. We look so alike that I can cycle through the compound gates on my bicycle without having to register. Once on my way out, a man stopped me and said, 'Why didn't you come up yesterday?' I had no idea what he meant so I mumbled, 'I've just come down,' and peddled away at full speed. When I told Liu Ren he said, 'That was the deputy chairman, you fool. There was a Party members' meeting on the third floor yesterday. I should have attended, but I skived off.'

'You seem troubled tonight. What's up?' I ask.

His nose twitches like mine. 'Nothing. Pass me a fag.'

He doesn't usually smoke, and his face goes red after just two sips of beer. When he has finished presenting his radio programmes, he returns to his room, sits in front of a picture of his wife and a photograph of the blind Borges torn from a literary magazine, and works on his short stories.

'Seen anything interesting today?' he asks. 'Oh by the way, I found these letters for you on Mo Yuan's desk.'

'Got hit on my back with a black stone,' I reply.

There are two letters. One from Li Tao and one from Fan Cheng. Yesterday I received a bundle of post that had accumulated for me in Chengdu. In the covering letter, Yang Ming said she has divorced Wu Jian and plans to study English and go abroad. Wang Ping has not replied to the postcard I sent her from Lijiang. I have not heard from her for four months.

'Ha! The sacred stone! Tibetans only visit that cave when they are sick. They believe the stone can strike disease from the body. You must be careful where you take your camera, Ma Jian. You can't go snooping around like that. Relations between Han and Tibetans are very tense. If you cause any upset the rest of us will have to pay the price. When I first came to Lhasa, the Tibetans held a water-splashing festival – completely bogus of course. No one has a water splashing festival in the middle of winter! It was just an excuse to vent their anger. If a Han walked past, they splashed him with water. It was very frightening. None of us dared go out. They dragged a colleague of mine off her bicycle and poured freezing water down her shirt.'

'I have been travelling for three years, but this is the first time I have sensed there are places on this earth where my feet should not tread. Perhaps that's how it feels for those people who go abroad. The Tibetans have been pushed to the limit, they have a right to be angry. Imagine if you invited some friends for supper and they decided to move in and take over your house. It is not the loss of power that hurts, it's the loss of dignity and respect. A man tried to steal my camera in the Barkhor today. The strap was tied to my hand, but he tugged and tugged. His friend tossed a yak hide over our hands so the police wouldn't see. The thing was still dripping with blood. In the end he gave up. I threw the hide off and held my camera in the air, daring him to have another go. But he just spat at me and walked away.'

I pour some hot water into a basin and wash last night's bowls and chopsticks. Then I sit down and take the clay tablets from my pocket. 'So how did the water-splashing festival end?' My ballpoint pen has leaked and Avalokiteshvara's faces are stained with blue ink.

'Same as usual. "Political power grows out of the barrel of a gun" as Old Mao said. The soldiers stood on the streets waving their guns and everyone went home. We bear the brunt of the anger though. Tibetans can spit in our faces but we're not allowed to fight back. They have huge daggers dangling from their belts but we can't carry so much as a fruit knife.'

The wooden chest I am sitting on is draped with a soft Tibetan rug. Liu Ren meets many Tibetan artists through his job and his room is crammed with their gifts of religious scroll paintings, opera masks, thigh bone horns and ritual conch shells. Liu Ren fetches the egg and tomato soup from the stove and pours it into wooden bowls.

'What have you gained from these four years in Tibet?' I ask him. He was assigned to the radio station after graduating from Shaanxi Nationalities Institute. At the time boys who applied for posts in Xinjiang or Tibet were the heroes of their universities, and were worshipped by girls for their bravery and self-sacrifice. But times are changing, and now the best students dream of moving south to make their fortunes in Guangzhou and Shenzhen. In the market yesterday I bumped into one of the Hebei boys I met in Golmud. He told me he likes his job at Tibet Press, but his friend found life too hard here and returned to China after the first week.

'Quite a lot. There are only two things people write about in China: the contradictions of market socialism or painful memories of the Cultural Revolution. Tibet has so much more to offer: relations between man and man, man and God, the primitive and the modern. *Tibetan Literature* is featuring our work next month. I think it will make a great impact. They have dubbed us the Asian Mystical Realists.'

'Sounds interesting. But be careful not to form a group or you will lose your individual voice. That Roots Group is a farce. They write stories about brave men killing wolves in the grasslands, but never mention communism, which is the biggest wolf of all.'

I remember the political argument we fell into last night, so I stop talking and take a chunk of beef.

'And what have you gained from your month here?' Liu Ren asks.

'I didn't come as a tourist, or a writer looking for exotic stories. I came as a pilgrim. I was hoping for a revelation, or confirmation at least, but now I am more confused than ever. I sense man and Buddha exist, but not in the same realm. I feel I have walked onto a stage. The people around me are absorbed in their parts, putting

296

on this great show, but nothing seems real. Every object looks like a prop. Since I have no part I am reduced to the role of a spectator, but there is nowhere to sit, so I have to mingle with the actors on stage. It is a terrible feeling.'

'It's not always a performance. The older generation worship the Buddha as sincerely as the Chinese used to worship Old Mao. For them life and religion are inseparable. The Buddha is in their every thought and move. I met some lamas in Drepung who have spent their entire lives in the monastery. Their souls are not human any more, they have reached a higher plane. Do you think the government can change all that?'

'Communism can wipe out individual rights, but it cannot destroy a nation's traditions. Although, when traditions are too strong, they can smother the individual as much as any political tyranny. This country is now caught between the two faiths. I saw little boys in Young Pioneer scarves drop their school bags in front of Jokhang Temple and perform five full prostrations.'

'Tibetans are different from us. They care little for material wealth. If you give them plimsolls and a packet of seeds, they will sell them the next day for beer money. But they are kind people, and when they accept you as a friend they will trust you with their lives. They are not as crafty or sly as the Han.'

'It's easy to be kind when you are poor. I've met a lot of kind people in my travels, but the cost of their kindness is exclusion from the outside world. As soon as a road is built, the kindness vanishes. The communists are pushing China into the modern age and our values are changing. Soon kindness will be perceived as a weakness. I came here hoping to see man saved by the Buddha's compassion, but in Tibet the Buddha cannot even save himself.'

Liu Ren picks the largest chunk of beef from the pot. The smell of meat has filled the room.

'For us Han Tibetophiles, Tibet is an escape from China, but we are drawn to it for aesthetic rather than religious reasons. So much of the culture is being lost, though. The Tibetans in our office are more westernised than us. They wear jeans and perm their hair. The only people left who can talk to us about art are a few mad painters hiding in the hills.'

'You shouldn't confuse art with religion. Buddhism is a very practical philosophy. Disciples have to abide by the rules and control their desires. But art requires you to push your individuality to the extreme and break all the rules.'

'What can I say to them, Ma Jian? I have a child, after all.' He changes the subject suddenly just as he did last night.

'What are you talking about?' I am slowly getting used to speaking to my mirror image.

'The work unit has received another vasectomy demand, and my name has come up. There are only three of us left to choose from and the other two have just got married.' He snorts, and I instantly think of the peasant I saw being sterilised in Guizhou.

'You can promise not to have another child, but don't let them operate. If I were you I would resign. You could go home, go travelling. No one is forcing you to stay here.'

'I like my job. You only have yourself to think about, but I have a family. Besides, I'm a Party member, I am expected to set an example.'

He is sitting on a wooden stool. The table is strewn with bones and half-eaten rolls.

Beimu has not barked for some time. I push the door open and peep outside. 'Oh no. Where's that dog gone?'

We run outside. The dog has vanished and so has the rope that tied her to the post.

My ears start ringing. 'Bloody hell. What's Mo Yuan going to say?' I grab a torch and run through the front yards shouting her name. The gatekeeper tells us he has just come on duty but has seen no one leave with a dog. We scour the office block, canteen, boiler room, water tower, then search the yards again.

'He gives me the keys to his room and I go and lose his puppy. What a disaster!' My throat is burning.

Back inside in the room, Liu Ren turns on the electric heater. 'Don't worry,' he says. 'She can't have left the compound. Maybe someone has stolen her. When everyone has gone to bed, we'll go out and have another look.'

A few hours later we creep outside and start whispering her name. Suddenly we hear a dog bark.

'It's her,' says Liu Ren. 'No doubt about it. That room belongs to Lobsang. He's one of our technicians.'

'Go and get her then. She might be hurt.'

'I can't. He's Tibetan, it could cause trouble. Let's wait for a while. He can't keep the dog in the room all night. He will have to take her out later and sell her in the market.'

'I'm not waiting!' I make for Lobsang's door, but Liu Ren pulls me back. We sit down and half an hour later the door opens and Beimu is dragged out. When I snatch hold of the rope, Beimu bounces at me and wags her tail.

'Why did you take this dog?' I shout. The man laughs awkwardly.

Liu Ren pulls me away. 'Please, Ma Jian. Don't make trouble.' He mumbles some placating words in Tibetan then tells me to take Beimu home. As I turn to leave, Lobsang whips his belt off and tries to hit me. I grab his hand but Liu Ren pounces between us and shouts, 'Ma Jian! Don't fight! You can run away, but the rest of us have to live here.'

Lobsang knows my hands are tied, so he catches up with us and starts thrashing Beimu with his belt. Beimu rolls to the ground and yelps in agony. I control myself and whisper, 'Stop, or you will get hurt.'

But he ignores me and continues to attack the dog. The people who have gathered to stare pull me back to Mo Yuan's room. I tie Beimu to the post, my hands still shaking. Then suddenly Lobsang runs up with a rock in his hand and throws it at the dog. It misses Beimu by a hair and smashes through Mo Yuan's wooden door. I untie Beimu and carry her inside, and tell myself if he comes at us again I will not hold back.

I lie awake for hours, smoking cigarettes. I have calmed down now, but Beimu has lost all her spirit. She is on the brick floor now, trembling with fear. Liu Ren brought her a plate of beef a while ago, but she didn't even sniff it.

Same Path, Different Directions

Three days after leaving Yangpachen, I am still walking south-west along the banks of a clear stream. The high plateau is covered by green grass and brown hills. The dark dips in the land are lakes.

As the sun reddens, wisps of white cloud drift to the horizon. I can tell the sunset will be beautiful. I check the view through my camera. There is no snow on the mountains to the east and the hills in the foreground make an awkward silhouette, I will have to climb the hill for a better shot. This region is wonderful for photography, but the land is criss-crossed with rivers and streams and it is easy to get lost. As I crest the hill the sun rolls below the horizon. I scan the grasslands in the fading light but see no sign of the pilgrims I have been walking with, or of their large white tent. I will have to sleep under the stars tonight.

I sit on a breezy slope and finish the biscuits I bought in Yangpachen. Then I dig into my pocket and pull out two lumps of dried yak cheese I pilfered from a stall in Lhasa. I pop one into my mouth. The taste is very sour at first, but as the lump softens it produces a comforting milky taste. I remember the girl I saw crouched below that meat stall on the dusty corner of the Barkhor: the lower rims of her eyes slightly swollen, cheeks blown purple by the grassland wind, forehead wrinkled in supplication. If someone stopped and looked at her with pity, she would cup her left breast and suck it, then smile affectionately. Her eyes were full of kindness and her smile was as pure as the grassland air. Dogs clambered over her feet, waiting for scraps of meat to fall from the butcher's knife. Now and then she chanted softly, 'Om Mani Padme Hum.' Can the Buddha really extinguish all suffering?

Before the wind gets up, I lay out my sleeping bag and snuggle inside with my shoes still on. I stare into the black sky and think about life and death. For Tibetans death is not a sad occasion, merely a different phase of the same reality. All that concerns them are the causes of death and the quality of the funeral. Where is the poetry in that? I think back on the lines of a poem I wrote a few days ago: 'In the silent graveyard/Let me, like the rain's song/ Dampen your shoulders again . . .'

Ma Jian, religion calms your spirit, but the Buddha does not fill your every thought, he has not entered your heart. Can you still call yourself a Buddhist then? No. All you believe in is a list of precepts and principles. My stomach feels empty. A cold wind passes straight through me. I roll onto my side and the hunger slowly subsides.

Today is 18 August. Three years ago in Beijing, I could never have guessed I would spend my thirty-third birthday alone in the wilds of Tibet. The pilgrim family I walked with today are trekking to Mount Kailash. The journey will take them six months, but their sheep are so thin they will run out of food well before then. The two yaks that carry their carpet and tent are as skinny as the sheep. The pilgrims wore tattered hides, I could not guess their ages. Last night I spotted their tent and went to ask them for some food. The man in the felt hat spat into a bowl, gave it a wipe with his sleeve, then filled it with ground barley and milk. This morning they folded their tent and continued along the pilgrim trail. I followed them all day, watching them chant with their hands in the air, praying for release from earthly suffering. They looked to heaven and saw liberation. I looked into the same blue sky, but saw nothing. The noon sun blistered my face.

I read in the newspaper that Liu Yu has reached Shanhaiguan. Now that he has finished walking the Great Wall, where will he go next? Everyone's lives are changing. Tian Bing wrote to say she is taking classes in qigong. Last year she thought it was superstitious nonsense and slapped me for giving a demonstration. Li Zhi, the underground poet I stayed with in Guiyang, is apparently a deputy to the People's Congress now, and has moved into a large government flat. I wonder what has happened to his kiln. The Daoist poet Yao Lu wrote and said his wife wants to leave the country and has filed for divorce. He asked if *Shenzhen Legal Journal* is still looking for an editor. When I told him about the vacancy last year he laughed and said Shenzhen was no place for intellectuals. I am still treading my path. But if it comes to a dead end, I suppose I could always go back to Beijing.

The Woman and the Blue Sky

Our bus grinds to the summit of the five-thousand-metre Kamba Pass. Behind us, a few army trucks are still struggling up the foothills. As the last clouds tear from the rocks and prayer stones and scrape down the gullies, Yamdrok Lake comes into view. When the surface of the lake mirrors the blue sky and bright snow peaks plunge head-first into the water, I am filled with a sudden longing to hug someone.

This is the road to central Tibet. When the bus descends to the foot of the mountain and careers along the shores of the lake, a foul smell of dank sheepskin wafts from the seats behind. I am squashed so tight my legs are numb. The girl next to me by the door is swathed in a thick cloak. She delves into its woolly folds and takes out hawthorn jellies and a pocket radio. Then she rummages again and pulls out a small sticky baby. She holds him up to piss on the floor then stuffs him back into her pouch. My shoes are splashed with urine. I try to shift my bag away from the puddle.

Outside the window the lake looks calm and wide. There is not a speck of dust in the air. I shout to the driver and ask to be let down.

August is the plateau's golden month. The sky is so clear you cannot feel the air. I walk to the shore, take the flannel from my bag and wash my face. A breeze ripples across the lake and sun rays shine on the pebbled bed. This is a beautiful place. In Tibet, since lakes are considered holy and the herders rarely bathe or fish, the waters are always pristine.

Nangartse town is still a few kilometres away. On a far mountain I see a cluster of adobe houses with prayer flags fluttering from each roof. Above them is a temple painted in bands of red, white and blue, and higher still, a freshly whitewashed stupa housing the ashes of dead lamas gleaming in the sun.

Below the village, by the edge of the lake, is a concrete building which I presume is the committee house. I get up and take out the introduction letter Liu Ren forged for me that says I am a guest reporter for Tibet Autonomous Region Radio. When I reach the house I discover it is an ordinary hut. A soldier opens the front door and speaks to me in a Sichuan accent. I hand him the letter and tell him I am conducting research into local customs. He invites me inside.

'This is a repair station. My name is Zhang Liming.' There is a rifle on his wall. The floor is littered with cable cutters, porcelain insulators and broken cardboard boxes. He is stationed here to service the army telephone line and maintain a smooth connection.

He looks delighted when I ask to stay. 'I have been here four years. If the telephone line is working, I fish on the lake or have a drink with the Tibetans in the village.' Or read books about ancient warriors, it seems – there is a stack of them on his desk, next to a dusty walkie-talkie, a cassette player, a few tapes and a tangle of red cables.

'Is there a sky burial site near here?' I ask, taking a wooden stool.

'Yes.' Liming is not tall. His cap has left a circle around his head.

'Any chance of a seeing a burial in the next few days?'

He pauses. 'There's one tomorrow. A woman died three days ago.'

'Really? What a coincidence. Do you think they will let me watch?'

He mumbles inaudibly, then says he needs to buy some drink for tonight. I take out some money but he pushes it away.

So I accompany him to the village. On the way I tell him about the changes taking place in China. Two years ago I passed through his home town, Zigong, and visited the new dinosaur museum. The huge unearthed beasts lay on the ground where primeval forests once grew. The buses outside ran on natural gas which was stored on the roofs in large black rubber bags that wobbled from side to side. Liming says he had no idea there were dinosaurs in Zigong. I mention my failed attempts to view sky burials in Lhasa. Either the ceremony was over before daybreak, or the locals forbade me to approach the site. Once they even threw stones at me. My friends said it would be easier to see a burial in the countryside.

'The people live differently here,' he says. 'There are a hundred families in the village, and in nineteen of them, the brothers all share the same wife.'

'You would go to prison for that in China. Although in Yunnan, I visited a Naxi village which still practises the Azhu system. Women can take as many lovers as they like. The more they have the higher their prestige.'

'Here a women's role is to mediate between her husbands and keep a good house.' He tugs at the brim of his cap.

'Sharing is a virtue that modern society seems to have lost. Could you take me to one of these families?'

'We are going to Sangye's house now. She is head of the village women's association and has three husbands. The oldest, Gelek, was the village's first entrepreneur. He built a grain mill last year and grinds barley for a living. He never charges widows or orphans. The middle one, Tashi, operates the village generator. He bought a truck recently and has started a delivery service. The third one, Norbu, is a bricklayer at Tashilhumpo Monastery. They live in the new house up there.'

I step inside their door and see a large poster of Chairman Mao, and on the lacquered chest below, a gold buddha surrounded by small incense burners and plastic flowers that are sold on every market stall. A few butter lamps flicker beside a photograph of the Panchen Lama.

Liming and I sit down. While he chats with Gelek in Tibetan I watch Sangye drop salt and tea leaves into a black kettle and carry it to the stove in the yard. When the kettle boils she pours the brew into a wooden churn, adds a dollop of yak butter, and stirs with a wooden stick. The liquid gulps and gurgles. Sangye is wearing a white shirt under a sleeveless robe that is tied at the waist with a striped apron. She knows I am watching her, she keeps turning round and smiling into the room. She brings the kettle inside and pours the tea into three wooden bowls. I take a sip. It is oily and salty but richer in flavour than the brew Tibetans served me from thermos flasks in Lhasa.

I take advantage of having an interpreter and ask Gelek about his family background.

He says that before Liberation his father worked for a living buddha to repay a ten-thousand-year debt. His mother's family owed the temple forty thousand jin of barley so she worked on their fields from the age of thirteen. When she was released from her duties in 1951 she met his father and got married.

'What is a ten-thousand-year debt?' I ask.

'It means you can pay back the interest but not the loan, so you are always in their debt.'

Tashi walks through the door smelling of petrol. He removes his sunglasses and white cotton gloves, extends his tongue in greeting, and takes the stool next to Sangye. The corner of her mouth rises towards him in a half-smile. Gelek explains his brother is just back from a trip to Shigatse.

I ask Sangye how much butter she uses for the candles. 'We are still quite poor. Yeshe's family has thirty-six candles. When they sheer their flock of sheep they can make two thousand yuan in a day. They invite lamas to recite scriptures every month.'

'Which scriptures?'

'We invite two lamas a year, three if we can afford it. We had two this year, they stayed with us for a week.' Perhaps Liming did not translate my question properly, or maybe it is not important what the lamas recite.

'We visit Tashilhumpo in the slow months,' Gelek says, picking a date from the table. He is on his second bowl of tea.

'If Tashi's business takes off, what would you spend the money on?' I watch Sangye's coarse hand stroke the corner of her prayer book. The red socks peeping between her trouser legs and black shoes are almost threadbare.

When the soldier translates my question everyone laughs.

'All his money goes back into his truck!' Sangye squeezes Tashi's leg. His eyes redden as he smiles. His speech is slower than his brother's.

'When we are rich, we will invite three lamas a month.'

'Wouldn't you like a wife of your own, your own family?' I ask Tashi. Liming fidgets with his cap, he looks uncomfortable.

'If we have too many wives it will split the family inheritance.'

'More wives mean more children, and children are expensive to keep.'

'Sons kill oxen and sheep, daughters tread on insects and worms, this is harmful to life.'

Before I have time to ask another question, Liming puts his cap on and stands up. Gelek goes to fetch us six bottles of beer. Liming places the money on the table and whispers, 'You shouldn't ask so many questions. They are not used to it.'

In the evening we open the beers and talk about sky burials. Suddenly he pauses and says, 'The woman was only seventeen. Her name was Myima. She haemorrhaged during childbirth. The baby is still in her womb.'

I crush my cigarette and watch his pale fingers rub the edge of the table. Five red stars and a regiment number are printed on the headboard of the single bed against the wall. Above his desk are posters of aircraft carriers and a photograph of a Japanese actress torn from a magazine. There is just one window in the room. The lower pane is pasted with newspaper. Through the top pane I can see the sky slowly darken. It has been hours since I heard a truck pass.

The soldier stands up, kicks an insulator out of the way and sprawls on the bed. 'You can go to the burial. The people are more relaxed here. Most of them have never seen a camera before. Myima's husbands certainly haven't.'

'How may husbands did she have?' As the question leaves my mouth, I realise how disrespectful it is. The soldier turns his radio down. A woman's voice sings through the speaker, 'You came to me with a smile but brought me only pain . . .' It reminds me of the Chengdu Ballroom and the girl in the red dress called Ding Xue. She was always humming that song.

'You will see her for yourself tomorrow.' He closes his eyes. 'Myima was not born here. She was a weak child, the youngest of eight. Her parents could not look after her so they sent her here when she was six. After a while she grew stronger, and even attended school in Nangartse – but that was before her adoptive mother died.'

'And what was her name?' I ask, opening my notebook.

'No. You mustn't write this down . . . Her adoptive father is a drunk. When he's had too much wine he starts singing and grabbing women. Sometimes he grabbed Myima. Everyone in the village knew. She was still a child. How could she defend herself?' His voice trembles, I can tell he is about to swear. When he was showing off just now, he let out a torrent of abuse.

'Fucking bastard! Wait till I'm out of this uniform!' His face flushes from red to purple and fumes with the stubborn rage typical of Sichuan men. I keep quiet and wait for his anger to subside.

He goes to the door to check the wind's direction. The telephone line is completely still. There are no mosquitoes up here, even in summer. Damp air from the lake rolls into the room and chills my bones.

'Will you take me to meet them?' I ask. He flinches, so I say, 'No, don't worry, it's not important.'

Without looking round, he puts his cap on, tugs the brim down, and takes the keys and torch from the table. 'All right then, let's go.'

We climb to the village again along dark mud-walled passages that are just wide enough for an ox to pass. My torchlight catches the straw and dung strewn along the paths. Behind the walls dogs begin to bark.

The soldier pushes through a gate and shouts towards a house with a lighted window. We step inside.

The men huddled by the fire turn and gape. The oldest one stands up and talks to the soldier, while the others continue to stare at me. I pass my cigarettes round, then light each one in turn. In the dark all I can see is the white of their teeth. I flick the lighter again and turn up the flame, and their jaws slacken. I hand the lighter to the man standing up. He takes it and sits down. Everyone's eyes focus on the lighter. They pass it round and smile at me. At last I feel I can sit down. The man on my right cuts me a chunk of dried mutton. I pull out my knife and take a slice. It tastes better than the meat I ate a few days ago in the pilgrims' tent. They pass us a bowl of barley wine. It is still green, there are husks floating on the surface. Perhaps Myima made it before she died.

The stench of dung smoke is so strong I can only take shallow breaths. As my eyes adjust to the dark, I look around the room. It is as simply furnished as most Tibetan homes, with whitewashed walls and wooden chests. Next to the front door is an opening into a dark chamber – Myima's bedroom, or the larder perhaps. Opposite the fireplace is a traditional Tibetan cabinet, a scroll painting of the wrathful Yama, Lord of Death, clasping a Wheel of Life, and a table draped with white prayer scarves.

The men eye me and nod. They are probably discussing my request to attend the sky burial tomorrow.

The soldier stands up and beckons me to follow him. He leads me to the dark chamber and shines his torch on a hemp sack that is tied at the top with telephone wire and stands on a platform of mud bricks.

'That's her,' he says.

I flash my torch on the sack. She appears to be sitting upright, facing the wall, head bowed low. Perhaps they had to push it down before they could tie up the sack.

Back in the soldier's hut, I lie on the bed, eyes wide open, thinking about Myima.

The living and the dead can only meet in the mind. I imagine her singing, like the Tibetan women I have heard in the hills, and in the backs of open trucks. I picture her bending over the fields, her long braids slipping over her ears. I give her the face of a girl I saw on a bus: large red cheeks, small nose, dark-rimmed eyes, round bosom. A bent paper clip holds her shirt together where the second button has come off. The dark dip inside trembles with each shake of the bus.

The soldier walks in from his nightly inspection of the telephone line. His face is blank. He lights a cigarette and lies down beside me.

Eventually he speaks. 'You'll be gone in a few days, so I might as well tell you. Besides, I can't keep this to myself much longer, the pain is too much.' I lift my pillow and sit up.

'Myima and I were very close, that is what kept me here so long. Most people would have applied for a transfer years ago. I first met her on that hill up there. I was walking to the hill behind to change a telephone wire. She had let her sheep out and was sitting on the grass. On the way back I was carrying a large roll of wire, it weighed a ton. I said hello and sat down beside her to rest. It was a hot afternoon. I was sweating even in my vest. She watched her sheep grazing in the breeze, then turned and stared at me straight in the eye. No woman had looked at me like that before.'

I remember the girl in the red blouse I saw in Maqu. She too stared at me like that before she escaped to the banks of the Yellow River.

'I told her I worked in the repair station. She didn't understand Chinese, and my Tibetan was still very poor, so I traced my finger along the telephone line to my house at the bottom. She laughed and turned her face to the Kamba Pass. She said she had seen me before, and asked why I had stayed here so long. Before I left her that afternoon, I cut her a long piece of wire and said she could use it to hang out her laundry or to tie things up with.'

'After that, we met quite often on the hill. She was the one who taught me Tibetan . . .

'Last year, at about this time of night, she came to my room and sneaked into my bed. She had never slept here before . . . She was the first woman I ever touched. In the morning she pushed me away and said she had to go home. Before she went, she took off the necklace she had worn since she was a child and put it under my pillow. The next day I heard she was getting married to Dawa and Dorje. If the army ever hear about this, I'm finished.'

I nod my head. 'Sleeping around on military service – they could lock you up for that.'

He pulls the necklace from a drawer filled with batteries and pencils. I study it under the lamp. It is a string of agate and wooden beads with a large turquoise in the middle. The stone is smooth and shiny, and still carries the milky smell of a woman's skin. My mind flashes back to the hemp sack on the platform of mud bricks.

'Did she visit you after that?' I want to say I will not to go to the burial tomorrow, but the words do not come out.

'I don't want to tell you everything.' He pulls the army coat over his face and rolls onto his side. I toss my stub on the floor, turn the light off and close my eyes . . . I sent my copy of *Leaves of Grass* to Ai Xin in Wushan and she wrote back from Beijing saying she was studying at Lu Xun School of Literature. At the end of the letter she wrote, 'I have a boyfriend now. A painter. He says he knows you. His name is Da Xian.'

Night and day are different worlds. At dawn, the winding passages have vanished and each path leads straight to a house. The night seems like a distant dream.

When I reach the sky burial site the sun is already up. This site is not a large boulder jutting from a cliff like the one in Lhasa, it is a broad gravel terrace halfway up a mountain between the foothills and the higher slopes. Dirty ropes hang from a metal post that is rammed into a crack in the ground. Beside it lie rusty knives, two hammers and a hatchet with a broken handle. The surrounding gravel is scattered with fragments of bone, human

311

hair, smashed plastic beads, scraps of cloth, and vulture droppings dotted with human fingernails.

The mountain is quiet. Black vultures sit perched on the peaks. In the valley below, ribbons of mist rise from Yamdrok and slowly roll into a single sheet that covers the entire lake. The mist then stirs and spreads, rising and falling over the foothills like a woman breathing, drifting higher and higher until it veils the blood-red sun. Three men emerge from the mist. Dawa, the elder brother, is lugging the hemp sack. The family probably could not afford to hire a body breaker. Dorje, the younger brother, carries a felt bag, a thermos flask and a flat frying pan. A lama in red robes follows behind. I recognise him as the man who sat beside me last night. Clouds of mist billow behind them. They smile at me.

The sack is opened and her body is pulled out. Her limbs are bound in a foetal position. The swastika carved onto her back has dried and shrunk. When the cord is loosened she flops to the ground. The brothers tie her head to the metal post and pull her body straight. She is lying on her back now, eyes fixed on the sky and the spreading clouds of mist.

Dorje sprinkles ground barley onto the flames of a juniper pyre he has just lit. The thick smoke merges into the mist. Dawa adds a dung pat to the fire on the other side, looks into the sky, then drops a lump of yak butter into the frying pan. The lama sits cross-legged on a sheepskin, counting his rosary beads over an open prayer book.

I study Myima through the lens of my camera: limbs splayed, breasts hanging to the side, palms upturned as if communing with the sky, belly still swollen with her unborn child. Her white feet are tightly clenched. The smallest toes are so short they have no nails.

It is a good thing the soldier is not here. He is probably upset I have come, or perhaps he wants me to be here, to say goodbye for him. I imagine Myima arriving at this mountain on horseback as a child of six, her little face peeping out from under her sheepskin cloak to catch her first glimpse of Yamdrok Lake. When she was up here last week tending her sheep, was she thinking of her home in the north, or of the soldier in the valley? One day she asked him, 'When will you take me to the cities where the houses are as tall as mountains?'

I press the shutter, but nothing happens. It is stuck. Suddenly I see the corner of Myima's mouth tremble very slightly. It was neither a smile, nor a sneer, but it definitely moved.

I tramp back to the fire and sit down. Dorje takes another dung pat from his bag and feeds it to the flames. Then he pulls out a lump of roast barley, blows the dung away and breaks me off a piece. I chew it greedily. There are raisins inside. He fills the lid of the thermos flask with barley wine. I grab it and down it in one, then take out my knife and hack at the dried mutton. The brothers smile at me. I smile too, perhaps, but my face is turned to the distant snowcaps that are reddening in the morning sun. The mist has gone now, and the lake is as calm and clear as yesterday, and as deep as Myima's turquoise. Dawa stands up and pours the lama some wine. The lama pushes it away and tells him Myima's soul has risen to the sky.

I follow the brothers back to the body. Immediately the sky darkens with screeching vultures that dive and wheel. Black crows cover the cliff waiting for their chance. The moment Dawa slits his knife through Myima's face and peels the skin back, I forget what she used to look like. Dorje chops her flesh into small pieces, hammers her fingers to a pulp and throws them to the crows. A pack of vultures fight over the intestines.

Myima's body disappears from the burial site. I think of the ritual bowl made of a human skull that I bought in the Barkhor. The bone is brown and burnished from years of use. It must have been dropped at some point in the past – the crack along the left side is filled with dirt.

313

At last Dawa staggers back to the fire, driving the birds away with a bunch of Myima's braids that are still tied with red thread.

I check my watch. I have been up here for two hours. It is time go down. The soldier is waiting for me in his room. He said he would borrow a boat today and take me fishing on the lake.

In the Sky, on the Road

When I leave the seat of Tingri county and set off for Everest on a path five thousand metres above sea level, I understand how hard it is for man to live in the sky. The air is so thin I have to breathe through my mouth. The ground seems to shake and the houses of the nearby village and the river beyond it appear to waver in mid-air. I think back to the show I saw a few days ago in Shigatse celebrating thirty-one years of 'peaceful liberation'. As soon as the Sichuanese troupe finished dancing 'Tibetan Girls Wash Clothes For Their Dear Friends, The PLA Soldiers' with beaming smiles, they rushed backstage and clamped oxygen masks over their faces. They travelled here on a political assignment, I came to find peace of mind. But Tibet's high plateau is no place for the Han.

I sit down at the village crossroads and try to catch my breath. Children slowly surround me. Some peer at my hair and face, others at my clothes, beard, camera. In the pauses between breaths I try to smile. Eventually I stand up and ask the way to the village committee house.

The village secretary attended Tingri county high school. In the time it takes to smoke a cigarette he reads my introduction letter. His face melts into a smile and five minutes later he looks up. I tell him the radio station has sent me here on a political assignment to climb Mount Everest. He is not interested in who sent me, but insists I cannot climb alone. A man started from here last year, and wrote a will before he left. When he returned two weeks later, his face was purple, his nose and ears lost to frostbite. He had to spend a month in the county hospital. The secretary rests his head against the wall. His dropsied face looks serene. 'Not everyone can touch Green Tara's face,' he says, very slowly. Then, after a long pause he adds, 'At the foot of Everest, is a river. If its waters do not freeze you to death, its ice rocks will break your bones.'

I gaze at the dusty willow in the yard outside and my heart sinks.

'There is a hill nearby you can climb, if you want a glimpse of Everest.'

'I heard expedition teams drive past here on their way to Base Camp.' I take out my fountain pen and mutter, 'I'll just fill up my pen if you don't mind.'

'But they are mountaineers, with professional equipment. That mountain is no place for tourists.'

'Well, are there any cultural sites near here?' When the cartridge is full I discover the ink is blue, not black as I had thought. I hate writing with blue ink. A wave of tiredness sweeps over me.

'I can introduce you to an eighty-three-year-old Nepalese silversmith. Two Lhasa journalists interviewed him this year. He's had his picture in the papers.'

'All right, I will see the Nepalese silversmith then. Is there somewhere to stay in the village?' My heart is still pounding.

'We have a small guesthouse.' He points to a string of keys hanging on the wall. 'But no restaurant, I'm afraid.'

So I stop and go no further. I will explore the village and head back to Shigatse tomorrow. When I collapse on the metal bed my mind turns to jelly. I open my map and notebook and try to organise my thoughts.

The village is not marked on the map, so I draw a red circle around Tingri. My path south is blocked by the highest mountain in the world. It was mad of me to come here. I have no equipment and no experience of climbing above the snow line. My notebook has lost its spine.

25 August. Gyantse. This morning I visited the huge, octagonal stupa also known as the 'Tower of A Hundred Thousand Images'. It was ransacked in the Cultural Revolution and the interior was cold and bare. The streets outside were empty, apart from a lone postbox at the crossroads. As I climbed to the fort behind the stupa it rained and I kept slipping down the hill. When the British force advanced on Gyantse in 1903, that hill was the main battleground. The Tibetan soldiers defending the fort were heavily outnumbered and many chose to jump to their deaths from the ramparts rather than die at the hands of the British.

Back in my hostel this afternoon, I met a living buddha from Sichuan who is travelling to Shigatse for a religious meeting. I fetched a prayer scarf and went to visit him in his room.

I told him I was a journalist and a Buddhist. He asked me who my teacher was, I said Master Zhengguo and he said he knew him well. He is 56 years old. At 8 he studied Buddhist scriptures at Sera Monastery and attended classes for young incarnate lamas at Drepung.

I asked him his views on the changes taking place in Tibetan monasteries. For example, in the past, the 1,200 monks of Tashilumpo Monastery relied on the community for their upkeep, but now the monastery has opened a Buddha Warrior Company and supports itself from the revenue of souvenir shops.

He said: 'The government has relaxed its policies on religion. Retired lamas receive a cadre's pension now and people are free to visit temples, give offerings and invite lamas to recite scriptures in their homes. But Buddhists are more concerned about the next world than the trivialities of the present. In the past, every Tibetan was a Buddhist and society was stable. But today's monks do not understand the scriptures. Their studies are poor. Their minds have been corrupted by the six dusts. All they seek is material comfort and this leads to suffering. There was more poverty in old Tibet, but less suffering than there is today. The more desires the deeper the pain.'

I said desires are not the only source of pain. Man can also suffer from a sense of helplessness, a feeling of being oppressed by society and having nowhere to turn. Then I asked about the punishments the religious leader Tsong Khapa stipulated for monks who violated Buddhist law: chopping hands, cutting lips, burying alive, drowning. I asked how a religion that promised release from misery could endorse such cruelty.

He said: 'Every religion has its rules. Those punishments only apply to the monastic order, and they are seldom carried out. In China, Daoist monasteries employ the death sentence. All suffering has its cause though, and man must learn to reap what he sows. Our punishments are the fruit of sins committed in previous lives. The only escape from a life of misery is to empty the craving from your heart. The Buddha said that the three realms of samsara are worlds of dust, filled with suffering. It is good to ask questions, but you should not be so concerned with success and failure. It will cause you much turmoil.'

I said: 'I became a Buddhist because I thought the world was full of pain and that Buddha offered a path to freedom. I was rebelling against the Party and all that it stood for. But now I see that although the communists have destroyed Tibet, lamas lay the blame on karma and the sins of past lives. The communists only allowed religion to return because it absolves them from responsibility for the pain they have inflicted. Buddhism is playing into the hands of the tyrants. And this has made me question my belief.'

He advised me to go back to my room and read the Sutra of the Pure Land.

27 August. Yatung. Met some Hong Kong tourists in Gyantse who were hiring a minibus south, so I chipped in and got a ride. On the drive down from the high plateau to the Yatung plain, the vegetation changed from grass to scrub to dense tropical forest. I met a man on the street today who works for the grain department. We started talking about poetry and he offered me a bed in his house. Yatung has wooden houses, and stands on a toe of land between the borders of Buthan and Sikkim.

30 August. Shigatse. This is the second largest town in Tibet. This morning I visited Tashilhumpo Monastery, the traditional seat of the Panchen Lama who is believed to be the reincarnation of the Buddha Amitabha. Beams of sunlight poured down the long red banners hanging from the wooden columns of the assembly hall. I saw an inner chapel filled with a thousand flickering butter lamps. A small girl was raising her hands to the gold buddha on the shrine. As the lama doused her with water from a silver jug, her eyes shone with devotion. Just as I was about to press my shutter, the lama jumped to his feet and shooed me away. I turned to leave, feeling guilty for disturbing the child. Then the lama shouted, 'Take picture, 20 yuan!' But I walked away and didn't look back.

The main chapel housed a 26-metre-high statue of Maitreya, Buddha of the Future. It was covered in gold and precious stones. The extravagance seemed offensive after the scenes of destitution on the streets outside.

On my way back to the hostel I saw the herder I met yesterday. He was sitting on the road begging, so I gave him a yuan. He told me he sold his hides this morning for a thousand yuan, and offered it all to the golden buddha. He will have to beg his way home now.

Is the Buddha saving man, or is man saving the Buddha? From now on I will hold to no faith. I can only strive to save myself. Man is beyond salvation.

I put down my notebook and stare outside the window at the grey sky above the grey wall. I wish I was in a room of my own. These four walls are splattered with spit and there are cigarette butts on the windowsill. In her last letter, my sister wrote: 'Some hooligan smashed your front gate last week, and seeing that it was left unrepaired, your neighbour took the opportunity to build a kitchen on one side of it and a coal shed on the other. He even had the cheek to nail his washing line to your front door. Don't pick a fight when you get back though. His mother belongs to the residents' committee.'

I pack my camera and go for a walk. There are very few houses at this altitude. That is probably a hamlet ahead, although it looks more like a sheep pen. The slate roofs of the stone houses nearly reach the ground. The path is soft and dry, each step I take lifts a cloud of dust that hangs in mid-air. A dog creeps under a fence and barks slowly. A girl looks out from under a roof, disappears, then emerges again with a mirror and sits down to comb her hair. The dusty path is scattered with broken slate. Behind me, girls approach carrying stones on their backs. They pass through my cloud of dust then stop to catch their breaths. Everything moves in slow motion: the clouds, sheep, dogs, prayer flags, me. My head throbs. A crack opens from one side of my forehead to the other and my crown comes loose. Soon it will lift like the lid of a space observatory. My memories start to slip away. The names Guoping, Xi Ping, Lu Ping, Wang Ping drift through my mind, but I cannot put faces to them. None of those women were perfect, but if one of them still loved me, I would not have to live this vagrant life. I have travelled for so long, to so many strange places, I have become a stranger to myself.

In the afternoon, the village secretary takes me to see the Nepalese silversmith. Apparently he can carve images of the horse-headed Hayagriva and the eleven-faced Avalokiteshvara with his eyes shut. There are no lights in his dark basement, so I never see his face. He spent most of his life in the confines of Shegar Chode Monastery.

When I return to my room my stomach tightens. I shouldn't have drunk that second cup of tea, the silversmith's yak butter was so rancid it singed my throat. I run to the latrine and empty my bowels, but when I reach my door I know I must go again. This time I take a jacket and torch. An hour later, I stagger out of the latrine and fall to the ground in agony. I scream my daughter's name and cry for help, but the noise shoots to my stomach. My hands grab at the night air as faces of wrathful deities flit before my eyes. At last I make it back to my room, but when I collapse on my bed and take a deep breath the gripes return. That yak butter was more poisonous than the water of Sugan Lake.

In the middle of the night, I lie awake on the metal bed under two thin quilts, shivering with cold. A wind howls through the rain and snow outside. This stinking body no longer belongs to me, my mind is as empty as a plastic bag caught in the high wind. Suddenly, I think of Beijing, and realise that although it is crammed with police, at least there is a bed and pillow waiting for me there. I came to Tibet hoping to find answers to all my unasked questions, but I have discovered that even when the questions are clear, there are no clear answers. I am sick of travelling. I need to hold onto something familiar, even if it is just a tea cup. I cannot survive in the wilds – nature is infinite but my life has bounds. I need to live in big cities that have hospitals, bookshops and women. I left Beijing because I wanted to be alone and to forge my own path, but I know now that no path is solitary, we all tread across other people's beginnings and ends. I have stopped here, not because the Himalayas stand in the way, but because my inward journey has reached its end. In fact, we all tread a path – the gold-digger, the coil-remover, Myima who left her turquoise behind and rose to the sky. We are just travelling in different directions, that's all.

This path has ended, but from now on, my journey will be much harder.

In the morning the village secretary rides me to Tingri hospital on the back of his bicycle. When the doctor says he has run out of anti-diarrhoea pills, I ask for an injection of glucose and salt water so that at least I will be able to stand up. He digs into a drawer of empty pill bottles, pencils, tweezers, batteries, finds a syringe and attaches a drip to my arm.

I lie in the hospital bed, and moan to the secretary, 'Look at the state of me! And I didn't even touch the hem of Green Tara's skirt.'

'At least you still have your ears and nose.'

Last week, I would never have guessed that a thousand-metre rise in altitude would bring me so close to death. I was at four thousand metres at the time, in the town of Lhatse, trying to hitch a ride west to Tsaparang to see the tenth-century ruins of the vanished Guge Kingdom. It was a seven-day drive into the desert. I started walking along the empty road, hoping a truck would pass. When at last I reached a point where there were neither huts, paths, nor prayer stones, I gave up and turned back.

In the evening I came to a petrol station which had a restaurant built at the back. I walked inside and asked the cook for a bowl of noodles. When he disappeared into the kitchen, I went to the counter and stole a copy of *China Youth*. I crouched in the corner and read the magazine from cover to cover, twice. I was so excited, I began to read the articles aloud. I had travelled so far that I had forgotten the sound of my own voice.

The village secretary returns from the bus station and says there is a bus leaving for Shigatse in the morning. I tell him I will take it.

Road and Direction

When I reach Lhasa, Mo Yuan is already back from Guangzhou. There is a girl with thick plaits standing behind him. He hands me a parcel from Lingling, and makes it clear my presence is not welcome. So I go next door to Liu Ren and resolve to leave Tibet as soon as possible. Liu Ren says Mo Yuan and Dali have hardly left their room since they got back. I say it is understandable, I would not have disturbed him if I had known she was there.

I remember him saying before he left, 'Last summer, Dali and I were standing at the back of a boat watching the waves break, and I felt a sudden longing to grab hold of her and jump into the sea. I'm so damn in love . . .'

Dali has graduated from university now and has moved to Tibet to be with him.

'Have you thought of transferring back to China?' I ask Liu Ren. I am afraid he will agree to the vasectomy just to keep his job.

'I am not as fancy-free as you. If someone pays for my food, I have to do as they say. I have a family to provide for. Anyway, I like Tibet.'

'You've had the operation, haven't you?' I watch my twin's face change.

'Yes.' He looks down, his nose twitching. 'The cop just left,' he says, changing the subject again.

'Was he asking about me?' Images of Beijing flit through my mind: police vans, housewives, the wind blowing through the lanes, heaps of cabbages drying on the roadside. I open Liu Ren's jar of Sichuan pickles and pull out a small gherkin.

'No. It was Tian Ge. The tall policeman with the Tibetan girlfriend who runs a snack stall. Don't you remember? He gave you those confiscated photographs of the Dalai Lama. Well, he and Drolma are escaping to Nepal. I am worried though. He has taken a gun.'

'They'll be fine. I walked along that road last week. You can travel for days without seeing a soul. Maybe they will find a guide to take them across the mountains.'

In the evening, after returning from watching television in Liu Ren's office, I sift through my pile of mail and finally find a letter from Wang Ping. It has travelled from America to Guangzhou to Lhasa. She says she is living in Chicago now and has already passed her driving test. I stop reading. I don't want to know any more. I had no right to expect any commitment when I was unable to give it myself. I should feel happy for her – this is what she wanted. But I can't just yet, because I had planned to travel to Hangzhou next week and tell her my mind is clear now, and I am ready to give her all my love.

Lingling's parcel contains a bag of dried potato, a new notebook and a yellow filter for my camera. I had asked her to send the filter because a friend had given me three rolls of night film which I wanted to use in daylight. But I lost the film months ago when I fell into the Nu River. She says she will be a mother in September. She thinks it's a boy.

Li Tao says he is taking Chun Mei to Jiuzhaigou next week and asks if we can meet up. I check the postmark and discover the letter is a month old.

Fan Cheng says Shenzhen is unbearably hot in summer and he is planning to spend his vacation in Beijing. Now that he has a respectable job and a good income he never talks of our plan to build a cattle ranch in Weichang. People are changing with the times. Everyone can see their paths. But society travels along an invisible road and no one can tell where it is going.

Hu Sha has taken a sabbatical from the Steelworks University and gone to Shenzhen to set up an editorial office for *The New Era*. He says it is much safer to publish it there. He is considering branching out into trade magazines.

It appears that Chen Hong is having an affair with him. She says she plans to transfer to Shenzhen: 'I don't want to practise medicine any more though. Hu Sha has introduced me to the director of a video company who wants an English speaker for his public relations department.'

Zhao Lan has sent me a blank introduction letter from the Federation of Trade Unions, and a wad of rice coupons. She tells me she is having an exhibition of watercolours at the American Embassy and asks if I could pop back to Beijing for the opening.

Meina, the Jinuo girl whose foot I healed in Xishuangbana, has sent me a thank-you letter. 'Dear Dr Ma Jian from Beijing. Thank you for helping me. You are my favourite doctor. I hope you will continue to make great contributions to China's Four Modernisations. Please visit me again when you are in Xishuangbana.'

As the bus pulls out of Lhasa, I take a last look at the Potala Palace. I never did go inside, because I knew that once I came out again, there would be nowhere left to go.

There are still many white mountains to cross, but I am on my way home. I am leaving the wilds and returning to the dirty crowds of the city. But I am not afraid of them any more. They cannot hurt me now. I have changed.

A young man sits down next to me. He clutches a bag on his lap and fixes his eyes on the road ahead. The skin behind his ear is stained with ingrained dust.

'Where are you going?' I ask.

'To the Beijing Nationalities Institute,' he mumbles shyly.

'Beijing? You're going to university? That's wonderful! Beijing is a huge city. You will see many new things. Your life will change. I live there myself, in a small house on Nanxiao Lane. Number 53.'